THE DRAMA WITHIN

Psychodrama and Experiential Therapy

TIAN DAYTON, PH.D.

Health Communications, Inc.
Deerfield Beach, Florida

Library of Congress Cataloging-in-Publication Data

Dayton, Tian.
    The drama within: psychodrama and experiential therapy /
Tian Dayton.
      p.   cm.
    Includes bibliographical references.
    ISBN 1-55874-296-4
    1. Psychodrama.   2. Experiential psychotherapy.   I. Title.
RC489.P7D39   1994   94-16374
616.89'1523—dc20   CIP

Publisher: Health Communications, Inc.
               3201 S.W. 15th Street
               Deerfield Beach, Florida 33442-8190

Cover design by Robert Cannata

OTABIND®

INTERNATIONAL

Dear Friend:

You may have noticed that this book is put together differently than most other quality paperbacks. The page you are reading, for instance, along with the back page, is glued to the cover. And when you open the book the spine "floats" in back of the pages. But there's nothing wrong with your book. These features allow us to produce what is known as a detached cover, specifically designed to prevent the spine from cracking even after repeated use. A state-of-the-art binding technology known as OtaBind® is used in the manufacturing of this and all Health Communications, Inc. books.

HCI has invested in equipment and resources that ensure the books we produce are of the highest quality, yet remain affordable. At our Deerfield Beach headquarters, our editorial and art departments are just a few steps from our pressroom, bindery and shipping facilities. This internal production enables us to pay special attention to the needs of our readers when we create our books.

Our titles are written to help you improve the quality of your life. You may find yourself referring to this book repeatedly, and you may want to share it with family and friends who can also benefit from the information it contains. For these reasons, our books have to be durable and, more importantly, user-friendly.

OtaBind® gives us these qualities. Along with a crease-free spine, the book you have in your hands has some other characteristics you may not be aware of:

• Open the book to any page and it will lie flat, so you'll never have to worry about losing your place.

• You can bend the book over backwards without damage, allowing you to hold it with one hand.

• The spine is 3-5 times stronger than conventional perfect binding, preventing damage even with rough handling.

This all adds up to a better product for our readers—one that will last for years to come. We stand behind the quality of our books and guarantee that, if you're not completely satisfied, we'll replace the book or refund your money within 30 days of purchase. If you have any questions about this guarantee or our bookbinding process, please feel free to contact our customer service department at 1-800-851-9100.

We hope you enjoy the quality of this book, and find understanding, insight and direction for your life in the information it provides.

Health Communications, Inc.®

3201 S.W. 15th Street
Deerfield Beach, FL 33442-8190
(305) 360-0909

Peter Vegso
President

Dedicated
with love
to
Mom, Dad
Nick, Kutzi and Becka.

I would not exchange the sorrows of my heart for the joys of the multitude. And I would not have the tears that sadness makes to flow from my every part turn into laughter. I would that my life remain a tear and a smile.

A tear to purify my heart and give me understanding of life's secrets and hidden things. A smile to draw me nigh to the sons of my kind and to be a symbol of my glorification of the gods.

I would rather that I died in yearning and longing than that I lived weary and despairing.

I want the hunger for love and beauty to be in the depths of my spirit, for I have seen those who are satisfied the most wretched of people. I have heard the sigh of those in yearning and longing, and it is sweeter than the sweetest melody.

—Kahlil Gibran
A Tear And A Smile

CONTENTS

Psychodrama Can Create New Learning • The Ritual Aspects
Of Psychodrama • What You Will Find In This Book

Psychodrama: Recreating The Interior Life • Respecting The
Protagonist's Reality • Surplus Reality • Spontaneity
• Catharsis

The Concept Of Role • How We Learn A Role • *Role
Diagram* • The Dynamics Of Psychodrama • The
Psychodramatic Theory Of Development

How Sociometry Works In Group Therapy • The Basic
Tenets Of Sociometry • The Social Atom • *Social Atom*
• Action Sociogram • *Action Sociogram* • *Spectrogram*
• *Role Analysis*

*Goodbye • Family Losses • Personal Burdens • Abortion
• Separating The Disease From The Person*

*Generational Social Atom • Deepest Childhood Wounds
• Separation—Parent's Inner Child To Child • Stages Of
Growth And Maturation • Empty Nest • Parenting Roles •
Parental Role Analysis • Projection Of Need • Relinquishing
Authority: Changing Roles With Changing Times • The
Fantasy Child I • The Fantasy Child II • Parental Fears •
Creative Visualization*

*Inner Face Versus Workplace Face • Personal Overview
• Role Reversal On Paper • Accomplishing A Task • Work Role
Analysis • Work Atom • Group Walk • Getting-The-Job-Done
Atom • Fantasy Atom • Project Atom • What's In The Way
Of Success*

Basic Method • Follow-up Exercises • *Role-Play Of Being
Mugged • Depression • Pressure To Use Drugs • Personal
Double • Hiding Behind A Negative Role*

The Alcoholic Family System • The Effects Of Growing
Up With Chaos • Shame • Isolation • Unresolved Grief
And Mourning • Developmental Distortion • Post
Traumatic Stress Reaction • Sober Versus Nonsober Thinking
And Behavior • Emotional Numbness • Disorganized
Thinking • Distorted Internalized Family System
• Distorted Parental Role Models • Difficulty In Forming
Empathic Bonds • Incomplete Individuation/Separation From
Parents • Parentified Children • Internalized Marital
Dysfunction • Inflexible Ego Structure • Physical And Sexual
Abuse • Dissociation • Grandiosity • Difficulty
In Clarifying Needs

List Of Figures

FOREWORD

There is no greater joy for a teacher than to have the experience of seeing a former student grow into a colleague and feel the essence of that colleague's teaching, in turn. Tian Dayton, in her own, very energetic, nay indefatigable, way, proves herself over and over to be a very skilled and sensitive guide in the mental health field. Such skills are very much needed in this troubled world of ours.

In this book Tian gives back to us, in a splendid fashion, all the learning and absorbing she has done.

Both in form and content, it offers the reader a variety of action approaches, covering not only the field of mental health as such, but also a wide spectrum including all areas of human interation.

Zerka T. Moreno
Beacon, NY
September 1993

ACKNOWLEDGMENTS

This book is the result of a decade of research combining the fields of psychodrama and addictions as safely and effectively as possible. Many fine people have touched these pages in one way or another. It is my wish here to thank them and to let them know that they have been important to me in this endeavor. Psychodramatically speaking, this book has three grandparents—the people who have had the greatest impact on my professional life: Sharon Wegscheider-Cruse, Robert Siroka and Zerka Moreno. I feel fortunate to have been mentored by three such skilled, loving and generous people; I will be ever grateful to them. This book is a distillation of material taught to me by them and others, my own further research and experience in the use of psychodrama in the addictions field and the other populations represented in these pages. I extend my gratitude also to professionals in the fields of psychiatry, psychology, psychoanalysis, education and addiction who have read manuscript and offered me valuable feedback—to Dr. Don Shapiro for his wise, paternal, caring guidance; to Dr. Peter Meyers for his brilliance and humor; to Dr. Robert Siroka for his conscientious and perceptive critique; to Dr. Ross Speck for his gently insightful input; to Dr. Alan Cauldwell for his brotherly and intelligent presence; to

Kathy Krauthamer for her kind and helpful feedback; to Ted Klontz for his camaraderie and strong vision; to Margie Zugich for her caring and willingness to experiment; to Claudia Blackburn for her excellent research on trauma; to Joseph Cruse and Jacqueline Siroka for their assistance and input; to George Legeros for his consultation on classical references and Beatrice Manley for sharing her excitement and brilliance in the field of drama.

I also want to take this opportunity to extend my heartfelt appreciation to my clients, my students at New York University and to members of the communities of Onsite, Canon Foundation and the Institute for Sociotherapy—all very special people and very important to me. Together we create over and over again laboratories for personal and professional growth where we learn from one another and grow together.

I extend a special thank you to the wonderful people at Health Communications, Inc.: to Barbara Nichols, Gary Seidler and Peter Vegso for their enthusiastic and generous support of this work, to Naomi Lucks for her sensitive editing and to Matthew Diener and Christine Belleris for their perceptive editorial assistance and for guiding this project along a complicated path. I also thank Mindy Wexler-Marx, whose patience and good humor in preparation of the manuscript were ever thoughtful and professional. And last but never least, I wish to thank my husband, Brandt Dayton, and our children Marina and Alex for their patience, love and support throughout this process, as well as to other family and extended-family members for their interest and support.

INTRODUCTION

It is through direct experience that we come to know ourselves. It is through full engagement in life that all our senses, feelings and thoughts come into play. Doing is knowing—what we do we come to know, and what we come to know is stored in our brains as our baseline of learning. We can talk about swimming, read books on the subject and learn strokes on dry land—but until we get into the water, we have no *direct experience* of swimming. So it is with life: until we *do*, we do not *know*.

Why should therapy be any different? Experiential therapy offers us a safe stage on which we can *do* and *know*, allowing our inner selves to come forward so that we can examine what we have accepted as true about a situation or ourselves. We often confine the idea of learning to a classroom setting; but from the point of view of how information is stored by the brain, all our life is a classroom. Often it is the emotional content of a given event or teaching that determines the impact of a particular learning experience.

Early learning forms the basis for later learning. What we accept as true about ourselves early in life becomes the foundation upon which we build the beliefs about ourselves that we carry into adolescence and adulthood. What we are told about ourselves while we are young, either through verbal messages or the emotional atmosphere, tends to form the beginnings of our own personal mythology.

The brain stores memories in clusters called cell assemblies, as interconnected or associated events. The activity of learning actually builds up and pares down cells, leaving a biological trail through the brain: in a period of from five to ten seconds, an event of one-half second has produced a structural or physical change in the brain. Not surprisingly, rich memories—the most colorful, the most ridiculous and the most painful—are those most likely to be recalled by the brain.

The high emotional content of traumatic events is a powerful learning experience, which in part accounts for the ease with which a person raised in a troubled family will turn to self-defeating behavior. A man may repeatedly become involved with women who leave him, or a woman may constantly, yet unconsciously, seek out abusive men. They are acting out the same old script, a script that is literally imprinted on the brain.

According to Daniel Alkon,

> *Individual brain cells, after repeated exposure to similar events, begin to react in the same fashion each time: In other words, they learn.*
> *The human brain then starts to categorize and [to] group images, and then we use these complex sets to make abstractions. This process, created and reinforced in childhood, creates memories, which rarely go away. They may be hidden from the conscious mind, but they remain locked in the brain, waiting for a trigger to bring them to the surface.*

Some adults suddenly "remember" vivid memories of childhood abuse, sometimes even after decades, while others develop new ways to hide from them. Theirs is akin to the stress syndrome experienced by soldiers who have survived the battlefield and by men and women who survived the horrors of the Holocaust. For many, bringing back the memories is too painful. Forgetting and inhibiting enables them to function. Sadly, unconsciously repeating destructive behaviors is part of the stress syndrome. Psychodrama offers people a way to change the self-defeating script, to reprogram old learnings through the creation of new experiences. Children under the age of twelve think in concrete rather than abstract forms according to Jean Piaget. Traumatized people tend to regress back to this thinking. Psychodrama is concrete operational so it provides a modality for accessing and working with experiences that occurred in these operational modes.

PSYCHODRAMA CAN CREATE NEW LEARNING

As human beings we live in space, time and circumstance. We take in information through all five senses. Many traumas are pre-verbal—experiences that occurred before we learned to express ourselves through speech. It is difficult to reach these wordless places and reflect upon them exclusively through the use of language. But when our bodies are engaged, we can move through the memory and show what happened rather than try to reconstruct it through words.

Psychodrama is inherently corrective: It creates an opportunity to do and say in the here-and-now what we could not do and say then, when it was too threatening or dangerous. Psychodrama allows an interior problem to surface, to be reconstructed and to be played out in the present moment, releasing the long-held feeling on both the psychic level and the cellular or body level. As children we may have been victims of our size, strength or position in the family, but as adults in a psychodrama we regain our autonomy and power by finally giving back the internalized pain to the source from which we received it. We can release the voiceless victim who lives within by allowing ourselves to speak. We can have the situation as we wish we could have had it to begin with, can say what we wish we had said and can do what we wish we had done.

When we "suspend our disbelief" in a psychodrama, we are doing more than entering a world of our creation: we are opening a door into our own unconscious, through which we can pass in either direction. We can reach out and make friends with the terrified child, the innocent baby, the playmate, the victim or the enemy that lives within. When we bring these parts of ourselves out into the open, they lose the hold on us they had in silence.

Psychodrama is a powerful action method with specific techniques. When used with care and with an overall treatment plan in mind, it can be very effective in helping clients to reduce trauma, release pent-up emotions and learn new behavior. It is a valuable tool for virtually all people in pain, and it is particularly well suited to people whose lives have been affected by addiction. In fact, during the 1980s experiential therapy became the therapy of choice in addiction facilities across the United States. Psychodrama can be incorporated into a variety of treatment situations, and its techniques can be used within other methods.

THE RITUAL ASPECTS OF PSYCHODRAMA

Psychodrama is not only a psychological tool; it can also work on the social, family and private rituals that connect the deeper self with the social self, the soul with the body. Such moments of transition, validation, bonding and deep connection are rites of passage—acknowledgment that the self is alive and awake.

For most Americans the idea of ritual is obscured by vague visions of ancient rites and elaborate ceremonies. We have, as a society, divested ourselves of cultural and family rituals, and thus may lack clear connection with our deeper selves, our spiritual paths, and the society in which we live. Our lack of meaningful ritual often causes us to reach for objects outside ourselves to achieve a sense of grounding; we seek a feeling of connectedness through mood-altering substances or through the brain-chemical high of compulsive behavior. Eventually, we may experience a spiritual crisis in which we lose our inner sense of being a part of something larger than ourselves.

Rituals in longstanding cultures are, in some sense, scripted psychodramatic events. We can use psychodrama in a similar way to ritualize or concretize an important passage, event or stage by naming it, setting the scene and moving through it in the way that we need to have it in order to mark the situation.

WHAT YOU WILL FIND IN THIS BOOK

Psychodrama is one of the most flexible and adaptable treatment modalities in use today. *The Drama Within* makes psychodramatic theory and technique easily accessible to the therapist working experientially because it is simply laid out to help you adapt action techniques to your particular needs. You will find information, both instructive and cautionary, to help you direct psychodramas that are effective and safe.

Part I, Understanding Psychodrama, explores the history and theory of psychodrama—how it came to be, why it works. In Part

II, Drama Games, you will learn step-by-step methods to safely structure drama games for a wide variety of clients and situations. Part III, Psychodrama In The Treatment Of Trauma And Addiction, addresses these issues directly and explores the growing use of experiential methods in the addictions field. The Glossary in the back of the book will help you become familiar with the terms used in this book.

I have tried to write the book that would have been helpful to me in my own process of demystifying experiential work. It is my sincere wish that it will be in some way helpful to you, the reader, along the way.

Page xviii: The brain stores . . . Daniel Alkon, Minneapolis Star and Tribune, August 1993.

Page xviii: Individual brain cells . . . Ibid.

PART I

UNDERSTANDING PSYCHODRAMA

If you see him riding on a bamboo cane,
say to him, "Good health to your horse."
—Moroccan proverb

Psychodrama is a method of treatment that follows people into their inner reality, allowing them to describe it and work with it as they see it. Through dramatic action the psychodramatist brings long-buried situations to the surface to relieve emotional pressure, creates a "holding" environment through sharing, support and acceptance, and then allows the natural healing forces of the psyche and the emotional self to continue to work. Although the psychodramatic process has at times an almost magical quality, it is not mysterious at all. It taps into our innate healing forces, uses its method to release them, then backs up and trusts that we will continue movement in our daily lives. Thus healing is not confined to a clinic, but is an ongoing process.

We know that we feel better after a good cry. According to Joseph Cruse, first medical director of the Betty Ford Center, tears shed in grief actually have a different chemical makeup from tears shed in joy. Our bodies are constantly releasing chemicals that we use internally to calm ourselves, invigorate ourselves, numb our pain and reduce stress. When we cry out our pain, we are experiencing a chemical release and expelling enzymes from the body.

In much the same way, psychodrama provides a safe environment in which painful stored material can be released within a clinical structure. Feelings that have been jammed down so that they are out of sight, but never completely out of mind, float up to the present. Psychodramatic action acts as the trigger, and the feeling becomes the conduit toward the illumination of the material that needs to be examined. It not only releases the feeling, it also allows the feeling to draw from the unconscious the events that are stored in the psyche. The brain can then reexamine and repattern the structure of the memory that has come into consciousness. The feeling is the indicator of how the psyche experienced the event.

The beauty of exploring the emotion through action is that the emotion can surface as originally felt, and can be understood from that perspective *first*—before it is edited or reflected upon in any way. This is the process of joining and moving into a person's inner reality, of validating it as it exists within that person, with no attempt to manipulate it to conform to other people's perceptions. Psychodrama also allows for an intentional reconstruction of an event if so desired, i.e., reexperiencing it in a reformed or desired state as a corrective role play of the original event. This provides new learning of emotionally laden behavior on an experiential level. Psychodrama permits action and production as a means to study behavior in its concrete form. Behavior is stimulated when the psychological environment in which that behavior was learned reoccurs. There are many legendary anecdotes of a person having had a hard night's drinking and waking up with no memory whatsoever of the previous night's fun and games. But later, perhaps the next evening when he gets drunk again, his memories come flooding back. This phenomenon was tested by giving people a number of tasks to learn—some while they were under the influence of alcohol, and some while they were sober. It was found that what was learned after drinking alcohol was remembered best when again under its influence.

Psychodrama as a life-producing physical event, is elucidated by quantum mechanics which tells us that it is physically possible for something to come from nothing, to manifest temporarily in the here and now and then to fade away again. Indeed, this process happens over and over again in our living universe. All living events follow the process of manifestation and transformation which allows us to experience the psychodramatic event or moment as real, a true corrective for the original event because it is, in and of itself, real. Producing it with surrogates on a stage gives us the opportunity to suspend it in time—as Moreno says, to "study it in its concrete form." Also, to learn from it, to grow from it, to experience it as real. It is the tangible production of a psychic reality.

1

The Basic Theory Of Psychodrama

The psychodrama is human
society in miniature.
—Jacob Levy Moreno

When Jacob Levy Moreno, the father of psychodrama, was a young psychiatrist in Vienna during the first half of this century, he was eccentric, exuberant and fascinated by people. He used to sit in the parks and watch children play, noticing how they spontaneously acted out their emotional concerns and feelings by constructing situations and playing roles. He immediately recognized that acting out situations about which they had strong feelings and taking on the roles of authority figures in their lives had great therapeutic value for the children.

Moreno envisioned that there could be therapeutic value for psychologically disturbed patients if they were allowed, like children, the freedom to play out roles and scenes relevant to their lives. They too might live out their psychodramas in a controlled, supervised environment where they could both discharge the feelings attached to various roles and correct the experiences by

5

playing it through as it was, as it might have been or as they wished it had been. Moreno believed first in life and then in pathology; he wished to be remembered as the person who brought joy to psychiatry.

In his autobiographical writings Moreno also describes his work with prostitutes in turn-of-the century Vienna, out of which grew his psychodramatic methods. He visited their houses, along with a physician specializing in venereal diseases and a publisher of a newspaper, not to "reform the girls nor to analyze them," but rather to return to them some dignity: "Because the prostitutes had been stigmatized for so long as despicable sinners and unworthy people . . . they had come to accept this as an unalterable fact." He met with the prostitutes three times a week in groups ranging from eight to ten. At first the meetings dealt with the problems of everyday life—"being arrested, being harassed by a policeman for wearing provocative clothing, being jailed because of false accusations from a client, having venereal disease but being unable to get treatment"; eventually, however, the prostitutes found that they were less isolated, able to share deep concerns and able to feel identified with each other. Moreno had discovered that the simple experience of sharing had a curative effect; his work with these prostitutes had convinced him of the healing power of a group.

Moreno formally introduced psychodrama on April 1, 1921, in Vienna. In the late 1920s, he emigrated to the United States and founded the Moreno Institute. Moreno felt that full treatment required a threefold system: (1) psychodrama, (2) group psychotherapy, and (3) sociometry. Incorporating these three approaches allows the person to begin to experience personal healing, to work out new behaviors and connections in a network of support and alignment, and thus to change and grow and learn new ways of being in the world. Moreno believed that in a group, each person becomes a therapeutic agent of the other. He viewed the group as rich in healing potential. His science of sociometry (see Chapter 3, Sociometry: How Psychodrama Works) explored the subtle and complicated connections among people, the vast body of relationships that create our society.

Moreno explained the clinical significance of his method: "Historically," he writes, "psychodrama represents the chief turning point away from the treatment of the individual in isolation, to the treatment of the individual in groups, from the treatment of the individual by verbal methods to the treatment by action methods."

As the original action-oriented technique out of which others have grown, psychodrama is an extremely flexible method. Today various forms of psychodrama, role-play and role-training are in use in such diverse venues as mental health institutions, law enforcement agencies, schools, rehabilitation centers and corporations. In fact, psychodrama is in worldwide use. According to the World Academy of Psychodrama, there are practitioners not only in the United States but in Australia and New Zealand; Japan; France, Germany, Switzerland and Austria; Greece and Brazil and Argentina. Moreno's books have been translated into German, Italian, Spanish, French, Serbo-Croatian, Turkish, Japanese, Russian and Portuguese. Psychodrama journals have been established in Britain, West Germany, Italy, France and Japan. Psychodrama, sociometry and group psychotherapy have truly come of age as methods of treatment.

PSYCHODRAMA:
RECREATING THE INTERIOR LIFE

Moreno established the science of psychodrama to offer individuals an opportunity to rework missed developmental stages by allowing them to experience and practice the dynamics of a given stage in a safe therapeutic environment. When the trauma and pain are released in this way, they can be understood in a new light, and the experience can be reintegrated into the unconscious. The psychodramatic action can also be reconstructive work, where surrogates in the group give the protagonist the emotional support he or she never received in the original situation. In this way release is accompanied by understanding and love, which promotes healing and a greater sense of safety in trying out new behaviors.

In this sense psychodrama recreates the ordinary. It gives us the opportunity to say what was left unsaid, and in this way to correct our original experience. It provides the pathway to bring our inner and outer reality into balance and accord. Society cannot always allow us to say what is in our hearts, but psychodrama can. It gives voice to our inner life, to the pain we are too ashamed to share, to the dream we hardly dare have. As Moreno once said, "The stage is enough." Psychodrama gives us the opportunity to walk onto the stage and into ourselves, to take hold of our own dark side and place it in the light in a way that feels natural and is safe and controlled.

RESPECTING THE PROTAGONIST'S REALITY

One reason psychodrama is so successful is that the roles we enact in psychodrama enable us to explore virtually every aspect of ourselves and our relationships with others. The basic roles in a psychodrama are the *protagonist*, the person whose story is being enacted; the *double*, the inner voice of the protagonist; the *director*, the person directing the psychodramatic action (usually a therapist); and the *auxiliary egos*, the people in the group who play the other characters in the psychodrama; and the *audience* or group. The use of *role reversal* allows the protagonist to play any role in the drama, in order both to see the self from the outside and to experience the self from the position of the other. (We'll explore the concept of role in Chapter 2, The Elements Of Psychodrama, and the roles themselves in Chapter 4, The Techniques Of Psychodramatic Enactment.)

The primary difference between true psychodrama and applying psychodramatic or experiential techniques on top of other therapeutic models is that psychodrama follows the lead of the protagonist. The director—the professional who leads the group—facilitates the protagonist's choicemaking, involving what material will be examined psychodramatically and how that enactment will take shape in time and space. In a sense the director takes a walk through the protagonist's *surplus reality*—that which we carry within our psyches as personal history, which affects the whole of who we are and how we relate. Surplus reality is important and it is real. What the protagonist says "is" simply "is," and the director works from there.

SURPLUS REALITY

Each of us has an intellectual, an emotional and a spiritual self, the inner workings known primarily to ourselves; yet even we have trouble understanding ourselves much of the time. We are always in search of ourselves. We are our own greatest mystery.

In this confusing pursuit we often project our inner reality outward, perhaps in an attempt to get a better look at it. Many times, however, we do not achieve that better understanding because we tend to project it and then see it as being attached to someone else and no longer to ourselves. We create a house of mirrors, in which we see ourselves reflected in a variety of distorted shapes. And if we project without awareness of what we are doing, we may lose a sense of where we leave off and everything else begins.

Though invisible to others, surplus reality has a powerful impact on our lives, one that it is difficult for the mind to see and reflect upon. Through psychodrama we can learn to observe the workings of our minds from a more objective perspective, through observation of concrete behavior.

The psychodramatic journey is the pilgrimage into our surplus reality. It is the brave and courageous walk into ourselves—through the deepest fear, humiliation, hidden shame, barely spoken hopes and dreams—and ultimately back out again. Psychodrama offers us a stage onto which we can lovingly place ourselves so that our surplus reality can be better understood. The method is gentle; it does not ask us to reflect until first our surplus reality has been seen. It offers a unique opportunity for producing the inner workings of the psycho-emotional self, with willing participants who help us recreate our own reality. In psychodrama we reach into our own experience and pull out ourselves. This is, in itself, healing—to speak the words we dared not speak but had shouting within us.

Because psychodrama heals so powerfully, the therapist must always keep respect for the client foremost. The danger of this method resides in the chance that the therapist will use techniques to push clients to where the therapist feels they should be. As therapists, when we enter into surplus reality, we are being allowed to go into the intrapsychic world of the protagonist—where angels fear to tread. We need to trust the process of our clients as being right for them, and understand that what is opening up for them is what their own psyche intends them to know at that time.

The protagonist is leading the director through the labyrinth of the protagonist's mind. The therapist is holding the protagonist's hand with one hand, and carrying a flashlight with the other—shedding light on what can be seen at that moment, knowing that it is not the whole picture. The therapist must always recognize that, when dealing with people's psyches, there is no such thing as seeing the whole picture. Failing to do so, the therapist may try to implement expectations that are invalid for the client.

Each person's journey is unique to that person; so therapists must make the therapeutic approach fit the needs of the client; if clients have to adjust their psychic functioning to fit our therapeutic bias, we will not tolerate growth outside of the parameters that we erect for them, even if that growth is what would be best for them. Moreover, it must be borne in mind that therapeutic norms are not necessarily consistent with social norms; and though a part of the process of therapy is a socializing one, there are many points along the way where the work might feel antisocial. The clients will be revealing those parts of themselves that they have kept closeted away in secrecy for fear that they are unacceptable to others. Often the problem is not so much what is being hidden, but the hiding itself. The therapeutic environment needs to first play the role of unconditional love, or the "maternal" function, before it plays the "paternal" function of setting limits and offering guidance.

According to Moreno,

> *Psychodrama puts the patient on a stage where he can work out his problems with the aid of a few therapeutic actors. . . . It can be adapted to every type of problem, personal or group, of children or adults. . . . Our deepest psychic conflicts can be brought nearer solution by its aid. The psychodrama is human society in miniature, the simplest possible setup for a methodical study of its psychological structure. . . . New dimensions of the mind are opened up, and, what is most important, they can be explored under experimental conditions.*

Moreno explains that the therapist does not participate in the production itself: "He is like a conductor in an orchestra; he does not play an instrument himself, but supervises, directs and observes. He keeps a certain distance from the patient." It is the protagonist who chooses auxiliary egos to role-play the people within his drama and who sets the scene and tone of the enactment, along with the director. An *auxiliary ego*, chosen from the group, safeguards the director's neutrality.

It is the surplus reality of the protagonist that the therapist and group see during the enactment, and the truth of the protagonist is the truth that the therapist deals with. The protagonist is allowed to hire and fire auxiliary egos and doubles if needed, and is encouraged to correct anyone, including the director, in order to portray more accurately his truth on the psychodramatic stage.

SPONTANEITY

Spontaneity is one of the central elements of psychodrama, and an ever-present goal in its use. When we were children, no one needed to teach us how to play, but unfortunately, most of us managed to lose this self-affirming, nurturing ability on the rocky path to adulthood. Psychodrama can help us get it back.

Play is about spontaneity. It is a deeply transforming activity in which the primary goal is involvement. When we play with people, we experience them and ourselves in a new way. We co-create a happening, entering willingly into unscripted territory, where each person's contribution is what creates the whole. Play, like psychodrama, is a spontaneous interaction of the parts toward creating the whole. It is filled with the full gamut of emotions, and we only understand it in retrospect, if at all. It is at that moment when the spectator in us is burned away and we become the action itself, when "as if" gives way to "as" and we are fully present in the moment.

Psychodrama is not far removed from ordinary life: every day we play a variety of roles—mother, father, lover, worker, boss. Every role comes with certain expectations, certain assets and liabilities. Moreover, we have a different set of feelings about each role we play. In some we feel very much ourselves, whereas others cramp our natural personalities and create problems for us. Some we overplay, and in some we are inwardly less present than we might like. Part of spontaneity lies in our ability to move in and out of roles with ease. Some philosophers suggest that we wear life as a loose garment. Perhaps we can also learn to wear our roles as a loose garment, not becoming overly attached to them and being careful not to let them bind us so that we cannot move freely. Life, after all, is to be lived, and some playfulness can help us to maintain that sense of purposeless purpose that is one of the paradoxes of existence.

Role-playing techniques such as drama games and psychodrama are very effective in the creation of new roles. When we take on a variety of roles and improvise them in the moment, we release our creative energies in new directions that our daily lives would not necessarily provide for. The structured format provides a stage on which our selves can spontaneously emerge in new and unexpected ways. The format also serves to maintain safety and continuity, to create a true laboratory of experimentation. What we learn through these activities can be quickly and naturally applied to our lives because it has been integrated into our behavioral repertoire.

In play and in psychodrama we experience a loss of self-consciousness and a deep sense of connectedness with those around us. We are at once vulnerable and powerful, and we move into and out of roles and identities that may confound us in normal life. Play and psychodrama teaches us the art of being alive. The roles in which we experience the most success and satisfaction are those in which we feel the most alive. These are the roles in which we are constantly renewing ourselves and our energy for life; where commitment gives way to passion and we feel ourselves to be genuine. The more that we can play a variety of roles with ease and spontaneity, and the greater our satisfaction within each individual role, the healthier and happier we will ultimately feel.

According to Moreno, spontaneity means that we are ready to respond to a situation as required by the situation. This ability must be natural: we cannot attain spontaneity by an act of will. If it is no longer natural, as it is with children, it must grow by degrees as the result of training in spontaneity, which psychodrama provides.

Psychiatrist Adam Blatner writes,

> *Spontaneity need not be showy or dramatic; it can be unassuming. It can be present in the way you think, walk, look at nature, dance or sing in the shower. . . . The essential qualities of a spontaneous act are an openness of mind, a freshness of approach, a*

willingness to take innovative action and an integration of the external with the internal.

Psychodrama defines three types of spontaneity: (1) a novel response without adequacy, or *pathological spontaneity*; (2) an adequate response without novelty and creativity, or *stereotyped spontaneity*; and (3) an adequate response with novelty and creativity, or *the spontaneity of the genius*. Spontaneity is closely linked to creativity. It acts as a catalyst or a companion to the creative process, however that creativity may choose to express itself. It may be in a way of looking at a paining, cooking a dinner, approaching a lecture, watching a film, entering a new situation, reading a book or writing a story. It is the creative underpinning of any endeavor, a way of living and interacting with life and the self. It is central to psychodrama as it acts to remove and resolve emotional and psychological problems that block it and demands, teaches and trains spontaneity by placing participants in situations that require novel responses. When our spontaneity and creativity can grow, healing occurs. We reconnect with life and self, a primary goal of therapy.

Over and over again, role-players in psychodramas are asked to call upon their creativity in order to provide the deep and complicated responses necessary to fulfill their roles in action. It trains people to think on their feet. It encourages risk-taking and allows a large enough margin for failure (or what might feel like failure) so that participants learn to move through situations that may have previously baffled them, shut them down or rendered them silent. It allows them to experiment with new behaviors, alternate responses and fresh points of view. Spontaneity occurs when the inner and the outer being meet freely and easily on the level of thought and action; it allows more of the real person to come through and acts as a deterrent to role fatigue, role burnout and rigidity. In dysfunctional families, identities tend to be solidified, enacted either in a repetitious, unfeeling manner or overly heated in comparison with the situation. Spontaneity lies in the middle. It is an adequate response, one that meets the situation with a serene aliveness, ready to act or not act as the situation demands.

CATHARSIS

The concept of *catharsis* as it is used in psychodrama comes from the ancient Greeks, specifically from Aristotle. He believed that "through the dramatic enactment and representation of a real life situation, violence within the soul . . . could be purged." The tragedies of the ancient Greeks dealt with a few basic themes common to all people, much the way psychodramas do. Native Americans also sought to effect a catharsis or psychic purging through the enactment of dreams. Dramatic enactments were used to bring complexes, problems and fears to a conscious level in order to effect a psychic purge.

Catharsis of the feelings is the first step on the way to a catharsis of integration, without which behavior will not necessarily change. Though the drama is not a spontaneous event for the actors who have practiced it again and again, it is a spontaneous event for the spectator, who experiences a mental and emotional catharsis as a result of being a member of the audience. This is one avenue of catharsis in psychodrama.

The audience moves through the pattern and gradually sees the pattern to be the same as its own personal one. Dramatic meaning is achieved as the actor moves toward the climax, the resolution of the action. And this is all-compelling to the spectator because there is a familiarity present in the story. The compelling notion is that this drama is my story, my history's meaning being ritualized before me on the stage. This play is a mirror of my meaning. Catharsis, here, is indeed dramatic clarification and explanation.

Psychodrama carries this one step further by providing a situation in which the role-play is a spontaneous enactment of the protagonist's real story.

Metaphorically katharsis *presents seven pictures. (1) In one ancient papyrus* katharsis *is "clearing," as when a person is clearing the land of twigs and stones. (2) In another papyrus* katharsis *is "winnowing," as in the thrashing of grain. (3) Diocles used the term as the image of "cleaning" when he described the process of cleaning food by cooking it. (4) Theophrastus, in his essay "On Plants," meant "pruning" when he used* katharsis *in relation to trees. (5) Both Philodemus in his essay "On the Freedom of Speech" and Epicurus in his Letters used the same word to picture the "clarification" achieved by explanation. (6) Galen, of course, used* katharsis *to signify the "healing" of an illness by the application of medicine. And (7) Chrysippus'* katharsis *was the "purifying" of the universe by fire.*

For substantial growth and movement, the client must experience a *catharsis of integration,* one in which not only a catharsis of feelings has been effected but also a cognitive and emotional shift in perception as a result of the catharsis. Ultimately, this is where the client will need to go for healing to fully take place.

A *catharsis of abreaction* is a reaction against—for example, a catharsis of hate toward one's father arising out of anger and despair is released. Any catharsis needs to be process-oriented rather than results-oriented. The therapist who pushes it, who asks for a particular goal, may arouse in the protagonist the need to be "good." Thus, though the feeling may be released, the co-dependency within the protagonist will be reinforced.

Psychodrama embodies both these forms of catharsis: a catharsis of "separation and clarification and a catharsis as unification and completion." It is the bringing of unconscious material to the conscious level that produces the healing effect, taking it out of the surplus reality of the individual and moving it into the collective reality of the production and of the group. An effective catharsis of *integration* returns us to a state of equilibrium and moves us away from the disequilibrium we were experiencing in our inability to respond adequately to life situations. According to Moreno,

However relieving [the] analysis of situations may be for the patient, for a final test he must go back onto the stage in a real life situation. There it may rapidly come clear that the equilibrium he had thought to have gained from the analysis is not adequate. [What seems lacking is a] binder between whatever analysis can give him in the way of equilibrium and in the action and movement of living. This binder is the spontaneity which the patient must be able to summon with split second swiftness when a life situation calls for it. Retest after retest must be made in order to assure the patient that the necessary catharsis has been attained within him. It is spontaneity in its various expressions which at last crowns the efforts of the psychodrama.

A mental catharsis can happen in three ways: (1) within the protagonist; (2) within the auxiliary who participates in the drama; and (3) in the audience that participates through identification in the experience of the enactment. Catharsis happens also on a physical level, cleansing the body, causing a cellular release of the held memory within the brain and body. Psychodrama assumes that a lack of spontaneity in a social setting provokes disturbances not only in the individual but also in the group. These disturbances increase as the deficit of spontaneity increases. A catharsis that is successful within an individual in the group should have the effect of increasing the spontaneity of the entire group, which should then reduce both the individual and group-dynamic disturbances.

It is the writer's belief that true catharsis actually alters the cell assembly in the brain, changing the person's record of learning. Fritz Perl's adage "insight is the booby prize" might apply here. If the insight does not provide a catharsis—that is, if the learning is not experiential—we may *see* an event differently but will not *be* different. Though the catharsis should be accompanied by insight in order to ground the learning on a cognitive level, the insight must be accompanied by experience in order to change behavior.

Page 1:   According to Joseph Cruse . . . Onsite, Rapid City, SD, November 18, 1988.

Page 2:   Similarly . . . J. L. Moreno, *Psychodrama*, vol. 1 (Beacon, NY: Beacon House, 1946).

Page 2:   The beauty . . . Ibid.

Page 5:   When Jacob Levy Moreno . . . J. Fox, (ed.). *The Essential Moreno: Writings on Psychodrama Group Method and Spontaneity by J. L. Moreno, M.D.*, (New York: Springer, 1987).

Page 4:   Angela Tilby, *Soul, God, Self And The New Cosmology* (New York: Doubleday, 1992).

Page 6:   Moreno formally introduced . . . R. F. Marineau, *Jacob Levy Moreno
            1889-1974: Father of Psychodrama, Sociometry and
            Group Psychotherapy* (London: Tavistock/Routledge, 1989).

Page 6:   His science of sociometry . . . J. L. Moreno, *Sociometry*
            (Beacon House, 1950, NY: Beacon).

Page 6:   Historically, psychodrama represents . . . J. L. Moreno,
            Psychodrama vol. 1 (Beacon, NY: Beacon House, 1946).

Page 7:   According to the World Academy . . . Dale Buchanan, "The
            Psychiatric Therapies: Psychodrama" American Psychiatric
            Association, Washington, D.C.

Page 8:   As Moreno once said . . . J. L. Moreno, *Psychodrama*, vol. 1.
            (Beacon, NY: Beacon House, 1946).

Page 8:   The primary difference . . . Ibid.

Page 8:   In a sense the director . . . Ibid.

Page 9:   It is difficult for the mind . . . C. Kris, Boston, July 21, 1991.

Page 9:   As therapists we need . . . R. Siroka, Psychodrama Training
            Institute, New York, 1989.

Page 10:   Psychodrama puts the patient . . . J. L. Moreno, Psychodrama
            and the psychopathology of interpersonal relations, *American
            Society of Group Psychotherapy and Psychodrama Journal* (1948).

Page 10:   The psychodrama is human society . . . Ibid.

Page 10:   "He is like a conductor . . ." J. L. Moreno, *The Theatre of
            Spontaneity* (Beacon, NY: Beacon House, 1947).

Page 12:   Spontaneity need not be showy . . . Adam Blatner, A. Blatner,
            Foundation of Psychodrama: History, Theory and Practice
            (New York: Springer, 1987).

Page 14:   Aristotle believed that . . . George Legeros, Minneapolis, MN:
            Lecture, August 16, 1993.

Page 14:   The audience moves . . . Joseph Campbell (ed.), *Myths, Dreams
            and Religion*, (Dallas: Spring Publishing, 1970).

Page 14:   Metaphorically Katharsis presents . . . Joseph Campbell (ed.),
            Myths, Dreams and Religion, (Dallas: Spring Publishing, 1970).

Page 15:   "Separation and clarification . . ." Joseph Campbell (ed.), *Myths,
            Dreams and Religion*, (Dallas: Spring Publishing, 1970).

Page 15:   For substantial growth and movement . . . R. Siroka, Psychodrama
            Training Institute, New York, 1993.

Page 15:   Your protagonist does not . . . Zerka Moreno, Highland Park, NY:
           April 16, 1988.

Page 15:   However relieving analysis . . . J. L. Moreno, *Psychodrama*, vol. 1
           (Beacon, NY: Beacon House, 1946).

Page 15:   binder between whatever . . . Ibid.

2
The Stage Is Enough: Concepts And Premises

*This laboring through what is
still undone, as though, legs bound,
we hobbled along the way, is like the
awkward walking of the swan.*
—**Ranier Maria Rilke**

Before we can explore the practical methods of psychodrama and drama games, we need to be familiar with the context in which the dramas are being enacted and elements that exist in psychodramatic role-playing interactions.

THE CONCEPT OF ROLE

No one is the same person all the time. We operate in life through a variety of roles—as parents, as children, as friends, as colleagues—and many of our feelings and behaviors tend to be specific to a particular role. Not all of our life roles, however, are equally successful. We may experience great success in one role, be moderately successful in a second, and fail miserably in a third.

For example, Michael is extremely successful in business, earns a great deal of money and is an excellent executive, but at home he is a relative failure as a husband, insensitive to the needs of his wife and the pressures on her. While he can negotiate a business-related situation brilliantly, he has no comparable skills to help him negotiate an evening at home with his family. Feeling unsuccessful, Michael begins to think that his family ought to be run as his office is run. And when confronted with the complicated and sensitive issues of inclusion and exclusion that are present in a family, he takes the same unemotional approach that works well in his work situation and applies it—very unsuccessfully—at home.

Psychodrama gives Michael an excellent chance to affirm his executive skills and work on his family life because it affords an opportunity to treat specific roles. His therapist can learn which roles Michael feels successful and alive in, and explore expansion within these roles. Together they can determine which roles in Michael's life are neglected or underplayed and explore them both psychodramatically and actually, they can look at Michael's life to see what should be added or reduced to create more balance.

Psychodrama gives us the valuable opportunity again and again to work through our most painful roles, those in which our power is blocked and our emotional selves remain both wounded and stuck. The boy who has been wounded by his alcoholic mother and her erratic behavior toward him can have an opportunity to meet her on the psychodramatic stage. He can release the anger he felt toward her but did not dare to express. He can push away her guilty attempts to repair the pain through excessive attention that made him feel smothered and emasculated. He can, at last, wrap his arms around her and tell her how much he needs her; he can express the filial love and affection that were previously blocked by fear of her overdependence on him or by the oedipal confusion he felt in seeing his adored mother in a drunken state. He can say what he was unable to say and ask for what he was unable to ask for.

The concept of treating the role, as used in psychodrama, is perhaps one of Moreno's most significant contributions to the field of mental health. He defined *role* as "the actual and tangible form which the self takes . . . the functioning form the individual assumes in reacting to a specific situation in which other persons or objects are involved. . . . Self, ego, personality, character, etc., are cluster effects, heuristic hypotheses, metapsychological postulates, 'logoids.' Role is a final crystallization of all the situation in a special area of operations through which the individual has passed (for instance the eater, the father, the airplane pilot)."

In *Psychodrama, A Rehearsal For Living*, Adaline Starr defines role as "a pattern of behavior that a person develops from his life experiences in order to cope with the situation he faces." In other words in our daily lives, we play roles that arise out of situations—that is, we play them for a reason. When we explore a role, we explore the reasons, the needs, the underlying fears and the secondary gains that lead us to play it. In psychodramatic role-playing we relieve repressed feelings associated with the role; we release and explore the role and the hold it has on us.

Psychological health is associated with the ability to move in and out of a variety of roles with relative fluidity. We become unhealthy when we get stuck in a role or two and cannot get out. When the role superimposes itself on our being, and we become the role, we lose our spontaneity and freedom of choice. Then the role plays us. What occurs is not only a shift in reality but also a shift in how we participate in reality: we falsely identify or overidentify with the role, and underidentify with the self.

Psychodrama offers us countless opportunities to play out roles—as the protagonist, the auxiliary ego or an audience member. The variety of role-playing opportunities provides situations in which we can explore any role that occurs to us. The more alternatives we are aware of, the more we are able to create solutions that are both adequate to the situation and novel. Knowledge of alternatives and security in a particular role naturally enhance the possibility of spontaneity and creativity.

Role Development

We pass through three stages in learning a new role: (1) role-taking, (2) role-playing and (3) role creation. *Role-taking* is the stage of imitation, or modeling, one of the deepest forms of learning. *Role-playing* is the stage of doing what we learned in role-taking while bringing something of ourselves to the new role we are practicing, experimenting with and making adaptations to. *Role creation* is the stage in which we recreate the role with a unique vision. We keep elements from the first two stages, while creating the role anew to suit our own talents, needs and desires—a self-validating creative process.

HOW WE LEARN A ROLE

Role-Taking

The process of role-taking is closely related to modelling. It is the taking on of a role through a sort of imbibing process as we immitate at the deepest level what we perceive or experience outside ourselves. There is generally little awareness of this process as it is happening. It begins in infancy: the way we are touched, spoken to and held, the way we are seen or not seen is impressed on our brains. When we become parents, this historic knowledge will be brought to the surface and acted out in role reversal if there is no conscious intervention in that process. The child is now the parent, and will do what was done to him—he will pass on what he learned. And so it is with a multitude of learning experiences.

Role-taking or modelling is perhaps the most powerful form of teaching, for role-taking forms a brain template that is referred to again and again as familiar. "Do as I say, not as I do" is meaningless in the face of the process of modelling. The truth is closer to "Do as I do," "Be who I am." And so we play out scripts for no apparent reason, because role-taking has formed a partially unconscious pattern of behavior.

Role-Playing

Role-playing operates at a more conscious level than role-taking, for we have already learned a role and are comfortable enough with it to try it our own way. We have some perception of what we are doing and an ability to bring pieces of ourselves to the situation and try them out in the role. One can observe early role-playing during latency years when it occurs to a child that he is a participant in determining who he is. One might hear him say, "I walk like this." "My friend likes brown chocolate, but I like white chocolate." "My mommy does this, but I do it this way." He is experimenting with adding to what he has learned of himself. He has discovered that he *acts on* the role as well as having it *act on* him.

The freedom with which we are allowed to experiment and the support of the people around us are very important in how we learn as children to bring ourselves to life. If we are not merely expected to behave in a prescribed way but rather encouraged to explore ourselves, we come to feel in the depths of our beings that it is all right to take risks and to be who we are in addition to meeting expectations—to become socialized, not as robots, but as individuals. If we are allowed freedom within clear boundaries we will know that we do not have to leave ourselves behind in order to live in the world, or to rebel—which is just another way of leaving the self behind. When the home is secure, the boundaries intact and the identities stable, the child has ample opportunity to learn how and where he fits into the scheme of things, and to learn how to fit in without disappearing.

Role Creation

Role creation can occur when the first two stages have been fully enough integrated to allow the most creative part of the self to be brought to bear on restructuring the role in a new and unique fashion. Consider the exquisite early drawings of Picasso—how fine his lines, how delicate and sensitive, his portraits, how he progressively mastered technique. And then he was in a position to throw away what he had learned, to toss it up in the air, into the universe, into the vast expanse of himself and let fall in a new and highly personal vision of his own uniqueness. Much in the same way we create ourselves out of the roles we play out in our lives. When they have been fully learned and experimented with, when something new has been created and something old blended in with the new—and when the security of those two stages is internalized—then we feel able to take on the ultimate challenge of experiencing our inner dimensions and reaching out for what is there. The creative act is everyone's birthright; to enter into our lives with wonder, firmly rooted but with arms open to what may be. After the actor has learned his lines and incorporated the blocking and after he has drawn out the parts of himself that relate to the role and integrated them with the playwright's conception, then he is in a position to role create, to bring to the character what has never been brought, to release what is known and walk into what is not known with the confidence that what is available to him will be all the accumulated knowledge of the script, the playwright's conception of the role and his own integrated perception—with the confidence to let it happen spontaneously within the moment. That is role creation.

Survival Roles

A child who is abused or traumatized when he is too young to protect himself may develop *survival roles,* a set of defensive behaviors designed to keep themselves safe. A boy who is scared may develop the role of a tough kid in order to hide his fear both from himself and from the aggressor. A girl who is sad may put on a happy face both to make herself feel better and to disguise her sadness from the world. A child who feels that his family is falling apart may become supercompetent as a way to cope with deep feelings of helplessness and to gain some sense of control.

The greater the painful feelings, the bigger the job of the survival role. A self-protective role—through being played over and over again—takes on a life of its own, and actually organizes the child's personality. The child feels, "I am my survival roles"—I am the bully, I am the fixer, I am the person who is relentlessly happy—and the child within the adult hangs onto these roles as if for dear life.

When, in the therapeutic process, we challenge the usefulness of these roles or personalities, we challenge clients at their core. The baby who turns away from affection because she fears rejection may become a distant, self-protective adult. The man whose role is that of the person who is always right rigidly plays out the role before he will risk letting his true feelings show. The more scared these men and women become, the more they engage whatever role or personality they have developed in childhood in order to cover their fear.

For a child terror feels life-threatening, and it is this feeling that is engaged in the frightened adult as well. While an onlooker may see it as a gross overreaction, the adult is truly in a state of terrror and fears for his life. The adult is right back in his early self and is experiencing life-threatening fear; when early trauma is triggered by present events, the trauma is experienced all over again.

Although survival roles may protect a child, they get in the way of adult relationships. Intimate relationships actually act as triggers for the old roles. The closer and more vulnerable and dependent the person feels, the greater the sense of danger and the stronger the impulse to call on the survival role to intervene, to take over and protect. An unpleasant survival role can have an actively destructive effect on interactions; instead of sharing real feelings of hurt or vulnerability, the person flips into rigid defensive behaviors that inhibit satisfying and constructive communication.

ROLE DIAGRAM

The following exercise is intended to familiarize participants in a psychodrama with the variety of roles they play. (You may find it helpful to make a diagram of your own life roles.)

Goals

1. To understand the number and variety of roles played.
2. To observe those roles in relation to one another.
3. To explore content and satisfaction within the roles.

Steps

1. Ask participants to get a pencil and a paper.
2. Ask them to put a circle somewhere on the paper with their name inside of the circle and extend lines like spokes of a wheel from the outside of the circle for about one and one half inches.
3. Ask them to write on each spoke the major roles they play in their lives, for example, mother, wife, daughter, daughter-in-law, writer, professor and so on.
4. Ask them to choose one of those roles they would like to explore or one in which they feel some conflict.
5. Ask them to place another circle somewhere on the paper and put the name of that role within the circle, for example, mother. Then, as in the previous diagram, ask them to extend the spokes from the outside of the circle.
6. Ask them to put on each spoke an aspect of the chosen role, for the mother role, for example, chauffeur, doctor, listener, cook, nurturer, playmate, executive planner, teacher and so on.

7. Next, ask them to write the following words in a column at the side of the page: taste, smell, color, movement, texture and sound. Then, after each word, the appropriate association with the word that would best describe or relate to the role they are exploring. (For example, the color that feels like the role of mother to me would be burnt orange.)

8. At this point you may allow some time for sharing, with the group or in pairs, the adjectives they have chosen to describe the various roles.

9. If you wish to move into action, the next step is to examine the diagrams to discover in which aspects of the role participants experience conflict or discomfort.

10. Set up two empty chairs or structure whatever scene feels appropriate, and ask participants to feel who comes up that they wish to speak to around the conflict or issues they are experiencing: that is, where and with whom does the unfinished business lie, or what aspect of themselves would they like to address by putting it into an empty chair or selecting an auxiliary ego to represent it.

11. Allow anyone who wishes to do vignettes in order to explore further the issue or conflict, using doubling, role reversal, interview, soliloquy or whatever technique might be helpful. The protagonist may wish to use an empty chair, or he may wish to chose someone to represent the person or aspect of self he is addressing.

12. Allow time for sharing after each vignette or for sharing as a group after several vignettes have taken place.

Variations

The exercise may be varied by rating the satisfaction within each role on a scale from one to ten in either of the diagrams, or by assessing the time spent in each role using a large circle and dividing it, each sector representing the percentage of time spent in a given role. If this is done, you may wish to use another diagram representing the ideal, that is, how the participants would wish the roles to be allotted if and when they could change them. Or a role might be put in an empty chair and the participant asked to stand behind the chair and double for the feeling present on the inside of that particular role. If this is done, he can choose an aspect of the role in which he feels a conflict or an issue, one in which he feels especially empowered or one in which change may be taking place. Healthy people tend to be able to move in and out of roles with relative ease, and happy people tend to play more than one or two roles; they have a variety of roles among which they travel easily and naturally. Getting stuck in a role can lead to fatigue, a lack of creativity and a sense of being bored or even depressed with life. In this case role work can help to gain perspective and a shift in awareness. If someone overplays a role until he feels burned out, he may need to add other roles to his life in order to provide new outlets for nurturing, creativity and growth. Though the answer may seem to lie in leaving the role in which he feels burned out, the solution may lie instead in adding new roles and expanding potential experience.

If role diagrams are used in couples work—the role would be husband or wife and the ancillary roles might be lover, friend, sibling, parent, child, in-law—the completed diagrams can be examined with a view to discovering which roles are compatible (as individuals as well as in partnership) and which are conflictual. The role of parent may or may not have conflict as that of lover or friend. It is useful for the couple to examine which roles are positive and going well and which roles need attention: it can be helpful in building on strengths and in revealing that while some roles in a relationship may need work, it does not mean the entire relationship is unhealthy or nonproductive. Role diagrams may also help the couple understand that a successful, long-term relationship requires significant role changes and shifts as the couple moves through their life stages, and that each life stage requires the playing of different roles. Successful couples can allow each other to change roles without losing the relationship. Long term, a couple experiences at least four major stages of life: couple, nuclear family, couple/extended family and old age. Each of these stages will require learning new roles and letting go of or changing the shape of old roles. Any stage of life can be examined in this way: for example, mid-life crisis can be examined from the role perspective by way of diagrams, exploring which roles have been under fulfilled and which roles need to be added to or expanded upon in order to live happily. The empty nest, retirement, loss of a loved one and other major life changes can be explored in this manner as well.

THE DYNAMICS OF PSYCHODRAMA

Each person's personal history is unique. Each interaction changes us. If there is a good feeling between two people, they are able to agree on a particular event as feeling good. If the feeling between two people is out of sync, they experience the same event quite differently. Each of us brings our accumulated history, neurochemical makeup and emotional development to our experience of all of life's situations.

Psychodrama offers the protagonist a safe stage on which to re-experience a traumatic event with safety and support enough to avoid freezing, so that he can feel, understand and know it, and thus come to closure. Then the traumatic event can be reintegrated into his being in a reconstructed form—given a context and meaning—and he can move on.

Psychodramatic representation helps people free themselves from their delusional systems. At first the auxiliaries are an extension of the protagonists' delusional systems, but the more frequently the protagonists can have or experience their auxiliary representations, the more easily they can let them go. They can relinquish them as extensions of themselves and see them as real people. They can finish their unfinished business.

To understand the dynamics of psychodrama, it is necessary to be aware of what is being played out on the psychodramatic stage, in particular *tele, act hunger, open tension systems, auto poesis, concretization* and the attendant *psychodramatic trance.*

Tele

We have all met people whom we seem to know and understand immediately, without even speaking. We encounter people with whom we are instinctively comfortable, and others from whom we instinctively remove ourselves. Such nonverbal responses are a part of tele, or a sort of telepathic sensory awareness.

Tele is characterized by Moreno as the simplest unit of feeling between two people. It is two-way empathy, a sensing the reality of who someone else is; it is the bonding that holds people together. It is *not* transference. The tele connection enacted within the psychodrama enables protagonists to remain within their own psychic reality by giving it shape, definition and connection.

Tele is a reciprocal process; it flows in two directions, describing the sense of connectedness between two people. In a group situation, cohesion is measured by the strength and number of reciprocal pairs, and tele is experienced as a feeling of nonverbal understanding—a sense of being seen and understood by another person.

Tele in action assumes a willingness to play the auxiliary role, combining both thinking and emotions in support of the protagonist's surplus reality so that he does not become detached from his own experience. Tele in action opens the door to trust by providing a real surrogate with whom to explore and test connections in reality. Tele allows the bringing of a delusional system into the here-and-now for examination, making the unconscious material conscious through experience in action so that it can be lived through again and resolved.

Act Hunger

The longing to take action toward completion is *act hunger*. Like the repetition compulsion, it can become a ritualized reenactment of the unsatisfied hunger. It stems from painful experiences, and not from pleasurable ones, for it is a manifestation of the psyche's desire to bring the trauma to a conscious level so that it can be mastered. Until it has been worked through or mastered, the painful experience is repeated, pressing for discharge through action.

Being engaged in a cycle of the repetition can actually be seen as a positive sign because it denotes an attempt at resolution. Sometimes referred to in the addictions field as "a cry for help," it manifests an inner desire to know the contents of the psyche fully, a wish that "the spirit be made flesh." The demand for action, the act hunger or the repetition compulsion supersedes the pleasure principle. If they go unresolved, they can preclude the enjoyment of pleasure.

Psychodrama offers a unique opportunity to personalize act hungers through the use of auxiliary egos, who play the roles necessary to bring the original situation into a concrete form. If the drive and need are sated in the enactment of the psychodrama, the behavior can be diminished. The psyche or brain accepts the auxiliaries as real, allowing the protagonist to rework the traumatic experience and become re-empowered. The psychodramatic enactment provides a context, and it allows the event to be restored in the psyche in a corrected, finished form, so that it no longer exists in a state of numbness or open tension.

Open Tension Systems

Open tensions systems are unresolved, open-ended experiences that we carry around in our psyches. According to Umberto Maturara, the brain operates on the principle of organizational closure: that is, it always seeks to fill in or finish the picture. If a situation comes to a satisfactory resolution, the brain has closure.

Each of us is an independent biological system complete onto itself, governed by the principle of organizational closure: we seek a state of closure and completeness so that we can live. If we fail to come to a satisfactory closure of an event, we are left with fear and anxiety. The brain tries to force closure so that it can live, and it will close well or badly because that is its nature: that is, it will close around whatever is there to close around, whether the conclusions arrived at by extrapolation from it are healthy and well organized or chaotic. Psychodrama, which offers the protagonist a way to re-enact an unsatisfactory, unresolved situation and complete it in the present, can help to resolve open tension systems.

Autopoesis

Autopoesis is our state of being alive in the environment. Whatever we do is triggered by our interaction with the environment, or the environment interacting with us; our reaction is a compensation designed to maintain our balance, or our state of being alive in the environment. While *autopoesis* is not a psychodramatic concept per se, it helps to illustrate why the dynamics of psychodrama mirror the dynamics of life.

Concretization

The purpose of the psychodramatic enactment is to *concretize* or give dimension and space to the intrapsychic drama of the protagonist. The drama gives the protagonist real people to deal with rather than imagined ones. What he has held in the form of ideas, body memories and flashbacks can be played out on the psychodramatic stage through the use of auxiliaries.

This process of concretization is, in itself, healing and cathartic. Simply to expose our inner reality in the present moment and in space brings it to a conscious level where it can be seen, felt and dealt with in new ways.

The nature of the psychodramatic enactment is to make the protagonist the center of his own drama. It offers him an opportunity to gain a sense of mastery over what has been inside, in order to achieve inner harmony. In the concretization the "inner spectator" is wiped away, and the protagonist becomes all action in the midst of act hunger. Situations in which the protagonist may have felt powerless or invisible are reproduced on the stage as they were originally experienced, so that he can explore his reality, truth and experience without having to entertain and work through other points of view at the same time. It is an opportunity to meet fully and deal with inner dimensions—act hungers, repetition compulsions, fantasies and dreams. It is a chance to make real what has felt unreal and to bring to the conscious level what has been swimming around the unconscious in a formless, shapeless state.

The entire process of concretization is designed to pull the surplus reality out of the psyche of the protagonist and to place it on the stage where it can be moved through in a safe and clinically appropriate manner. The warm-up process helps to bring it forward to the conscious level in the mind of the protagonist; the enactment puts it onto the stage, transforming the then-and-there to the here-and-now.

Psychodramatic Trance

When the "as if" falls away to "as" in a psychodrama, the protagonist may enter a psychodramatic trance state somewhat akin to a dream state. According to the "era-sure" theory put forward by Crick and Mitchinson, the activity of the dream state allows the brain system to "rid itself of its parasitic oscillations . . . [and] along with these would go unwanted memories, especially those of a potentially pathological nature such as obsessions, hallucinations, and delusions." J. Allan Hobson writes, ". . . we not only appreciate dreams as they happen to us, but can actively enter into our dream experience. We can enhance recall and even change plots so they become more enjoyable." During psychodramatic trance we may have the opportunity actually to alter our memory of experience and focus new learning as we almost walk through a waking dream. And it is this writer's belief that what occurs during this state in terms of brain repatterning accounts in part for psychodrama's mysterious healing potential.

When we experience a traumatic event, we have a tendency to freeze. When we freeze, our brains do not function normally. We are not understanding or knowing the experience and integrating it. As a result, when the experience is triggered, a full integrated memory cannot come back; what comes back is the unresolved state of frozen needs. Thus in a psychodrama it is important that the environment and action be safe so that when the trauma surfaces, it can actually be experienced and felt, known, understood and integrated.

THE PSYCHODRAMATIC THEORY
OF DEVELOPMENT

Moreno outlined four major stages of development related in name to his action roles: the double, the mirror, the auxiliary ego and role reversal. The stage of the *double* begins to build our core as we move through the *mirror*, or the stage at which information from the outside contributes to the formation of the self. Next comes the stage of the *auxiliary ego*, the dawning of an awareness of separateness: we become aware that the world is not only an extension of our self, but is also shared by other people who are completely apart from our self. After this comes the stage of *role reversal*. This is the beginning of empathy, when we are truly able to stand in the shoes of another person and see the world as they might see it.

Psychodrama integrates a variety of approaches—cognitive, emotional and behavioral—that offer the opportunity to integrate these elements of the self. The three parts of a person's personality are the *director* (who controls action), the *spectator* (who monitors it) and the *actor* (who does it). Psychodrama offers a stage on which full participation of all these parts can take place.

We live in a context. As children we do not develop in isolation; we are members of a system of people and relationships that live, always, within our psyches in some measure, and that we are influenced by and that we influence. In the same way, the developmental stages are not discrete, and though we need to deal with them fully and fulfill them, we never fully outgrow them. All of these stages remain functioning and present for us as adults.

People who have passed satisfactorily through the developmental stages as children will know when these areas are not operating well as adults and will set about to reorganize their lives to fill in the gaps. People who have not passed through them satisfactorily will experience confusion over many issues. As Robert Siroka says, "They will experience an inner void, a lack of sense of self, an anxiety that seems to have no foundation, a hunger that cannot and sometimes will not be fed." They will push away what they need, not because they are full, but because they are starving: just as victims of starvation must begin to take in a little food at a time, people seeking to recover unfinished developmental stages need to do so slowly, so that the material can be digested.

The Developmental Stage Of The Double

Psychodrama calls the initial stage of development the stage of *the double*. This is a period in which the child's self is undifferentiated from the self of the mother or primary caregiver. It is a seemingly timeless period of oneness and unity, a flowing in and out of energy. The baby feels as if the parent were a true extension of herself. Closeness to the parent or caregiver is all important. This is the stage of "marsupial mothering." At this stage of development, a mother, father or caretaker senses the need of the baby to be almost in a pouch (to address this need we now have front packs, backpacks and side packs in which to carry infants). The natural rhythm of the parent becomes the beat by which the child lives; the parent's voice, sound, smell, breathing and feelings are shared by the baby, taken in as if there were no beginning or ending between the two.

This is how humans learn to trust. When the baby is hungry, food is provided; when the baby is wet, loving hands make her dry and comfortable; when the baby hurts, attempts are made to alleviate her pain; when she needs comfort, gentle hands caress him and a soft voice coos to her. Thus she learns trust—and if these things happen often enough for the child's development to progress in a healthy way, she has had, as D. W. Winnicott puts it, a "good enough parent." When they do not happen enough, children learn to see the world as unable to understand them and unwilling to meet their needs; sometimes they feel that their needs are unmeetable and incomprehensible to others.

During the first few months of life, the human infant feels undifferentiated from the rest of the cosmos. There is a sense of oneness, no "I-You" relationship—no sense of any person, place or thing that has a position outside the perceiver. The double in the first universe is really an extension of the infant, but it encourages a bond. Later the double is an internalized sense of being seen, understood and learned through the compassionate care of the parent or caretaker.

The Developmental Stage Of The Mirror

The mirror supplies information from the outside, not necessarily congruent with an inner voice. If the mirroring is sensitive, it can provide a safe crossing from the self to the larger group or society, helping us to understand not just how we see ourselves on the inside, but how we are perceived by others. If the mirroring is harsh and punitive, it distorts the pathway from the self to the outer object; it is difficult for a child to experience and understand himself in the larger context when feedback from the outside world feels judgmental and threatening.

If a child has been sufficiently doubled within the family, he can effectively use mirroring as it comes to him. When the mirroring is sensitive—when what is said strikes a chord within—he feels a sense of connectedness, of being seen and understood by the world outside. If harsh things are said that feel consistently incongruent with his inner feelings, he develops a sense of never being seen as he is and feels unable to connect to or satisfy outside expectations. His sense of self is slowly eroded, and his connection to the world is weakened.

Mirroring plays an important role in how the growing, changing child learns to perceive himself.. In the same way that two-year-olds work so hard for physical independence, saying, "I can do it myself," adolescents work for emotional independence or a differentiated self. Their cry is clear: "I am not you"—not my hair, my clothes, my likes and dislikes, my friends. And as we give two-year-olds age-appropriate tasks to develop their sense of autonomy, adolescents need age-appropriate responsibilities and freedoms to develop their separateness.

The two-year-old is saying, "Let my body be separate," let me lift my own fork to my mouth and move my own chair to sit on. The adolescent is saying, "Let my self be separate," let me follow my own course of action, pursue my own likes and dislikes, and experience life through a self that is centered, not within my parents, but within me. If a society is restrictive, an adolescent need not act "far out" in order to differentiate; in a permissive society he must go a little further to differentiate himself from the norm. The adolescent must make the break in order to seek a rapprochement or to return as a separate person whole onto himself.

The Auxiliary Ego As A Developmental Stage

The developmental stage of the auxiliary ego heralds the child's awareness of "the other," of something beyond his narcissistic needs and wishes. He has a dawning awareness that the world is filled with other people who are separate from the self. And if he has been adequately doubled and mirrored, he has developed a strong enough sense of self to be able to empathize with the other.

Through successful doubling, children learn that they are not alone and that the universe is a friendly place where their needs are seen and met; they learn that self is a place within, from which they can gain sustenance and grounding and from which they are free to come and go without its disappearing. In its turn sensitive mirroring provides safe passage from the inner world of the double to the outer world of the other; it provides the child reflections and information about the self that he can use in patterning himself to fit into a social network.

Then, with awareness of the other comes an ability to live as a being among beings, to take one's place as a member of society. By this time the ego should be strong enough to tolerate the "slings and arrows that the flesh is heir to." The child has learned to choose and be chosen, to give and take and to have compassion for those other than himself. He has learned that his point of view is not the only point of view, and that balance, empathy and fair play are required to live happily among others. The stage of the auxiliary ego is a stage of entering into society, having internalized the double or the home, the mirroring or the reflected self, and taking those secure awarenesses into the world at large.

The Stage Of Role Reversal

The stage of role reversal comes when the self is complete and separate enough so that the individual is able to stand on his own and face another, for it is only then that a person is truly able to stand in the shoes of another.

A person who is able to reverse roles is in a position to balance his needs, desires and wishes with those of another, recognizing that people are not islands unto themselves but live in the context of others. It is the time, as Moreno says, when "I will see you through your eyes and you will see me through mine." More than empathy, however, it is the ability to feel and experience momentarily from a position outside one's self, even to look back at one's self from there. It is one of the purest forms of communication between two people because one is not only communicating from one's self to another, but from the interior of the self, one can stand beside another self and communicate as one. (This only really works when the self of each person is intact and the boundaries of each personality are well in place.)

To reverse roles is not to disappear into the self of another. Rather it is to enter willingly into the heart and eyes of another person, to see the world from the point of view from which he might see it, knowing it to be a journey inward and then back out again, a momentary visit into another universe.

This stage of role reversal, then, is one in which the self has been sufficiently developed and accommodated so that it can tolerate a temporary journey from itself. It is an ultimate act of trust, not necessarily in the other, but in the sense of solidity and solidarity within the self. Role reversal enables people to see life and themselves from another perspective: "The son, who is still himself," says Zerka Moreno, "must now warm up to how his mother may be feeling and perceiving himself; the mother, now the son, goes through the same process."

The Stages In The Psychodramatic Enactment

All the major elements of development are built into psychodramatic treatment: the double, the mirror, the auxiliary ego and role reversal. The double, for instance, supports the inner experience of the protagonist, or a new double is created within the psychodrama if the person's original double was less than sat-isfactory. Also the psychodramatic action itself acts as the double as it joins unquestioningly the reality of the protagonist.

After the action, the doubling continues as people share iden-tifications evoked in them, either as players or as witnesses to the action. Mirroring comes into play as others share with the protag-onist a variety of different images of the action. The stage of the auxiliary ego, or the other-than-self, becomes illuminated while, in the course of group interaction or sharing, the protagonist comes to the realization that there are things happening for peo-ple that have nothing to do with her, are completely separate from her own experience and do not reflect upon her in any way. This is part of the developmental stage of separation.

After the protagonist has successfully assimilated these stages and established an inner anchor, she may be able to reverse roles with another in the group, to leave herself behind momentarily and adopt the role of another person. This is part of the stage of rapprochement, the moving away from and returning to the moth-er or caregiver. In this way the client learns to temporarily put herself into the shoes of another without becoming the other.

A need to *see* the self in action may be met through using a per-son who functions, literally, as the client's "mirror." Moreno writes, "When a patient is unable to represent himself, in word or action, an auxiliary ego is placed on the action portion of the psy-chodramatic space . . . The auxiliary ego represents the patient, copying his behavior and trying to express feelings in word and movement, showing the patient 'as if in a mirror' how others might experience him."

The mirror can be a powerful technique for protagonists who are unable to tolerate the intensity of playing themselves in a drama and who need to feel one step removed in order to feel safe. It provides an opportunity to view from a less heated posi-tion, and with the support of the director, a traumatic or perplex-ing event. It can also allow protagonists to gain perspective on their own behavior by watching rather than being.

Role reversal is perhaps one of the most important elements of true psychodrama. It allows protagonists not only to project onto or empathize with another person (the auxiliary ego) in their dra-mas, but to actually experience being that person. Not only does this increase their understanding of the other, but it also allows them to view themselves from the other person's position.

When the child is safely centered in her own skin, she will have passed through the stage of the auxiliary ego. She is a separate ego and is now able to reverse roles with the "other." In this new-found ability to be a separate person able to empathize or reverse roles with another person without becoming them, that is with the self remaining intact, a closeness can take place that was not possible before.

When we are not able to pass through these stages of individuation, we go through life as an incorporation of the parent, ever feeling a need to attach to any object outside ourselves, person, place or thing. This, of course, is co-dependency, or the undifferentiated self looking for a self to attach itself to. In treating co-dependency it is necessary to return to the stage of the double and work through the double, mirror, auxiliary ego and role reversal, reconstructing and reliving what did not fully happen. The group is crucial at some point in this process, because it is in an arena of people that we live our lives.

Page 19: We operate in life . . . R. Siroka, Psychodrama Training Institute, New York, 1993.

Page 21: Moreno defined role as . . . J. Fox (ed.), *The Essential Moreno: Writings on Psychodrama Group Method and Spontaneity by J. L. Moreno, M.D.* (New York: Springer, 1987).

Page 30: According to Umberto Maturana . . . Cuernavaca, Mexico, October 1990.

Page 32: Moreno outlined four major stages . . . R. Siroka, Psychodrama Training Institute, New York City (19 West 34th Street), 1988.

Page 33: "They will experience an inner void . . . R. Siroka, Psychodrama Training Institute, New York City (19 West 34th Street), 1988.

Page 33: a "good enough parent . . ." D. W. Winnicott, *The Child, the Family and the Outside World*, New York: Pelican Books, 1964.

Page 34: It becomes difficult . . . R. Siroka, Psychodrama Training Institute, New York City (19 West 34th Street), 1988.

Page 35: A child who is adequately doubled . . . R. Siroka, Psychodrama Training Institute, New York City (19 West 34th Street), 1990.

Page 36:   "I will see you . . . ." J. L. Moreno, *Psychodrama: vol. 1*, Beacon, NY: Beacon House, 1946.

Page 36:   "The son, who . . ." J. L. Moreno, *Sociometry and the Science of Men*. Beacon, NY: Beacon House, 1950, p. 241.

Page 37:   "When a patient . . ." Ibid., p. 240.

Page 37:   Role reversal is perhaps . . . Z. Moreno, Highland Park, NY: Lecture, July 3, 1990.

3
Sociometry: How Psychodrama Works

and if i ever touched a life,
i hope that life knows that i know that
touching was and still is and always
will be the true revolution.
—nikki giovanni

Though J. L. Moreno is most remembered for creating the "science" of psychodrama, he felt that his greatest contribution was sociometry, which is essentially the science beneath the science, or the empirical study underlying the effectiveness of psychodrama. Moreno felt that working through sociometric alignments was where true healing lay.

An essential element of sociometry is its overt incorporation of projection and transference, which it takes as a given. It takes into account the projection and transference that arise inevitably in a group. And it provides for the playing out of projections psychodramatically, as group members play out the roles of significant others.

41

Sociometric exercises done in a group are designed to make the unconscious dynamics of the group become conscious. And asking specific questions that involve specific answers is one of the active aspects of sociometry: "Whom should I choose to play an old friend?" "Who intimidates me?" or "Which person would I like to know better?" The questions are powerful and threatening, and would only be used in a group where members are ready to confront one another honestly in order to grow both individually and as a group. Moreno notes that these exercises have wide significance: "The number of interrelations among these individuals (in human society) influence the total world situation in some manner, however slight."

Sociometry also explores the roles we choose in a situation and the way in which we play them, as well as parallel phenomena in the world at large. Essentially, we bring our full interior sociometry (our internalized original cast of characters and states of relatedness with them) to any situation, and that particular sense of who we are in relationship to others interacts with another's interior sociometry. Psychodrama always sees a person in his full sociometric context, even in a one-to-one therapeutic situation, and even as an isolate in a context. None of us was born by himself into nothing; we were all born into the larger group.

We can most easily understand sociometry as a science dealing with the connectedness or lack of connectedness among people. It moves from the vast connections between nation and nation, race and race, sect and sect, to that between two people. The system of attractions and repulsions, the vast network of interrelations and the dispassionate reporting of the quality, intensity and type of connections between people is the work of the sociometrist. *Tele*, the simplest sort of feeling between people, is at play in the understanding of the connectedness between people (Chapter 2, The Elements Of Psychodrama, discusses tele in more detail). The level of identification is a strong component of why we choose certain people and why we do not choose or are actively repelled by others.

Sociometry, though appearing complex, is actually simple, for it is the study of *what is*—the observation of attractions and repulsions on all levels of social interaction, from the family to the classroom to society at large. Further, it is analyzing the data gathered from that study to see what might work best in organizations from family systems to schools to corporations to government. If we organize ourselves according to mutual attraction (special interest groups), will things run more smoothly? If we are able to allow maximum flexibility within these organizations, will we then be able to engage more of the person and encounter less resistance?

HOW SOCIOMETRY WORKS IN GROUP THERAPY

Our sociometric alignments resurface in the group therapy situation.

We carry our attractions and repulsions with us from group to group; also our alignments and our assessments of sociometric status. Our assessments of our sociometric status are represented by the roles we assume, and role-playing is the enactment of those roles. And to the extent that our assessments are real and accurate, so is our sense of being well-related.

Children play this out naturally. In grade school they have layers of friends—first best, second best, third best and so on. In adolescence they constantly compete for more subtle forms of status, based not only on personal choice but also on acceptance by the group at large. Those chosen "most popular" have qualities most group members wish they had, or that best embody the values of the group. Or they may be chosen because they act out for the group somewhat antisocial behavior. As the values of the group shift and mature, the social structure shifts, as do the people unconsciously chosen by the group to represent them.

Sociometric theory can be applied on several levels:

1. *In the mind of the therapist.* The therapist is constantly observing and assessing attractions, repulsions, mutual pairs and the various levels of interrelatedness with the group.

2. *The leader can use the family-of-origin social atom as a tool to ground early work.* Each member makes a social atom of his family of origin (social atoms are discussed later in this chapter), shares it, works it through in action and uses it as a reference point when powerful feelings are aroused in or out of the group. The group member can ask, "Who is this person representing for me from my original social atom?"

3. *The leader can ask the group sociometric questions that further illuminate the above two points.* For example, "Who in this group could play your sister (mother, father, grandparent)? Who do you feel a kinship to in this group? Who most bewilders you? With whom might you be guarded in what you say? With whom would you open your heart?" Once choices are made (by walking over to the person and placing a hand on his shoulder), each choice can be shared with the person chosen—the inner workings of the chooser or the feelings of the chosen.

4. *The leader can explore sociometric questions on behalf of a group member.* Such questions might include "Where am I on this continuum? How close or how far do I wish specific people to be from me? How and whom do I choose or not choose? Why? What are the origins of the attractions and repulsions that influence my choosing on the outside, affect the inner organization of my self-system and vice-versa?"

In psychodramatic enactment, we explore roles that we play with one another: the mother talks to the daughter, the husband to the wife and so on. Many of our personal self-definitions are wrapped around a particular role. When we work with the role, we shift the internalized criteria and attached feelings. As Siroka said, "The role is the enactment of a status within the system. Consequently any role work is by nature a systems intervention."

THE BASIC TENETS OF SOCIOMETRY

Sociometry, according to Moreno, incorporates the following basic tenets and naturally follows along these lines:

- *The Sociogenetic Law:* The highest forms of group organization have evolved from simple ones.
- *The Sociodynamic Law:* The income of choices is unevenly distributed among members of a collectivity, regardless of the size of the group or its kind. (Groups tend to be stratified with respect to relevant sociometric criteria rather than fairness.)
- *The Sociodynamic Effect:* There is an unequal distribution of choices among people in the group—the chosen get chosen more, and the isolated will be more isolated. The

over-chosen individuals will accumulate a surplus of choices if the number of permitted choices are increased.

• *The Law of Social Gravitation:* People from one community will move toward people of another community in direct proportion to the amount of attraction given and received, and in inverse proportion to the rejection. The process of differentiation draws the groups apart; the process of transmission and communication draws the groups together.

• *Group Cohesion:* The larger the number of mutual pairs, the higher will be the rate of mutual interaction and the probability of a high group cohesion. The larger the number of individuals involved in positive tele communications, the greater the group cohesion.

THE SOCIAL ATOM

The social atom is a diagram or picture that represents the nucleus of all individuals toward whom we are emotionally related. The study of these atoms and their interrelations is important in understanding the relationships we have with the significant people in our lives; hence it is of great significance in any attempt to understand and modify personality disorders.

A social atom offers the opportunity for us to see ourselves. This clear, concise and objective feedback to the self helps to bypass our resistance because it is in fact produced by us. It is a useful referent for change if done every so often throughout the treatment process. We can use it as a guide toward that change by asking questions like, "What would I like to be different on my social atom? What aspects of this might I choose to change? What are the parts of my social atom that I am bringing from my childhood into the present that might not be helpful today?"

The social atom is useful both in individual therapy and in a group context. Used collectively, clients may take time to do it on their own and may share it, either with the large group or in smaller subgroups. It can be shared in the past or in the present moment. For example, a person who is doing a social atom of herself as a child may wish to share it from the position of that child: "I am eight and this is my mother." Social atoms are an extremely flexible and adaptable tool of measurement that can be helpful in exploring a wide variety of circumstances.

Figure 3.1. Notational System For Social Atoms*

◯	=	female
△	=	male
☐	=	genderless (to represent problem, obstacle, pet and so on)
◌	=	deceased female
△ (dashed)	=	deceased male
———	=	mutual attraction
- - - - -	=	mutual rejection
··········	=	mutual indifference

* This is the most basic notational system; many more variations are possible. For more information, see Chapter Notes. *Conducting Clinical Sociometric Explorations: A Manual for Psychodramatists and Sociometrists,* Royal Publishing Co., Roanoke, VA. James Vander May, "A Perceptual Social Atom Sociogram," in Anne E. Hale, ed., vol. 28 (1975), 128-134.

SOCIAL ATOM

Goals

1. To make conscious the unconscious patterns of repulsion and attraction that form a person's social network.

2. To provide a map of interrelations that the leader and group member can refer to throughout the treatment process.

Steps

1. Have participants get pencil and paper.

2. Tell them to make an atom of their current lives. Say, "Using circles to represent females and triangles to represent males, first locate yourself on the paper, anywhere that feels right to you."

3. Continue, "Now locate your important relationships or significant tele relations as close or distant from yourself as you feel them to be, and in the size or proportion that feels right. You may include pets, in-laws, grandparents, friends and so on. Use a broken line to represent anyone who is deceased. Write the name of each person next to their symbol."

4. Once all the symbols are on paper and the atoms feel finished, people can begin to share them, either in the large group, with a partner, in small groupings, or with the therapist one-to-one. Remind them that these atoms are only a current reflection, they are always subject to change.

5. Sharing the atom may bring up many feelings toward or about those present on the atom, and in reference to clarifying the reality of the interrelationships, the attractions, repulsions and relative size and importance. Allow plenty of time for sharing all these potentially strong feelings.

6. After the sharing is complete, you may (a) move the social atoms into action (see Action Sociogram, as follows), or (b) keep them and refer to them as a measurement of growth.

Variations

1. *Family-of-origin atom*. It is useful for clients to make family-of-origin social atom. They can share it from the present point of view ("This is me when I was eight, and this is how I saw my father") or as if it were in the present ("I am eight and this is my father"). This helps to make the past current. You can also move the atom into an action sociogram (discussed later in this chapter). Clients may keep these social atoms and use them as treatment maps or referents for resolving life transferences. For example, the therapist can say, "Who is this person for you on your social atom and what do you have to say to him?"

2. *Developmental atom*. People can make developmental social atoms representing various stages of life—as a child, adolescent, teenager, young adult, householder, elder and so on—in order to examine any stage along the way when development was impaired.

3. *Sober vs. nonsober*. Participants who were raised in addicted families can make atoms showing how their family life was organized while the addict was sober, and how it was organized while the addict was using. (Chapter 11, Using Psychodrama With Addicts And ACoAs, discusses special issues of this group.)

4. *Food atom*. Participants can locate themselves on an atom along with people, places, things and actual foods, so that connections can be made between eating patterns and how they get triggered.

5. *Sex atom*. Participants can make atoms that locate them in relation to sexual encounters that feel significant and that have formed their overall attitudes about sex.

6. *Substance atom*. Participants can make atoms that locate them in relation to any substance, person, place, or thing that might be used compulsively or addictively—work, cocaine, sex, food, exercise, cigarettes and so on—so that connections can be made between compulsive or addictive patterns and how they are triggered. (Chapter 11, Using Psychodrama With Addicts And ACoAs, discusses special issues of this group.)

7. *Medicator atom*. Participants can make atoms locating themselves and around them anything they might use to medicate feelings—from Valium to television to work or busyness—in order to gain insight into how these are used and how much they take over their lives.

8. *Cross-cultural atom*. People from two cultures can make cross-cultural atoms—one representing how they operate in their own culture as compared with another representing how they operate or who they are in their adopted culture, and their relative positions and sociometry in each culture. They can first locate themselves then around them the important players or aspects of the particular culture.

9. *Adoption atom*. Protagonists who are adopted may wish to make fantasy atoms of their birth parents, just to see what they carry inside, or an atom of their birth parents when the protagonist was born.

10. *Parents' atom*. Making a parents' atom can be a powerful tool when made for a time during which the parents' life situation may have complicated the life of the protagonist. It is also useful to make a parents' social atom at the time of their marriage, or at the time of the birth of the protagonist. Making generational atoms like these can help people reconstruct their history and illuminate what was passed down through the family system.

11. *Parent-child atom*. Parents who are having difficulty with a child at a particular time can make a social atom of what their own life was like at the age that their child is at present, in order to separate their own history from what they perceive to be their child's problems.

12. *A high and a clean atom*. Recovering addicts can make a

"high" social atom reflecting relationships when they are using their substance and a "clean" one when they are abstaining. Then they can compare those two atoms. Chapter 11, Using Psychodrama With Addicts And ACoAs, discusses special issues of these groups.

13. *A wish atom.* Participants can make atoms representing their social atoms as they wish they were.

14. *A fantasy atom.* Participants can make atoms representing their fantasies, first locating themselves on a piece of paper and then locating their various fantasies as close to and as far from the self as feels right, along with their size and intensity as compared with the self.

15. *Generational social atoms.* These can be useful in looking at the ways in which habits of behavior and mind are passed down from generation to generation. It may be useful for a client to make a personal psychological social atom; she can also make social atoms for various times of her development, for one or both parents and for siblings at the time of the birth of the client and at other significant periods. The client can make her parents' social atom at the time of their marriage or at a time that was particularly traumatic for her, in order to elucidate what might have been going on in her parents' lives at difficult times in her life.

These are some suggestions. The social atom can be adapted in any way that feels useful and appropriate.

Reading The Social Atom

Most people have from five to twenty-five people on their present-day atoms. A person who has less than five may be depressed. A person who has more than twenty-five or thirty may have more superficial relationships and fewer close ones. These amounts only apply to atoms of one's current life.

Here are some things to look for when you read a social atom:
1. *Erasures, changes.* These indicate that there is unfinished business or anxiety where the dramas will need to be explored.
2. *Large and distant images.* These are concerns with authority figures.
3. *Small and distant images.* These tend to represent negative transferences or competitive sibling figures, particularly if they are very small.

4. *Overlaps.* These may indicate relationships in need of differentiation, if they are not otherwise explained.
5. *Horizontal or vertical bisections.* If a vertical or horizontal line bisects a symbol, note whether there is a difference between what's on the left and on the right in the eyes of the client: for example, past and present, male and female.
6. *Omission.* Is there anyone who is conspicuous by her omission or absence?
7. *Multiple lines.* Look for anxiety connected with that relationship.

ACTION SOCIOGRAM

The action sociogram is a social atom that is put into action. After a protagonist has completed her social atom, she is invited to put it on the stage. The full social atom or a portion of it can be cast by choosing members of the group to play the necessary auxiliary roles. The protagonist may wish to begin by reversing roles with the people on her atom in order to role train or to show the auxiliary egos how the people appeared in real life or to her. The protagonist may interact wherever she feels drawn, or she may wish to mill around among the characters to discover at what point she is prompted to address someone on her atom—and then to do so. From this point the techniques of role reversal and doubling can be brought into play wherever appropriate. (See Chapter 4, The Techniques Of Psychodramatic Enactment).

This family-of-origin social atom provides a map of the original cast of characters to which both the therapist and the client can refer, when needed, throughout the therapeutic process. If there is a strong transference within the group, the therapist might ask, "Who is this person representing for you on your original social atom?" and they can work out the transference from there (for example, "What do you need to say to that person?"). The action sociogram provides a concrete picture, both in the mind and on the stage, helping the protagonist to better understand where she came from. The social atom is the visible constellation of the tele range of an individual; the nucleus of all individuals to whom a person is emotionally related at the same time. It reaches as far as tele reaches and it represents relationships that are near, far, alive and dead. It is the sum of interpersonal structures resulting from the choices and rejections of a given individual.

The following are different levels of social atoms:

1. *The psychological social atom.* This social atom is composed of the people who are most intimately connected with us, with whom we have the strongest tele connection. It represents, visually, an individual's tele range.

2. *The individual social atom.* This atom represents the smallest number of people we require to be in balance. It changes as our level of spontaneity changes.

3. *The collective social atom.* This atom represents the smallest number of groups and collectives that we require to be in balance. It includes the formal structures that provide us with opportunities to express various sides of ourselves, such as family, job, school or hobby groups. It can be called the cultural atom.

4. *Emotional expansiveness.* On any given atom, these are the people with whom we have some emotional recognition and connection. Emotional expansiveness measures the emotional energy that enables the individual to "hold" the affection of other individuals for a given period of time.

5. *Social expansiveness.* On any given atom, there are people with whom we are not intimately connected but nevertheless feel a tele connection; they are more than distant acquaintances.

6. *Acquaintance volume.* This might represent anyone with whom we have come into contact and become acquainted with. The acquaintance test measures the volume of "social" expansion of an individual, or the range of his or her social contacts. Social expansiveness differs from emotional expansiveness. On any given atom, there may be people with whom we are acquainted though not connected, reflecting by their number the range, but not the depth, of our emotions.

ACTION SOCIOGRAM

Goals

1. To concretize the social atom.
2. To offer an opportunity for interaction with real people.

Steps

1. Ask group members to draw their social atoms.

2. Choose a protagonist, then ask the protagonist to choose a person or various people to play any one role or various roles, depending upon how elaborate you wish the psychodrama to be.

3. If you feel the auxiliaries need to find out more about their roles, you may ask the protagonist to reverse roles and show the group a little of what the roles are like.

4. Ask the protagonist either to go where he is drawn to interact or to mill around the whole picture until he feels drawn to a particular person—at which point he may begin to speak to that person.

5. Allow the protagonist, if he wishes, to step out of the picture and take a full view of the setup and see how that feels. He may even wish to choose someone to play himself and watch his own drama, reversing roles with himself or doubling for himself where motivated.

6. Move through the enactment, allowing the protagonist to express his feelings freely to any and all characters, using all techniques appropriate, such as role reversal, doubling, interviewing and so on. (See Chapter 4, The Techniques Of Psychodramatic Enactment).

7. Ask the protagonist to finish the scene in any way he wishes including, if he wishes, "correcting" the scene by structuring it as he wishes it had been. You may offer him the choice of having "reformed auxiliaries" in order to get what he wishes he had had—he can ask for what he needs and receive it.

8. Leave plenty of time for sharing what came up for group members and what the auxiliaries felt while playing the various roles.

Variations

Protagonists may wish to warm up by walking around the "sculpture" (see Chapter 4, The Techniques Of Psychodramatic Enactment, for details on doing family sculptures) and soliloquizing about the feelings they are experiencing. They may wish to end the enactment in the same manner or simply back up and talk to the sculpture at large for closure.

It may be useful to include intergenerational scenes to gain perspective on the generational chain of dysfunction and to promote understanding that parents, for example, passed on what they got from their own parents, concretizing a chain of dysfunction composed of learned behavior patterns. Thus clients are helped to feel less singled out for abuse and realize that they were victims of generational patterns. It also empowers them to choose to do things differently.

SPECTROGRAM

Goals

1. To make unconscious material conscious.
2. To provide a method of action sociometry.

Steps

1. Draw an imaginary line dividing the room down the middle, showing group members where it is as you do so.

2. Tell participants that each end of the room represents an extreme and that the bisecting line is the midpoint between, for example, hot and cold, comfortable and uncomfortable, very much and very little, good and bad or one and ten.

3. Now ask a series of questions that apply to your particular subject criteria and ask participants to locate themselves at whatever point along the continuum that best describes their response to the question. For example, say that one side of the room represents very good and the other very bad, with the midpoint represented by the line, and the question is, "How are you feeling about your work life?" The person who was recently fired might go to the extreme edge of the very bad side, while the person for whom work is not an issue might stand close to either side of the midpoint.

4. Allow people to share spontaneously feelings that come up for them while doing this, either with one another or with the group at large.

5. Continue to share feelings within the group at large.

Variations

Use questions that are relevant to anything that will be helpful to the group, for example, "How do you feel in this group? How do you feel about your body? How do you feel about your recovery? How do you feel about your work life, personal life, family relationships?" Such questions bring up information for processing and also allow people to discover shared feelings.

ROLE ANALYSIS

As we have seen, we play many roles in life. We tend to take most of them for granted, but we can bring them to consciousness through role analysis, whether they are past or present.

Feelings and behaviors tend to be role specific—for example, we act one way in the role of parent to our own children and in another way in the role of child to our parents. So when we bring a role to consciousness, we also make conscious the healthy and unhealthy dynamics associated with that role. The following exercise can be used as a warm-up for experiential work, to bring up hungers and tensions associated with a particular role.

Goals

1. To understand more fully the roles we play and how we play them.

2. To examine where we are stuck in our roles and where we can exercise choice.

Steps

1. Ask participants to choose a role that is important in their lives—a primary role, such as wife, husband, mother, father, daughter, son, worker, and so on.

2. Ask them to list the people who see them in this role and are a part of the world around the role—family, in-laws, coworkers, children, friends, and so on.

3. Ask them to make seven separate columns and head them with these words: (1) Rhythm, (2) Taste, (3) Smell, (4) Texture, (5) Sound, (6) Motion.

4. Ask them to list adjectives about the role as they come to

mind in each category, such as stiff, bent, slow, jerky, bitter, sweet, stinky, floral, rough, wet, crazy-making, supportive, hurting, warm.

5. Ask them to make another category called Tensions and list the tensions present in the role—power struggles, financial problems and so on.

6. Ask them to make a final category called Hungers and list what they hunger for in the role—love, understanding, appreciation and so on.

7. Ask them to look at their list, think about what it tells them and share their feelings with a trusted person or with the group.

Page 42:   The number of interrelations . . . J. L. Moreno, 1937, cited
           in Fox, 1987, page. 20.

Page 44:   The role is the enactment . . . R. Siroka, Psychodrama Training
           Institute, New York City (19 West 34th Street), 1990.

Page 44:   The Basic Tenets of Sociometry . . . Quoted by Z. Moyal,
           New York City, Psychodrama Training Institute, Lecture,
           June 10, 1991.

Page 45:   The study of these atoms . . . J. L. Moreno, *Sociometry,
           Experimental Method and the Science of Society,* 1951,
           Beacon, NY: Beacon House.

Page 48:   Sex atom . . . R. Siroka, Psychodrama Training Institute,
           New York City (19 West 34th Street), 1988.

Page 48:   It is also useful . . . Z. Moreno, Highland Park, NY: Lecture,
           November 19, 1988.

Page 50:   It is the sum . . . Z. Moyal, Highland Park, NY: Lecture,
           November 26, 1988.

Page 52:   Acquaintance volume . . . Carol Hollander, *A Process for
           Psychodrama Training: The Hollander Psychodrama Curve.*
           Denver, CO: Snow Line Press, 1978.

4
The Techniques Of Psychodramatic Enactment

*There is a deep meaning
in children's God-playing. As a student
(1908-1911), I walked through the
gardens of Vienna gathering children,
forming groups for impromptu play.
I let children crusade for
themselves for a society of their own
age, their own rights . . .
Children took sides against adults,
grown-ups, social stereotypes, robots, and
for spontaneity and creativity,
I permitted them to play God
if they wanted to. . . .
I began to treat children's problems
by letting them act extemporaneously, a
sort of psychotherapy for fallen Gods.*

—J. L. Moreno

In psychodrama we bring our inner reality outside, where we can take a clear look at it, re-experience it, reframe it and bring it to completion and/or resolution. When we are fully present in the drama, we are no longer watching ourselves, but rather experiencing ourselves. We enter the moment, and the moment has the power to transform us—a moment of catharsis and transformation, a true spiritual awakening. Buddhist thought says that it is only when the mind stops that we can experience true enlightenment—and such a moment occurs in psychodrama when the mind slows down and we become the act itself in space and time, when the "as if" falls away and becomes the "as." For this reason psychodrama has the power to transform us spiritually.

In this chapter the practical aspects of the psychodramatic enactment will be explored—and it should be kept in mind that the context of psychodrama is space which is considered to be a dynamic principle in the therapeutic process. It should be kept in mind also that when the intellect takes over and becomes the primary source of functioning, with no action occurring, the individual's spontaneity is greatly reduced.

In psychodrama space is considered to be a dynamic principle in the therapeutic process. We operate in the context of space at all times: what happens to us occurs in space. In psychodrama, when we explore and rework those situations that we are seeking to illuminate and correct, we simulate the physical situation in which they first occurred; in this way, access to our feeling reality can be as full as possible, with all our senses operating as they do in daily life. The process of *acting out* rather than *talking out* places the intellect in its proper relationship with the senses.

THE STAGES OF PSYCHODRAMA

Moreno delineated three principal stages of a psychodrama: warm-up, enactment and sharing, with a possible fourth stage of analysis. Here we examine them further.

Warm-Up

A warm-up is any clinically responsible discussion or event that brings people to be present in the "here and now" and puts them in touch with their feelings or personal story so that their entry into the enactment phase will feel like a natural step. The purpose of a warm-up is to help clients get truly connected to what they need to work on and the depth to which they wish to go.

A warm-up is not only a set piece: it can consist of whatever works in a clinical setting to allow people to get in touch with their inner feelings. For example, talking about what came up during the week, what was present after the previous group and what is going on in the present are all part of warming up. Other subjects for the warm-up phase may include talking about current social or political issues, describing how one person's issue brought up feelings in another member, any feelings concerning group size, group cohesion, situations that occurred in group and so on. A warm-up engages the brain in a search process. "According to search theory, as with interference theory, forgetting occurs as more and more memories are accumulated without sufficient cues to differentiate among them. Thus it becomes harder and harder to find any one particular item in memory." Therefore the enactment may be a metaphor for an event, a composite memory or an actual event.

You may also use structured exercises and guided imageries. Exercises that focus on particular issues or times in the protagonist's life can be very useful in allowing situations and related feelings to move from semiconsciousness to consciousness. People often experience structured exercises as a sort of "safe passage" between their outer and inner worlds, leading them to inner spaces that they do not normally go to. Anything that allows clients to warm up to their internal reality and encourages them to feel the depth and breadth of the associated feelings can be considered a warm-up.

The sociometric task of the warm-up phase is to clarify the structure of the group by looking at the role relationships within the group. The director observes who is at the sociometric center of the group that day, that is, who represents the central concern of the group and is therefore a sociometric star. In director-selected dramas (discussed in Selecting a Protagonist on page 67), working with that person who is at the sociometric center will accomplish three things: (1) it will enable the group to be more supportive of the action because it is also concretizing some of their own concerns; (2) the work will have sufficient support and identification from the group in order to go deep; and (3) each individual will get personal work done through identification with characters in the drama. If the director chooses an isolate to work with in order to bring that person in, it is best to do that work as a vignette (discussed in Vignettes on page 70) and then move back into the sociometric center of the group.

It should be noted that a protagonist who is too "hot" may experience a useful cathartic release but may also become overwhelmed by emotion. A protagonist who is too "cool" will not be able to engage on an emotional level with the action. An optimum level of warm-up is one at which the protagonist can engage, release and interact in a useful way, at which the cognitive and emotional are both engaged.

Enactment

The enactment, or action phase, is the actual psychodramatic event in which the protagonist's inner reality is structured and enacted on the stage. It creates the opportunity for the expression of all that was left unsaid and for the protagonist's complexes, fantasies, act hungers and open tensions to be explored through action in a safe, structured environment.

The role players or auxiliary egos produce, in the present moment, the interior life and reality of the protagonist. The action has the timeless quality of a dream. It is a metaphor of the protagonist's inner life.

Enactment begins when the director invites the protagonist to choose group members to represent the people from her own life. The director helps the protagonist to set the stage and interact with role players as if they were the real people that they represent. Techniques of talking to the role players, reversing roles and interviewing (discussed below) are all part of an enactment.

Before you can direct a psychodrama, you will need to experience being in them many times, as protagonist, auxiliary ego and audience, in order to become comfortable with the level of intensity that takes place. Participating in the enactment can feel like "time traveling" as you speed through the varied worlds within the psyche that are acted out on the stage. As the director, you will need to have a good deal of experience with your own process so that you can remain fully present with the protagonist, without your own internal process interfering with the work.

Sharing

The sharing phase allows the protagonist to experience being identified with and supported, and it permits group members to express their thoughts and feelings about the action. The director asks participants to share what has emerged for them from their own lives as a result of watching or participating in the action, or to say what they felt while playing an auxiliary ego in the drama.

Sharing is also a way for group members to emerge from their roles and come to closure or to de-role. After a psychodrama the protagonist may feel exposed and vulnerable. When group members share what comes up for them from their own lives through watching or participating in the action, it reduces the isolation of both the protagonist and the participants, and reintegrates the protagonist into the group.

The protagonist should be encouraged to listen and take in what people are sharing as she continues to silently process the feelings that were mobilized as a result of her drama. It's very important for the group members to have ample opportunity to express their feelings fully; it is what makes one person's psychodrama a potentially healing experience for the entire group. The action that has taken place anchors the sharing because group members have shared a common experience. Sharing further connects them through identification with a common situation, and gives each sharer an opportunity for his or her own healing.

Sharing through personal identification also protects the protagonist from any potentially painful mirroring or harsh feedback. It allows the group to heal together through identification and support. It provides a cool-down period after the heat of action, so that people can begin to integrate their learning and normalize their state of mind before re-entering their day-to-day lives. One of the easiest mistakes to make in psychodrama is to allow too little time for sharing. Ideally, it should go on until every feeling possible is out and witnessed by the group.

Analysis

Moreno felt that a stage of analysis should be part of the continued healing, but he never formally incorporated it into the psychodrama process. I include it here with the suggestion that it take place not necessarily as part of the psychodrama process, but in the mind of the therapist. The therapist who remains aware of this portion of the process will be able to insert it wherever it would be most useful to the protagonist in the overall treatment.

Generally, protagonists are in too deep a feeling state—too open and vulnerable—to be able to use this type of cognitive feedback after a drama, and may even experience it as intrusive and unhelpful. When the time is right, however, cognitive information can help protagonists to use the emotional learning and awareness gleaned from the psychodrama and anchor it on a cognitive level. It can help them identify the source of destructive behavior patterns and make conscious whatever complexes they bring from the past that they may not wish to keep in the present. It can also help to empower them to make healthy choices in their current lives.

Analysis is useful if it is timed well, and if it is handled so that it feels helpful and interested, and not judgmental. The most effective analysis arises from the protagonist's own awareness, underlined and reinforced by an observant therapist.

(Figure 4.1 summarizes the stages of a psychodrama.)

THE ELEMENTS OF A PSYCHODRAMA

The main characters in a psychodrama are the director (the therapist), the protagonist, the double, the auxiliary ego or egos, the reformed auxiliary ego and the audience (the therapy group). Here we take a closer look at each of these roles.

The Director

The director of a psychodrama is the professional therapist who leads the warm-up, action and sharing. He also facilitates the choice-making process of the protagonist, the decision involving what material will be examined psychodramatically and how that enactment will take shape in time and space.

The psychodramatic director has three functions: producer, chief therapist, and social analyst. According to Moreno—

Figure 4.1. The Stages Of A Psychodrama

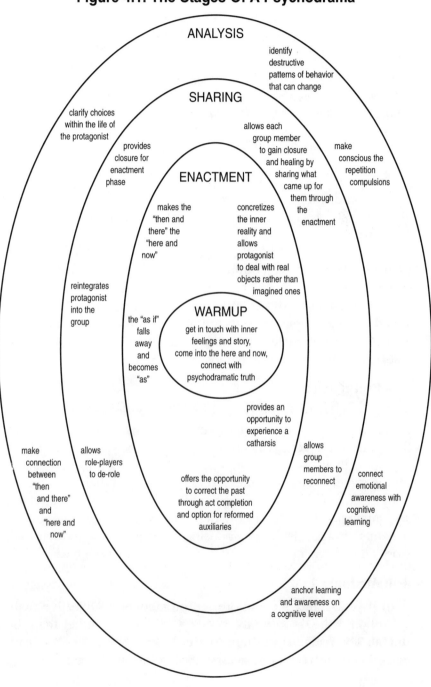

> *The director should work with the minimum expenditure of emotional energy. Once a production has begun he should leave its development to the subject. When and where guidance is required he should leave this to the auxiliary ego co-acting in the scenes. . . . This has the advantage that he is left out of transference and tele relations but he can watch and correct transference and tele relations which develop between the subject and auxiliary egos on the stage in the course of action. . . . There are emergencies, however, when the director has to come to the rescue as a person, but this is considered as an exception.*

The job of the director is to follow the lead of the protagonist in the production of the protagonist's surplus reality, always allowing the protagonist to define that reality as he sees it and being willing to go where the protagonist feels internally led. It is also incumbent upon the director not to "pre-script" the work, but to have ready the skills and knowledge to move quickly and spontaneously into the script that emerges, at times with split-second speed. Obviously prescripting and imposing the director's agenda on the drama prevents the protagonist from enacting what is coming up internally, and may even retraumatize the protagonist by producing the original event in an intolerable manner.

The Protagonist

The protagonist is the person whose story is being enacted or told, the person who, de facto, represents the central concern of the group. Protagonists need to work with the director in warming up to their own scene or story and allowing it to be enacted on the stage. Their willingness to fully engage in their own drama with the auxiliaries, and to move with the action and the director, will influence where and how deep the work will go for all participants. Protagonists are responsible for staying true to their own story and engaging in the action as honestly as possible.

The Auxiliary Ego

In psychodrama we explore the protagonist's subjective reality and offer the opportunity to deal with the real rather than the unreal. The reality is brought to life through the use of auxiliary egos or improvisational actors chosen by the protagonist to represent particular people in her life. These auxiliaries have five functions: (1) to represent the role required by the protagonist; (2) to approximate the protagonist's perception of the person being portrayed; (3) to find out what is really going on within the interaction; (4) to role reverse and understand the inner world of the protagonist; and (5) to provide contact with real people rather than imagined people, thereby enabling the protagonist to begin making a connection that is real.

The Stage

The stage in psychodrama is any space that has been designated as one onto which the protagonist may safely place her surplus reality. As Moreno said, "The stage is enough." To give someone the stage is to give her the opportunity to take a journey inward, with the support of the director, auxiliary egos and audience, and to meet herself. It is to provide a place or a platform where her voice or story can be heard and witnessed by others.

Reformed Auxiliary Ego

Once the protagonist's complexes, wishes and desires have been worked through psychodramatically, and feelings such as anger, pain and rage have been expressed, it can sometimes be useful to offer a corrective experience in the form of a reformed auxiliary ego. Until this point the protagonist has used the auxiliary ego to live out the unlived portions of the situation that have caused problems. Next the auxiliary ego can be given back to the protagonist in a reformed sense or as a wish, that is, as he "wishes it had been." This offers the protagonist an opportunity to tolerate the feeling of getting what he always wanted. Paradoxically, it can be very painful to finally receive what has long been wished for.

The reformed auxiliary ego is a useful model for the protagonist to take into life so that he can begin to know what it feels like to have what he wants, and to learn to accept it in small doses within a safe structure. It may also be useful for the protagonist to interact with the reformed auxiliary as a form of role-training.

The Double

The double speaks out the interior reality of the protagonist— gives voice to what is unspoken in the drama. The double should feel like an inner voice to the protagonist—one that makes the protagonist experience a sense of being seen and understood. The double helps to bring the protagonist to the threshold of his or her own experience.

If the protagonist experiences the double as discordant with her inner feelings, she should be allowed to correct the double. When the director is the double, he or she can encourage this by simply saying "Does that feel right?" or "Correct me." A good double can be very effective in moving the action to a deeper level by giving voice to that level of depth within the protagonist. Other group members can spontaneously double when they identify with the protagonist, by standing behind her, saying what they wish to say and then returning to their seats. It is also possible for protagonists to double for themselves.

The double speaks the unconscious of the protagonist, bringing the material that is lodged in the background to the foreground. Doubles are an optional part of an enactment, that is, the director may allow members of the group to stand behind the protagonist and double for them when they feel warmed up to what might be going on within them. It is also helpful to double for the inner life of the auxiliaries to further the action.

The Audience (The Group)

The group is the therapeutic context in which the protagonist enacts their drama. But group members are not there simply as context: deep healing work can be done within the audience role. Through the process of identification, the feelings that arise in those watching an enactment can be as powerful as those of the protagonist. Good audience members learn to use those portions of the enactment with which they identify to concretize their own internal dramas so that related feelings can become conscious and available to them.

It is important that audience members have plenty of time to share all that emerged for them during the enactment in order to complete their own catharsis and healing. When the audience members share what came up for them with the protagonist, it reduces the isolation of the protagonist, reconnects the group and allows new connections to be made. (The notion that dramatic representation of tragedy produces a catharsis of pity and fear goes back to the fourth century B.C., to Aristotle's *Poetics*. The plays centered around a few deep concerns and complexes central to all people. Through identification with the action a person could experience a spectator catharsis affecting a purge of their own painful feelings and deepening their understanding of a life dynamic or situation.)

SELECTING A PROTAGONIST

Protagonists can be selected in four ways: by the group, by the director, by the person who feels ready to be the protagonist and by a participating institution. Let's take a look at how each selection method works.

Sociometric Selection: Selection By The Group

In sociometric selection the protagonist is selected by the entire group. After the warm-up the director invites group members who wish to work, to share about what they might like to work on. When all who wish to speak have had a chance to do so, the director then asks the other members to select the person who they would like to see work. They do this by walking over to the person whose drama they most resonate with and either placing their hand on the person's shoulder or standing behind the person. This method of selection is often used in psychodrama.

In sociometric selection the protagonist is not chosen because the group members would like to see her work or because they feel she needs to work, but because *hers is the drama to which they feel most drawn.* Answering this inner pull is what makes this a sociometric selection, because it indicates the amount of support, identification and transference that will be available to the protagonist from the group. The stronger the selective identification, the greater the support. Not only will this enable the protagonist to work at a deeper level, but it will also concretize the inner drama of those identifying with the protagonist, allowing their feelings and concerns to surface throughout the protagonist's drama, which can later be expressed during the sharing phase.

Director Selection

Director selection comes from the therapist or director of the group. The director may feel that a particular person is warmed up to work, and will follow through on that by asking this person if they would like to work on a particular issue. The advantages of this method of selection are twofold. One, the director can address particular issues that he feels are important to the growth of the group member; and two, the director can bring isolates (people who tend to isolate themselves in a group) forward and provide an arena in which they can self-disclose, so that people can come to know and identify with them. The greater the true self-disclosure, the higher a person's sociometric position or status within a group.

The disadvantage of this method is that the director's selection may not represent a central concern of other group members, or the protagonist may shut down or not be present throughout the process, sabotaging the enactment.

Self-Selection

In self-selection, group members essentially select themselves by saying that they feel a need or a desire to work. The advantage of this method is that it allows someone who wishes to work the freedom to declare that. The disadvantage is that the self-selected person may or may not be supported by the other group members during the enactment.

Systems/Institutional Selection

When a client is referred to psychodrama by the caregiving system—by a person who deems it necessary, such as a supervisor or referring therapist in a clinic or hospital situation—he may come with what is essentially a prescription. For example, a therapist may ask the director, "Could you please help John work on his issues with his father?"

The advantage of this method is that it allows the client a safe space in which to work through an important issue experientially. The disadvantage is that, any time work is prescribed, there is the risk that it does not truly come from within the protagonist, that it does not arise from the inner depths and wisdom of his psyche.

PSYCHODRAMATIC TECHNIQUES

Just as in conventional drama, psychodrama uses a number of dramatic techniques in order to structure and frame the action and move the story along in meaningful and insightful ways. Commonly used psychodramatic techniques include role reversal, vignettes, time regression, mirroring, future projection, soliloquy and interview.

Role Reversal

Role reversal is a central concept of true psychodrama. It is one of the most important elements of psychodrama because fully reversing roles enables us to see life and ourselves from another perspective. Protagonists go beyond projecting onto or empathizing with an auxiliary ego: they actually experience being that person. This experience not only increases their understanding of the other, but it also allows them to view themselves from the other person's position. "The son, who is still himself, must now warm up to how his mother may be feeling and perceiving himself; the mother, now the son, goes through the same process."

The first purpose of experiential therapy is to elucidate the inner world, to bring light to that which has been held in darkness, and to see and understand ourselves in that new awareness. Another purpose of the method is found in the playing of different roles, allowing a situation to be seen from a variety of perspectives, which automatically shifts awareness, increases spontaneity and provides relief from our own roles. A person who is not able to role reverse may have a fragile self that is not intact enough to be able to leave its usual identifications. This person needs to work in more dramas in the role of protagonist to build a sense of self and ego strength.

When one is actually able to stand in the shoes of another and see things from the other's perspective, a true role reversal has occurred. It is different from empathizing or understanding. It is *trading places* momentarily with another person, stepping out of one's own skin and into another's, and seeing things through his eyes. We are limited in walking through life with only one set of eyes.

Psychodrama, by its very nature, gives us the opportunity to practice leaving the self, moving to other places and coming back again. Role reversal gives us a way of speaking, not for another person, but *as* another person. It is an exercise through which a true understanding of another person's mind can occur.

Vignettes

A vignette is a small psychodramatic scene comprised of one person talking to an empty chair, to another person or to more than one person. Vignettes can be a very effective way to relieve feelings and move through emotional blocks without mounting a full scene. It can also be a way to deal with the sociometry of the group and member-to-member transference.

Vignettes can also provide an opportunity for several people to work in one session. They provide a simple structure that can be moved into easily, as soon as a protagonist feels warmed up, because they do not require scene-setting or a buildup for action.

In one-to-one work, vignettes can be done with empty chairs. The director might double momentarily for an auxiliary, being careful to stay as far out of the transference as possible. The director may also use role reversal (into an empty chair) and the interview technique (discussed as follows) to deepen the scene. More than one chair can be used, and inner parts of the self can be represented by empty chairs—for example, rage, weight, the drunken self, the despised self, the grandiose self, a body part and so on.

Time Regression

Time regression is used especially when a client is tormented by a past, usually traumatic, experience. There is therapeutic advantage to reliving the past in a safe setting, and the time-regression technique allows a protagonist to do just that. It is the most common of all psychodramas. According to psychologist David Kipper,

> It requires the protagonist to recreate, through role playing enactment, significant events from his or her past and act them out as if they are occurring in the present. The rule that every simulated role-playing scene is portrayed by making the "then and there" the "here and now" has an important implication as far as Time-regression is concerned. All the participants—the protagonist and the auxiliary(s)—must use the present tense. For example, the protagonist will say: "I am doing it because . . ." rather than "I did it because . . ." The use of the past tense tends to put the actor in the role of a spectator whereas the use of the present tense makes him or her an involved partner.

The Mirror Technique

The mirror technique can be powerful for the protagonists who are unable to tolerate the intensity of playing themselves in a drama, who need to feel one step removed in order to feel safe. In this technique an auxiliary ego plays the protagonist, expressing the protagonist's feelings in word and movement. The protagonist thus see's himself "as if in a mirror": a living representation of himself.

The mirror technique provides a protagonist with an opportunity to view from a less heated position, and with the support of the director, a traumatic or perplexing event. It also can allow the protagonist to gain perspective on his own behavior, by watching rather than by being.

Future Projection

Future projection allows the protagonist to play out an anticipated, desired or feared event in order to feel it before it happens, to reduce the anxiety connected with it (common in job interviews) and perhaps to decide more wisely whether or not to go through with certain plans. For example, the man who wishes for a divorce may experience, through psychodrama, ramifications he has not anticipated and put off his decision in favor of continued work in the marriage, or a woman who wishes to have an affair may discover her real reasons for wanting it through future projections rather than having to live out the experience in real life.

Soliloquy

A psychodramatic soliloquy can be used as a warm-up to the enactment. After a scene has been set up, the director may wish to pull the protagonist aside, take a walk with the person and ask him or her to soliloquize, to talk freely about what is going on inside at the moment. Soliloquizing helps to bring the protagonist to the "here and now" and to warm up to the scene she has constructed.

Sometimes during a psychodrama protagonists may seem as if they need to talk about what is going on within themselves. In this case the director may ask them to soliloquize, or simply to step aside and speak out about what is going on within them.

Zerka Moreno describes various ways of structuring soliloquies:

The protagonist may be engaged in a solitary activity such as walking home, winding down after an eventful day or getting ready for an event in the near future. It might involve giving words to bolster courage or reproachful criticism. Variations include having the protagonist soliloquize with a double as the two of them walk around, having the protagonist talk to a pet or converting the inner dialogue into an encounter with an empty chair or an auxiliary playing a wiser future self or another part of the personality.

The soliloquy allows the protagonist to walk along and, in a sense, talk to herself at an appropriate time during the enactment, letting the audience in on what is going on within her. It can be used as a warm-up to action, or a break in action that allows the protagonists to share her internal dialogue with anyone who may be listening.

Interview

In the psychodramatic interview, the director asks the protagonist questions that help illuminate what is going on internally. This technique can be used with protagonists in their own role, protagonists in role reversal or the auxiliaries in a drama. The director can use it before the drama in order to gain information that will help to focus the work or during the drama to draw information from the various characters. The technique goes deep when used properly, and it can be an awakening experience for the protagonist to be interviewed while in role reversal. For example, if the protagonist is playing her father, the director can ask questions of "the father" as he is being played by the protagonist. The protagonist's experience of being in the role of her father is enhanced by answering self-referential questions from that role. The full parent can be brought to a conscious level, so that he can be further known and seen and so that the protagonist can detach from the idea that her father's actions were related exclusively to her. The interview allows the protagonist, in the role of her father, to play out the parental introject through psychodramatic action.

Generally, in life situations, we play out the internalized parent unconsciously. The interview technique helps to ground and hold protagonists in the role of the parent so that they can act out the introject in a clinical setting, where it can be both informative to them and cathartic. This affords them the opportunity to identify those aspects of the internalized parent that they are acting out in life in nonproductive ways, and it gives them the opportunity to change their behavior. Answering questions while in the role of another person can be enlightening and can provide protagonists with more pieces of the puzzle of their own inner lives.

AUTODRAMAS AND MONODRAMAS

In addition to the classical psychodrama—which includes director, protagonist, auxiliaries and audience—psychodramas may also be structured as monodramas in which one person plays all the parts, or as autodramas in which there is no director.

Monodramas

Monodrama comes from the Greek root word *monos*, meaning only or one. In a monodrama there is only one participant— which is to say, one person plays all of the roles. It may consist of empty chair work, in which the protagonist addresses the person she imagines to be sitting in the chair—a unique opportunity to explore the self-system without interruption from the points of view of the auxiliaries.

Using role reversal in a monodrama can facilitate the protagonist's understanding of her drama from another point of view. It is also a useful place in which to use the technique of interview. For instance, if the protagonist is addressing her mother, the director may ask her to role reverse. The director can then interview the protagonist in the role of her mother. In this way the director can explore the protagonist's internalized mother, or maternal introject.

The opportunity to spend time in the role of another person and be interviewed in that role can have various beneficial effects:

1. It is a source of information about the person being played.

2. It offers the protagonist an opportunity actually to experience being that person, to understand her from the inside out rather than the outside in. It allows the protagonist the freedom to see that what happened in the relationship was not necessarily directed at them personally but was a result of who the person was within their own self-system.

3. It allows the protagonist to act out the parental introject in a clinical setting so that he can identify the areas in which he may be acting out this introject in his own life.

4. In such a monodrama much unconscious material comes to the surface: the protagonist learns a great deal more about how he actually experienced the parent than he would by talking about him, for the parent will come to the surface in the heat of action in exactly the way in which he was experienced and stored in the psyche of the protagonist. Protagonists can play out as many auxiliary roles as they need to in order to fully explore their drama. If it seems indicated, the director is free to double for any of the roles in order to deepen the enactment or further the cause of the protagonist, though the director must be careful not to take on a role with too much negative transference.

Monodramas also offer a comfortable opportunity to explore intrapsychic realities. For instance, a protagonist may wish to encounter his own depression, putting the depression in a chair and talking to it, reversing roles with it or even doubling for his depressed self, standing behind the chair. An addict may wish to put his substance into an empty chair and speak to it from his point of view, and from the point of view of the substance in role reversal. A woman who has had surgery might put the part of her that she lost into an empty chair and allow the drama to unfold from there. A man who has lost an important person to disease or death may benefit greatly from saying what he never finished saying in life to that person.

Autodramas

An autodrama is a drama that does not use a director. The protagonist sets the stage, chooses auxiliaries if desired and directs the action from the role of protagonist. Because there is no director the action goes only as deep as the protagonist allows or directs. Autodramas can be very useful warm-ups to deeper action. Autodramas can also help people who are new to psychodrama to become used to the feeling of being a protagonist, without the added pressure or worry of being "pushed" by a director—for, though directors go where the protagonist leads them, initially people can be afraid of having their deepest feelings exposed, both to themselves and to others. Autodramas reduce that threat by removing the director.

Because autodramas provide a nonauthoritarian structure, they are useful for people who have an issue with authority. Autodramas can also have a playful, enjoyable quality; the material itself can be imaginative, and people can take turns in doubling for any character with whom they identify.

Learning how to have easy, supportive, spontaneous fun that does not become chaotic, threatening and out of control is important in the treatment of addicts and co-dependents, who experienced little fun while growing up. Their families may have used sarcasm and graveyard humor—but there is a real difference between being funny and being able to have fun; the emphasis on creativity, spontaneity and the "here and now" in psychodrama can help addicts and co-dependents to learn to have fun.

Adults who have grown up in addicted or otherwise chaotic environments tend to forge their strongest bonds and friendships through the sharing of mutual pain, and it is an important part of treatment to learn new ways of bonding and feeling close to people. Bonding through joy and fun can be a bittersweet experience for such people because it triggers fears of loss. It feels more familiar to bond through pain than to allow feelings of calm, safety and trust back in. The pain of losing safety and calm over and over again in childhood makes it difficult to trust these experiences. It takes time to rebuild the damaged self and resolve painful issues to a point at which a comfortable, pleasant life can be tolerated. Psychodrama provides a safe environment in which to do so. (Chapter 11, Using Psychodrama With Addicts And ACoAs, addresses the issues of this group.)

A protagonist may wish to put herself into an empty chair at a variety of ages—as a young child, as an adolescent, as a teenager, as a young adult—any time in her life that she feels a need to re-encounter herself in order to work something through. This could also be considered inner child work. It offers access to a wide range of developmental stages, so that the work can be tailored to a specific stage of development at which maturation was adversely affected. This gives the inner child a chance to begin to move through the missed developmental stages and grow up to maturity. Arrested development needs to be returned to and reworked. If we move the inner child work along through the necessary developmental stages, we will avoid the risk of overempowering the recovering inner child which would cause her to become stuck in her development rather than moving through it to the next stage.

There is a difference between being childlike and childish. Some people have been so damaged in their child selves, often having missed the opportunity to be a child, that it is tempting in recovery to get lost in "being a child" when they finally gain access to the repressed inner child. We all need to have access to our child selves in order to be happy, creative and loving people. And this is the ultimate goal of inner child work—to re-awaken the frozen child and work through the complexes on the road to full maturity, so that the inner child can come to life and be integrated into the adult where they are safe and available to feed and nurture each other.

A MONODRAMA WITH THE SELF

Goals

1. To bring forward the inner self at various stages.
2. To work out unfinished business from the past.

Steps

1. Ask group members to close their eyes and relax, and then to contact a point in their lives when some major change took place or something important was going on. Ask them to summon up the person they used to be, the one to whom they would like to speak.

2. Choose a protagonist and ask her to bring that person onto the stage into an empty chair.

3. Ask the protagonist to reverse roles and show the group how that person sits and looks. She may begin talking from that role or from where she is today.

4. Ask the protagonist to say what she would like to say to that person from her current vantage point knowing what she knows now.

5. Encourage the protagonist to speak freely to this part of himself, reversing roles if he chooses.

6. Ask the protagonist to end the scene in any way he chooses.

7. Let the group share with the protagonist what came up for them.

Variations

This exercise can be done over and over again for a variety of powerful moments at any age in the life of the protagonist. It is useful in individual or group therapy and offers people a way to empower themselves by contacting themselves at moments in their lives that they feel a need or pull to encounter.

DIALOGUE WITH A CHARACTERISTIC

Goals

1. To expand auxiliary ego options.
2. To reduce the sense that someone else is to blame.

Steps

1. Allow the protagonist to choose one or more characteristics—anger, regret, shame, grief, guilt, resentment or whatever he wishes.

2. Ask the protagonist to place these characteristics where they seem to be in relationship to himself.

3. Let the protagonist place them in any way, relate them to one another or sculpt them in ways that physicalize their inner meaning and impact.

4. Now ask the protagonist to relate to or talk to these parts of the self and reverse roles or use whatever techniques are helpful.

5. Allow time for sharing.

Variations

This can also be done in one-to-one work with an empty chair. It provides an opportunity to explore and relate painful, withheld feelings.

EXTERNALIZE THE PROBLEM

Goals

1. To move outside internal self-abuse.

2. To bring out the internal object of abuse so the healing can begin.

Steps

1. Choose a protagonist who seems to be constantly beating up on himself or open the idea for self-selection.

2. Allow him to warm up to his own drama by sharing.

3. If you feel that he is extremely hard on himself, check it out with him. You might say, "Let's see, do I have this right? You're telling me it's your fault." From the double position, you may continue with what you hear: "I never do anything right. No one does what I do. Things I do turn out wrong," and so on.

4. If the protagonist acknowledges that you are on the right track, ask him to take that part of himself that he is beating up on and put it in the chair.

5. Now tell him to give himself a really bad time, or just double for him in order to help to get him started, using all the cruel, punitive inner voices that he uses on himself. Let him chew himself up on the outside the way he chews himself up on the inside.

6. After most of the feelings have been released, let the protagonist say the last things he needs to say to close the scene for the time being.

7. Now let the protagonist share about anything he feels as a result of doing the same; or, if you are in a group, let the group share what came up for them while watching.

Variations

Role reversal is appropriate any time during such a scene. The idea is to externalize the inner object. Just the act of externalizing will cause it to move to a different place. This can be done as many times as necessary to allow the client relief and give him a chance to see how the abuse process works within him. The process of externalizing the internal battle is in itself healing, both in relieving pent-up feelings and in making conscious and overly dramatic what is happening on a subtle level much of the time.

FAMILY SCULPTURING

Sculpturing is the psychodramatic technique most often used in the addictions field. The client chooses group members who can represent important people in his life, and the therapist assists the client in creating a "family sculpture." This technique can be broadened into a fuller and more useful experience.

Stage I

A family-of-origin social atom (see Chapter 3, Sociometry: How Psychodrama Works), can be created by each group member, and, once it has been fully processed and fully shared, it can serve as an intrapsychic map throughout the therapy process. When issues come up during treatment, it can be referred to in order to trace the possible origins of the problem. Also, when the client has problems with other people, either in the group or in everyday life, the therapist can ask the client who that person might represent for him on his social atom and attempt to resolve the transference through sharing or role-play.

Stage II

Through one of the four selecting processes discussed earlier, one person can be chosen to move his social atom into action (see Action Sociogram in Chapter 3, Sociometry: How Psychodrama Works). Allow the client to move through and around his family sculpture, feeling the feelings that arise as he does so. He may soliloquize as he walks, and he may begin to speak with whomever he feels pulled toward; he should be allowed to say fully what he needs to say or was never able to say, when he feels drawn to do so, using role reversal and doubling whenever appropriate. He may choose someone to play his inner child or his stand-in so that he can watch himself in the context of his family. He can reverse roles into and out of these positions.

Such a first step toward healing family-of-origin wounds will also provide a map for further treatment, making evident where continued work is necessary and what may be involved in that work. It is important to allow a great deal of time for sharing after each person's work. The sharing should not be in the form of feedback—"What I saw you doing was . . ." It should arise from personal identification with the process that has just happened—"What came up for me from my own life as a result of watching and being a part of your work was . . ."

Through psychodramatic family sculpturing sociometric connections can be brought to a conscious level within the group, and any one person's work can have healing potential for anyone in the group. When group members share internal dramas that become real and felt during another person's enactment phase, they complete their own healing and catharsis. No matter whose work is being done, the potential for catharsis for group members through participation and identification is always present.

Playing out auxiliary roles also allows for the possibility for inner movement. The therapist can ask, "How did it feel to play the role?" or "Do you need to say anything that has arisen from playing the role?" And as part of emerging from the role, auxiliaries should be allowed to speak from the role so that they can let go of it and reintegrate into the group as themselves. Over time, each person can revise his social atom and action sociogram, sharing each one.

Stage III

Once the basic architecture of the "inner family" is established, the skill, knowledge and imagination of the therapist and group members must be relied on for continuing the work. The therapist can continue to work with sculpturing as the central psychodramatic technique, or expand into others. A wide variety of psychodramatic techniques—large dramas involving many people, vignettes, empty-chair work, monodramas and autodramas—will continue to provide vehicles through which act hungers, open tensions and transferences can be explored and resolved. The sociometric connections, identifications, transferences and projections (see Chapter 3, Sociometry: How Psychodrama Works) within the group will be a part of this process, as each person becomes the therapeutic agent of the other. Within the addictions field, with its preponderance of group therapy and 12-Step support, it is important that the therapist understand not only the use of action-oriented work but also the dynamics of the family system, and how they play out within the group and in the present-day lives of members.

Stage IV

Step IV includes role-training behavior modification and re-education, so that the client can understand the effects of living in a dysfunctional or addicted system. Having learned to identify and work with his early traumas and grieve their losses, he will now explore and practice new behaviors, learn new roles, make new connections and begin to let go of his past. The model of group therapy and 12-Step work will provide a laboratory in which to learn and practice new behaviors during this transitional period of letting go, coming to terms with the past and finding meaning in it. The format of psychodrama, group therapy, sociometry and one-to-one therapy supports and promotes this process while a new self is emerging.

Stage V

Throughout the shedding of an old self, a new self emerges that contains aspects of both the previous self and the new self. As this happens clients gain further access to their inner being and a deeper level of spontaneity and creativity. New roles are possible, through which to channel energy and creativity. It is important that clients be in a continuous process of rebuilding a self parallel to the therapeutic process of dismantling. And if the therapy has been successful, they will become familiar with themselves and begin to tailor their lives to suit their individual needs and wishes. They will come to accept the past as what got them to where they are, and they will no longer wish to "shut the door on it" because they realize they would be shutting the door on themselves. They will be in a position to use what they have learned to help themselves and others, through family life, friendships, and in twelfth-step work. (People in 12-Step groups may find that a relationship with a higher power as an internalized presence helps to dispel an earlier sense of separateness. They may experience themselves as co-creating a life with a higher power.)

The stages outlined are not necessarily discrete and may overlap. They merely provide a general framework for the therapeutic process of recovery, during which, when one-to-one therapy is needed to help contain the process and offer an opportunity to rework early distressed and distorted bonding, it should be undertaken. It is important, however, that the one-to-one therapist be supportive of the process and helpful to the client in working through the deep and confusing feelings that arise throughout.

GUIDELINES FOR THERAPEUTIC SAFETY: FIRST, DO NO HARM

When using experiential techniques to make unconscious emotional and psychic material conscious, there is a significant risk that the client might be retraumatized unless specific safeguards are respected. Here are some guidelines for safety:

Do not pre-script material. Therapists who decide beforehand where they want clients to go run the risk of pushing them beyond their ego strength and emotional capacity in order to get there. The lead of the protagonist should be followed and the direction checked out with him along the way—"Are we on the right track?" or "Does this feel right?" Also the therapist must be willing to be made wrong and to adjust his approach in midstream. Pre-scripting can also inhibit feelings from arising in a spontaneous manner.

Do not use psychodramatic shock techniques. If the therapist sets up a potentially powerful or frightening scene without the client's knowledge or input and then suddenly exposes the client to the fully set scene, the client may go into shock or be retraumatized. Sometimes such an occurence may not show, but it will have lasting effects.

Remain with the protagonist throughout the work. There should be one steady director who remains closely in touch with the protagonist from the beginning of the work throughout all that is done. As the director, even if you are in close physical proximity you also need to be in close psychic and emotional proximity, so that the client can feel your presence and support.

Use stand-ins for severely traumatic events. In the psychodramatization of severely traumatic events, such as early sexual abuse, rape or physical trauma, there is a risk that the protagonist will be retraumatized. One way to mitigate such potential risk is to give the protagonist the option to play herself and allow her to witness or co-direct her own scene if she wishes using an auxiliary to represent her. Moreover, in cases of trauma, one of the most important elements of healing is the telling of the trauma story and having self and others bear witness. These ends may be better accomplished through this format than by putting the protagonist in a situation that may cause her to re-experience the trauma directly. The protagonist can sit with the feelings that come up as she bears witness and verbalize them to others while being supported by group members or one or two chosen people. This becomes a vehicle for telling the fully story. It also allows the protagonist to connect with her extreme help-lessness and develop compassion for herself as a victim, which allows her eventually to bring closure to her victim self and move beyond the associated feelings. (Chapter 12, Trauma, covers this subject in more detail.)

Allow plenty of time for sharing. Sharing is extremely impor-tant to the emotional safety of the group. Sharing is not feedback; rather it is the continued expression of vulnerable feelings related to whatever the group process and psychodramatic enactment are bringing up within each person self-referentially. Each member of the group should have the time he needs to share his story and have it witnessed, so that his pain can be contained and brought to closure. Everyone is working at all times in an experiential group: the enactment is designed to bring up feelings not only for the protagonist but for everyone in the room. This is how the process works to bring issues and unconscious feelings to the sur-face. The sharing acts as the safe container for the material so that it can be held and witnessed by others in safety, without judgment or analysis at that point.

NEAR-PSYCHODRAMATIC TECHNIQUES

Near-psychodramatic techniques do not involve the full action of a classical psychodrama as previously described. They are not necessarily protagonist-centered and do not attempt to fully pro-duce the larger reality of the protagonist onto the stage, though they do work with the inner life of each person, in some way bringing unconscious matter to the conscious level for further exploration. Using these techniques, clients may address a need or a wish to receive or give something that was never obtained or given, such as a letter that they felt they deserved to receive or wished they had sent.

Near-psychodramatic techniques often involve the use of paper and a pencil. Guided imagery, letter-writing, journaling, drawing or painting can be used, as can any emotive technique that lacks full action. A social atom that is not acted out in the form of an action sociogram can be used as a near-psychodramatic technique. Family maps, role analysis, diagrams and sociograms not only warm a person up to further enactment but also are in themselves a way of cleansing the internal system and offering opportunities for growth and change.

These techniques can be very helpful in one-to-one sessions during which no auxiliaries are available to role-play in a classical sense. When used in a group, they can be very bonding, as group members use them individually and then share the results with one another. In a large group, the sharing can take place in dyads, triads or small groups, encouraging connection and enhancing group cohesion. Though these techniques do not necessarily lead to enactment, they are powerful in and of themselves and should be used carefully in a highly structured and focused manner, and ample time should be allowed for sharing what comes up. Confronting one's reality on a piece of paper, such as in a social atom, draws much material from the emotional and psychic self.

Letter-Writing

Letter-writing can be useful as a closure technique; that is, if a lot of feelings have come up for group members during a session, they can choose people to whom they feel they have something to say and take a few minutes to write letters to them—not to send, but to use as a psychodramatic release. After they have finished, they can (1) share the letters with the group; (2) form pairs or subgroups and share the letters; (3) choose group members to play the people to whom they have written the letters and then read the letters to them or experience the letters being read to them in role reversal; or (4) share the letters with a therapist in one-to-one work.

Clients may also write letters that they wish they would receive from someone. They may then (1) choose group members to play those people and experience the letters being read to them; (2) share them with the group; (3) share them in pairs or subgroups; (4) share them with the therapist in one-to-one work; or (5) choose other group members to play themselves and read their own letters while playing the other people. Letters written and read in a group offer many opportunities for identification, both helping members to see themselves in other people and breaking down a sense of isolation.

WRITING A LETTER

Goals

1. To work with feelings about another person without involving that person.

2. To work with feelings about the self in a structured way.

Steps

1. Ask participants to decide which type of letter to write (see "Variations" below).

2. Ask them to begin with "Dear So and So," and end with an appropriate closing and sign their names.

3. Encourage them to write anything that comes to mind. This letter is not meant to be sent, but to release their feelings. It works best to write quickly, not thinking about how it sounds or imagining that anyone will read it. Writing letters can be a useful closure activity to finish expressing feelings that have been stirred up through psychodrama.

Variations

A participant may write any type of letter he can think of to anyone he wants. Here are a few common ones:

- a letter of forgiveness to himself
- a letter asking forgiveness from someone else
- a letter expressing anger toward someone
- a letter from someone expressing sentiments he wishes that person had expressed
- a letter from someone who has hurt him, asking for his forgiveness
- a letter telling someone about a hurt

- a letter to someone expressing a desire for reconciliation
- a letter to someone expressing understanding of what that person went through
- a letter from someone expressing understanding of what the participant went through
- a letter to his disease self from his recovery self.

This is an endlessly useful exercise:

- It can help confront feelings that are too threatening even to speak about. Some people may even wish to dictate the letter if it is too difficult to write it, or merely to speak a letter without writing.
- It is a safe way to relieve anger, express it and let it go.
- People can share these letters silently or read them aloud with a safe person. They can share in dyads or in the group. A person may also choose someone to play the recipient of the letter and read it, or choose someone to play himself while he reads his own letter (to "himself") in role reversal.
- A letter can also be used to give a gift to oneself of good things that were never said.
- Letter-writing helps clients move closer to forgiveness and letting go.

Working With Photographs

Photographs can contribute wonderfully to warm-up for sharing material or setting up a scene, in a variety of ways. The client's choice is in itself a diagnostic tool. Generally, it will be a photograph that speaks to them in some way. The director may ask, "What does this photograph have to say to you? What does the child—teenager, adolescent or adult—in this picture wish you to know about him?" Then the protagonist can reverse roles and speak as the person in the photograph. Or the director can ask, "What do you wish to say to the person in this photograph from where you are today? What do you wish him to know that you now understand?" An empty chair may be used to represent the person in the picture, or a person can be cast in that role and a psychodramatic vignette can ensue.

A family photo can be used in much in the same way as an action sociogram. People can be asked to play the various roles that are in the picture. The psychodrama can be set up according to the positioning in the photograph and enacted as usual. If a family photograph is used, after the enactment is complete and all of the feelings of the protagonist have been played out, there is a good chance to do some reconstructive work. The director can ask the protagonist to reshape the photograph as he wishes it had been, and also ask him what he would like to say to the people in this picture or how it feels to look at it the way he wishes it had been. If the photograph is of another person, the director can simply ask the protagonist what he wishes to say to the other person, using an empty chair or a role-player, and the vignette can proceed from there.

The director can ask the protagonist what he imagines a person in a photograph is feeling and allow the protagonist to reverse roles with the person in the picture. The director can interview the protagonist as that person to illuminate further the experience the protagonist has internalized. If the photograph is of a house, the director can ask the protagonist to walk through the door of that house into his favorite room and show on the stage what that room looked like and how it feels to be in it again. If he chooses a room in which he feels he has unfinished business, in order to revisit the room and finish the business, it is important that he describe and set up the room in as much detail as possible. Then role-players can be included—or the drama can simply be the soliloquy of the protagonist.

The photograph might be of a nanny, housekeeper or houseworker who was important to a child while growing up. Though these are not family-of-origin members, strong bonds can exist between people who helped a child to feel less alone and from whom a child learned how to be a person. It is important to establish real contact with these positive role models, bringing them back into the present and using them in the process of healing, incorporating them as useful surrogate parents or companions.

Pets that appear in photographs are also important, for they may have been experienced as close, protective angels by a child who felt forgotten; the child may have felt more doubled by the animal than by those with whom he lived. All of these scenarios are well worth exploring if they seem to bring forward more of the real person.

What follows is an example of an exploration of a photograph through writing. In response to the assignment, "Find a picture of yourself when you were a child that you feel connected to." Here is the soliloquy one man wrote about a photo of himself as an infant.

> *The earliest photograph is of an infant. I'm being held over the shoulder of Mrs. Buffington—or is it Aunt Eunice? No, it's Mrs. Buffington, which means I was under six months old because she had to pass me along, when she got pregnant herself, to Aunt Eunice. The infant boy is cross-eyed and covered with spots—I had developed impetigo shortly after birth. Truly an appalling baby. Maybe his mother was right to take one look and say, "I'd rather be dead," as an unethical psychiatrist once suggested, working on rage and self-esteem . . .*
>
> *When Mary, my nine-years-younger half-sister, got married, Mrs. Buffington and Aunt Eunice were both there. I was 35. We three were talking and they were reminiscing and laughing. Aunt Eunice says, "Remember when you gave him to me, Lois, he had impetigo and he had to be rubbed down with olive oil; and you said, 'Be sure not to get it mixed in with the salad dressing!' and both ladies roared with laughter at the memory of their reality, as the man looked on, bemused in his surplus reality.*

Dream Work

A psychodramatic representation of a dream can concretize the protagonist's inner use of symbol and metaphor and thus be a vehicle for self-examination. A rock, a stream, a demon or an angel can be cast and played out as it appeared, acted and interacted in the protagonist's dream. And through role reversal the protagonist can enter into and give voice to all aspects of his dream, speaking, for instance, *as* the rock or *as* the angel, seeing what they wish to express as entities or symbols and experiencing what they may wish to say to him in role reversal. Dream work provides an opportunity for the creative self to emerge in artistic metaphor.

Structuring dream work is similar to structuring any psychodrama. The protagonist chooses the auxiliaries and sets the scene as usual. Because the dream is an extension of the protagonist's inner world, all the auxiliaries in a dream enactment are also extensions or representations of the protagonist. For this reason it is useful for the protagonist to reverse roles with any and all elements in his dream.

THE INNER LIFE OF A PSYCHODRAMA

It is one thing to read about psychodramatic theory in a textbook, and it is quite another to actually participate in an enactment. What follows is a unique opportunity to experience some of that emotional power. These are Carolyn Charnock-Atkinson's reflections on the process of her own psychodramatic enactment. They clearly delineate the inner life of a psychodrama and the depth and process of the experience of the protagonist.

The protagonist warming up to her own story internally.	Sitting here . . . trying so hard to fight for control, wanting to give in, yet not wanting to lose; but needing so much just to simply give up. My legs crossed, head bent with so much guilt, so much shame.
Inviting the protagonist to work. The sense within the protagonist of "time traveling."	I am always running, always running from the Shadows. You reached out for my hand . . . offering me willingly your help, offering me trust, offering me hope, and with that one small effort, like a child's reaching out for a mother's hand, I gave Her to you with total acceptance, and we began to travel to a place I so needed to go. A room that was so dark . . . the shades pulled down . . . so cold . . . so alone . . . so full of hidden hurt, all of my hurt that was not allowed.
Scene setting and description of characters in the psychodrama.	There was blackness with only shadows not to be filled. I was there with my Hurting Child; she looked so alone, trembling with fear.
Silent communication between protagonist and auxiliary she chose as her mother, now in role reversal.	I reached toward her with my eyes to give her a chance to let the mask down, to let her arms slowly unfold from the heaviness of guilt, lose the shame of feeling so unloved by this Shadow with a name called Mother, and so hurt by her Daddy.

Protagonist's wish to keep director as therapeutic ally.

I cried out for you not to leave me because this place hurt me so bad; my little girl's heart feeling broken, afraid of being alone again.

So we traveled some more paths of my pain . . . pictures in my head, memories buried so long ago. Total recall of hurt.

Fully contacted traumatic reality and memories.

The Child was beginning to feel her grief. I felt so sorry for her reliving some terrible places on this long journey.
I had to hide in this room . . . you helped me stay there, in this place that was hurting me. But it had to be done.

Protagonist's request to "make it all dark." We attempted to get it exactly as she needed it to be, including the reconstructive work of building in warmth and support.

My head bursting with pain . . . unbearable pain . . . She used to leave me with pain . . . so still I was by myself. I cried for the darkness; they closed the drapes, everyone protected me and helped keep darkness locked in. I needed it to keep hiding so I could let go of all my tears, my shame, my guilt of simply needing to be a little girl who was loved by a Mother. Everyone made a nest around me . . . creating warmth, and I cried once again for you to stay and not leave; you promised me you wouldn't. This room I was in was so full of emptiness, so full of my hurt that I could never speak of. But now I could sense something different. This time I could feel warmth reaching to me out of this black place, this silent place of a child's unshed tears, untold nightmares . . . a place that no sound could be heard. I was 14, I was 15, even three or four on this journey we traveled, and I was with Her at each Hurt.

Contact with real people, making the "then and there" the "here-and-now" . . . the auxiliary approximating the protagonist's actual experience.

I cried for Her.
And then we spoke to my Mother.
I told her how she had hurt me . . . how she had made me feel . . . and why did she keep leaving me.
So much to remember, so much to forget.
But my Mother yelled back my failures, cursing

me again. I could not look at her, but I knew her voice well . . . feeling her anger, her disgust. I hated her; yet a part of me did not want to hate . . . creation of guilt within me still.

The need of the protagonist for a reformed auxiliary to give her what she never got— protagonist asked for what she wished she had gotten from her mother.

All I wanted was to be held, to be loved by a Mother so this place that hurt me so bad inside would go away. I wanted my Child to be happy . . . to laugh, but still I could not find her.

And when she was still struggling so hard to speak of secrets . . . of guilt, when she was still needing to hide in the darkness, you were there protecting, giving warmth, giving comfort with an arm around me, rocking, I could not seem to stop rocking with the pain.

All my protectors were whispering in clear soft voices what a wonderful Child I was, telling me I was lovable, how warm and how pretty I was.

Creating such warmth, over and over the voices coming around in all directions.

Whispers of hope in my darkness . . . and I was still curled up hiding . . . but beginning to unfold like the infant I was, reaching into a warm world this time.

Role reversal into the role of mother giving herself what she needed from the role of mother.

Very quietly you offered for me to speak to Her, to tell her what she needed to hear, so sitting across from my Child I told her of the beautiful parts inside her—all her possibilities, things, dreams, that a Mother should give.

When I was done giving to my Child there was the greatest need inside of me . . .

Reformed auxiliary

a terribly sweet pain of wanting a Mother to hold me as the Child I was.

With this thought, you offered her to me without my needing to speak.

This was a time in my darkness I would have died for.

This woman who became my Mother sat me in her lap . . . rocked me, held me tightly and soothed me.

Reforming a "place called mother," the experience of a holding environment of unconditional acceptance, and reforming the hostile maternal introject.

So much given to me in this moment.

So much shame, so much guilt washing away as this Mother loved her little girl.

This little girl who was so willingly accepting, so eagerly taking what was hers to begin with.

I felt and knew this was mine . . . I did not want to ever let go; it felt so warm, so safe, *this place called Mother.* Being held, being truly loved, being so gently spoken to. She was telling me how beautiful I was, how it felt so wonderful to hold me, kissing my head, caressing my hair with a gentle touch—such a loving touch that only a Mother can give.

And all the while steadily rocking me . . . a gentle rocking meant only for a Child.

Internalizing a new self-concept of being good—first she needed to feel that her mother saw her as good.

Unspeakable words, feeling so good, so wonderful, so warm, and so Clean.

I was such a good little girl this time.

Why should my Mother not love and hold me.

I knew and felt I had never been cared for and held like this. It made me so sad. *(Beginning to mourn what she never had)* I stayed in this place for as long as I could, then it was time for me to go.

But this gift, this privilege of being in a Mother's arms gave me enough warmth to leave for a while *(the power of the reformed auxiliary).*

I crawled out of my Mother's lap . . . you were waiting.

In this case I asked the protagonist to sit next to me for the sharing phase so that she would continue to feel safe, and to afford her a safe place from which to experience and reconnect with the group.

You knew without my speaking the fear of abandonment. You knew I still needed the comfort of closeness—the cocoon of love that had been created for me.

You allowed me to be the special little girl I was, asking me to sit next to you while everyone shared their feelings about my journey, that was their journey as well.

My tears were not the only ones shed . . . we did this together.

I can remember holding your hand and playing with the rings on your finger, feeling so safe, so warm . . . such gentleness in this place my Child was.

New awareness of self. Identification with other people's experiences.

Such acceptance from need of closeness . . . the sweetness of total innocence in the newness of what she had been given.
How could anyone not have seen Her?
With each bit of sharing, and more hugs, more tears of what this journey had created for others.

Once she had finished her unfinished business with her mother, she was able to "have" her father —she did this from a vignette, then continued.

So I began . . . finally . . . to learn to grieve.
The beginning of a new Healing.
Then you allowed me to speak to my Father.
He was such a kind and gentle man with so much laughter in his eyes, teaching me so many wonderful things.
And I could look him in the eyes this time.
I saw and felt his love . . . felt the guilt over my hurt.
He said he was sorry and it was wrong what he had done to me.

Hearing what she needed to hear from an auxiliary to resolve the open tension of having no memory of saying goodbye to her father.

He also shared his joy and pleasure in being my Daddy, in being his little tomboy.
I think I told him that I knew he did not mean to hurt me and that he was probably drinking, but he said he was wrong and that drinking was no excuse.
He told me he loved me. I cannot remember all of what was said, but I had so many warm and gentle feelings while speaking with him.
And I reached another place where I could leave.

Coming to an inner resolution through psychodramatic action.

So I hugged him and told him I loved him. This little girl was warm and quiet, she was comfortable with going away.

Return to continued sharing/integration.

I returned to all of these wonderful friends who had shared this tremendous journey; this day with me.

Return to continued   I returned to all of these wonderful friends
sharing/integration.   who had shared this tremendous journey; this
                               day with me.

Page 58:   The purpose of a warm-up . . . This and the following discussion
           are based on lectures given by R. Siroka, 1987-1992, at the
           Institute for Sociometry in New York and by Z. Moreno, 1988-1991,
           at Boughten Place, Highland Park, New York.

Page 64:   The director should work . . . . J. L. Moreno, vol. 1, p. 258. Beacon,
           NY: Beacon House, 1946.

Page 66:   The double helps . . . Z. Moreno, 1990 (see page 58).

Page 66:   The group is the therapeutic context . . . Z. Moyal, Highland Park,
           NY: Lecture, 1990.

Page 69:   Role reversal is one of the most important . . . Z. Moreno, Lecture,
           same as page 58 (one month later).

Page 69:   Role reversal is . . . Z. Moreno, Lecture, 1988.

Page 69:   "The son, who is still himself . . . J. L. Moreno, vol. 1.

Page 70:   It requires the protagonist . . . D. A. Kipper, *Psychotherapy Through
           Clinical Role Playing*, New York: Brunner-Mazel, 1983, p. 194.

Page 71:   The mirror technique provides . . . Z. Moreno, Lecture, July 2, 1990.

Page 72:   The protagonist may be engaged . . . A. Blatner & A. Blatner.
           Foundation of Psychodrama: History, Theory and Practice.
           New York: Springer.

Page 75:   Psychodrama provides a safe environment . . . Moreno, vol. 1.
           Beacon, NY: Beacon House, 1946.

Page 78:   The process of externalizing . . . R. Siroka, Psychodrama Training
           Institute, New York City (19 West 34th Street), 1988.

Page 82:   "In cases of trauma . . ." Judith Herman, *Trauma and Recovery*,
           New York: Basic Books, 1993.

Page 88:   The earliest photograph . . . John R. Hawkins, from my psycho-
           drama class at New York University, May 22, 1992.

PART II

DRAMA GAMES

The art of life is to show your hand.
There is no diplomacy like candor.
Nothing is so boring as having
to keep up a deception.
—C. V. Lucas

Deep in the mind lie what the Hindus call *samsaras* or mental impressions, what Plato likened to impressions in a wax-like substance and what today we call old tapes or memory traces. Each experience that we have leaves an impression within us. These impressions form what we refer to as our body of experience. Wired up to each impression stored in the brain are our sensory memories surrounding the experience and our emotional reaction to the experience. When we contact any one part of a memory, the rest of it tends to come along with it. It's like pulling weeds up from the bottom of a lake—once we hook a corner of it, the rest follows.

There are many memory doors into a stored impression. Perhaps a smell (olfactory stimulation), a scene (visual stimulation), a sound or song (audio stimulation) or a tactile sensation (tactile stimulation) will remind us of something long ago. That one memory door, when released, opens others, and slowly or quickly the rest of the memory surfaces and becomes available to us in the present moment. Often, if the memories are important, we will re-experience them powerfully in the present moment. Drama games are small structured, psychodramatic events that provide a safe structure through which this unconscious material can be made conscious. The action itself becomes the focus, and everyone's attention is drawn to the present moment.

We make the "then and there" the "here and now" when we bring our surplus reality to the psychodramatic stage. During the process of experiential therapy we suspend our disbelief and become freely engaged in the surplus reality or psychodramatic moment.

Drama games make action-oriented role-playing methods available to a wide variety of people in many settings. The games, which can be structured for focus and safety are clearly laid out with a beginning, a middle and an end. In Part II you will find games that address family of origin, grief and mourning and parenting, and games that can be used in the institutional settings.

A NOTE ABOUT GUIDED IMAGERY

When guided imagery is included in warm-ups and drama games, it is helpful to turn down the lights or play some soft sounds or instrumental music to create mood and increase focus. Encourage people to be very comfortable. As your situation allows, they can sit comfortably in chairs or lie on the floor on their backs. Speak with an even, steady tone of voice, loud enough to be heard but not intrusive.

You may use the imagery as a warm-up to psychodramatic action or as a stimulus for getting in touch with and sharing feelings that arise. If desired, participants can use journaling or letter-writing after the imagery. The journaling can be impromptu, whatever the person desires to write, and a letter can be written (with no intention of mailing it) to any significant person in the imagery or to oneself from anyone in the imagery (a letter one might wish to receive).

Guided imagery can also be used toward therapeutic ends in and of itself. It's use may help to reduce anxiety by allowing the protagonist to imagine a dreaded circumstance and desensitize it by imaging it out again and again either in its desired form or with the protagonist successfully coping with the situation. Such guided imagery uses "effective imagination as a way of gratifying wishes including wishes to avoid painful states that are imagining (the wishes) as gratified."

A person's self-image is a form of mental set. The person who has a low opinion of himself, say, as someone who never really succeeds, is set to notice his failures more than his successes. He notices those aspects that reinforce his self-image and, believing himself to be a failure, puts little energy into trying to succeed. Conversely, someone who is optimistic about his potential will be quick to notice his successes, slow to notice failure and less put off by failure—the basic principle behind the many techniques of positive thinking.

Essential to positive thinking is setting goals and then imagining them to have been achieved. But it is not just a matter of setting goals: they must be seen in the mind's eye as fulfilled. The importance of this can be understood in terms of mental set. If the goal is merely a thing to be desired in the future, then the set remains negative—it has *not yet* been achieved—and experiences will be unconsciously selected that support that set. Imagining as strongly as possible the fulfillment of his dreams as already having occurred sets the person positively for events and opportunities that will support the goals.

Most systems recommend that such imagination be undertaken while in a relaxed state, either while sitting quietly and sinking into a dreamy, peaceful state or while in that no-man's-land between waking and sleeping at night and in the morning—the hypnagogic and hypnopompic states.

Page 95:   It's like pulling weeds . . . C. Whitfield, Lecture, New York City, January 22, 1986.

Page 97:   "effective imagination as . . ." Marshall Edelson, "Defense in Psychoanalytic Theory: Computation or Fantasy?" from Repression and Dissociation. Edited by Jerome Lisinger, University of Chicago Press, 1990.

5
Group Warm-Ups

The real voyage of discovery
consists not in seeking new landscapes
but in having new eyes.
—Marcel Proust

The purpose of the warm-up is to put group members in touch with their own inner stories, which they will later translate into scenes. It makes the transition into action feel compelling, allowing the suspension of disbelief to occur smoothly as the protagonist's surplus reality becomes real on stage. At that point the "as if" falls away and becomes "as," and the protagonist interacts with surrogates as if they were the real people. The past becomes the present.

SUBPERSONALITY I

Goals

1. To get in touch with various parts of self.
2. To clarify the relationship of one subpersonality to another.

Steps

1. Participants should all have paper and pencil.

2. On the paper, have participants make a list of four subpersonalities that they connect with as being a part of themselves, i.e., the angry one, the efficient one, the controller, the victim.

3. Ask them to give each personality a name.

4. Instruct them to use stick figures to locate each personality on a large sheet of paper, in the same relation to one another that they feel the personalities are within themselves.

5. Next to each stick figure, ask them to write the subpersonality's name and a few descriptive words or phrases. They can write as much as they want about any subpersonality that particularly stands out to them.

6. Allow time for group sharing.

Variations

A number of other near-psychodramatic techniques can be used to follow up this exercise.

1. Write a letter to any part of yourself, from "you," and then share it with the group.

2. Mentally reverse roles with any aspect of the self and write a letter from that aspect to your real self.

3. Mentally reverse roles with any aspect of the self and journal as that part of the self: for example, "I am insecurity, and I . . ."

4. Journal in the third person about an aspect of self: for example, "She is anger, and she . . ."

5. Write a poem related in any way to this exercise.

6. Write a scene in which all these aspects of the self interact.

SUBPERSONALITY II

Goals

1. To clarify inner dynamics.
2. To have a dialogue with various parts of the self.

Steps

1. Conduct a brief guided imagery session, leading people first toward relaxation and then centering on their breath. Ask group

members to close their eyes, relax, go into a quiet space and allow an aspect of themselves or subpersonality to surface. A subpersonality might be an angry child, a victim, an aggressor, a scapegoat, a lost child, a mascot and so forth.

2. Ask them to give this personality a name if they so choose.

3. Set up an empty chair.

4. Invite anyone who wishes to put her subpersonality in a chair.

5. Ask the person to stand behind the chair or next to it and introduce her subpersonality to the group by name and tell the group about it from the role of herself or another subpersonality within herself.

6. Allow time for sharing.

Variations

This exercise can be an entertaining way to explore aspects of the self that people do not usually express. Just the act of bringing this part of the self out in the group will be enlivening, relieving and informative.

SUBPERSONALITY PSYCHODRAMA

Goals

1. To get in touch with various parts of the self.

2. To gain perspective on how those parts of the self interrelate.

Steps

1. Participants should have paper and pencil.

2. Instruct them to make a list of four or so subpersonalities. These can be from the list in Subpersonality I, or they can be any others that people connect with as being a part of themselves.

3. Choose people to play each personality. Have the protagonist either tell them, in two or three sentences, about themselves or reverse roles and show them how they sit, act, look and so on.

4. Give the personalities a situation—they are in a waiting room together waiting for the doctor, a job interview, the roof to fall in, the second coming, spring or in any other situation.

5. Let the characters relate to each other while the protagonist

watches, with the director. The protagonist may double for any of the personalities at any time.

6. The director can ask the protagonist to reverse roles with any one of the subpersonalities that merits looking into.

7. The director can question the protagonist about the inner worlds of the personalities, using the technique of interview in order to investigate further what is being felt inside.

8. When the action seems near closure, you can ask the protagonist to end the scene from each role (in role reversal), or with a sentence or two to each role-player from his role.

9. Allow plenty of time for group sharing.

Variations

This exercise can also be done using empty chairs to play all the roles and by asking the protagonist to reverse roles with each subpersonality. It can be used in one-to-one or group work.

INNER-CHILD INTRODUCTION

Goals

1. To bond the group.
2. To introduce inner-child work.

Steps

1. Instruct the group to walk around the room.

2. Ask members to remember how they felt when they walked as children.

3. Encourage them to remember the name that they were called in childhood and to recall what they wanted to be when they grew up.

4. Tell group members to find another person, share this information with him and then begin walking again. Repeat this process with other questions—about favorite foods, favorite toys, what they did not want to be when they grew up and so on. Each time, have them choose a person to share the answer with.

5. End here or move into another activity, or ask members to share their discoveries with the group.

Variations

The group may wish to think of more things of a deeper nature to share about childhood—their fears, frightening or embarrassing experiences, feelings for a best friend—or move into sharing, or progress to an enactment phase.

PUTTING THE INNER CHILD IN A CHAIR

Goals

1. To get in touch with the child within.
2. To share information with the group.

Steps

1. Ask participants to set up a single chair.
2. Ask participants to stand behind or next to the chair.
3. Say, "From the role of your adult self, introduce your inner child to the group and tell the group something about him."
4. Use role reversal where appropriate.
5. End the scene in any way the protagonist wishes to.
6. Allow plenty of time for sharing.

Variations

The group leader may wish to ask a question or two of the person speaking to further the action or deepen it. He may also instruct the speaker to reverse roles and actually sit in the chair and speak from the role of the inner child. The director may wish to interview the inner child in the chair.

INTRODUCING YOURSELF
FROM THE ROLE OF ANOTHER

Goals

1. To share personal information with the group.
2. To get in touch with feelings associated with the self.

Steps

1. Set up an empty chair in the group.

2. Ask group members to think of a person they would like to have introduce them to the group. Then ask them to reverse roles with that person.

3. Have the protagonist stand behind the chair, using the empty chair to represent himself. Then, in role reversal, he introduces himself (represented by the empty chair) to the group. (For example, "I am Jack's Uncle Bill, and I would like to introduce Jack to you and tell you about him.")

4. The group leader can ask the protagonist to reverse roles with himself in the chair.

5. The group leader may question (interview) the protagonist in either role. Questions that require only short answers are best.

6. When the protagonist is finished, thank him and let him sit down.

7. Allow time for group sharing.

Variations

Reversing roles and asking interview questions deepens the action in this exercise quite a bit, and it becomes a minipsychodrama. The group leader can double for the protagonist if it seems helpful.

SHADOW-SELF PICTURE

Goals

1. To warm up to the shadow self.
2. To create a visual image of the shadow self.

Steps

1. Ask participants to get large pieces of paper and crayons or markers.

2. Instruct them as follows: "First, just scribble on a sheet or two of paper to loosen up and lose self-consciousness in drawing."

3. Continue with, "Let an image of your shadow self appear on the paper. It may be an outline, scribbles or very clear—anything is okay. Your shadow is a self that's somewhat hard to see, out of vision or a dark and disowned side you may wish to hide."

4. Then tell them, "Look at it, and allow the feelings it evokes to surface."

5. Finally say, "Write any words or phrases that feel descriptive on and around your picture."

6. Allow time for sharing, in dyads or in small groups.

Variations

You may wish to do the next exercise, Your Shadow Self, right on top of this one or use the picture to look at while doing Your Shadow Self. If more than one shadow self emerges, that's fine. Just follow the same procedure for each self.

YOUR SHADOW SELF

Goals

1. To bring into light the self that is kept in hiding.

2. To release some of the energy that has gone into keeping this opposing self in hiding.

Steps

1. Ask participants to find paper and pen.

2. Say, "Either using your shadow-self picture or just working from your imagination, write or share out loud descriptive adjectives or phrases that describe this part of yourself you wish to keep in hiding."

3. Say, "You may wish to include the names of people that you feel embody these hidden parts of yourself or identify situations that you get into because hidden parts of yourself are being played out."

4. Participants can share this information with another person or with the group.

Variations

Participants may wish to elaborate on the situations that get them into trouble from this point of view. (When we find ourselves being very judgmental of or hooked by someone, and can't let it go, it is possible that he embodies some part of us we don't wish to see in ourselves. This is not always true, of course, but it is worth checking out.) An empty chair or auxiliary can represent the shadow self, and a vignette can ensue.

A LETTER TO MY SHADOW SELF

Goals

1. To gain insight into the shadow self.
2. To release feelings tied up with the shadow self.

Steps

1. Ask participants to find paper and pencil.
2. Say, "From the point of view of your persona, or your outward, presented self, write a letter to your shadow self. You may either give your shadow self a name or write, 'Dear Shadow Self.'"
3. Then, "Write fully all you need to say without editing. Then conclude and sign the letter."
4. Participants can share the letter with a safe person or with the group.

Variations

Such a letter may be written any number of times for any part of the self. Say, "If you have carried feelings for parents or another person—feelings that they denied and you felt 'for' them—you can write a letter to the part of that person that lives inside of you. If there is a person you always felt you were supposed to be and feel less than because you never became that idealized person, you can write a letter to that introjected self. Or if there was a negative image projected onto you that you didn't know what to do with, but have carried in fear of its being true, you can write a letter to that self."

A LETTER FROM MY SHADOW SELF

Goals

1. To release stored feelings around internalized selves that are not especially useful.
2. To free the negative part of that self so that useful parts can be integrated.

Steps

1. Ask participants to find paper and pencil or pen.

2. Say, "From any part of your self that feels as if it needs to be released (see Variations from A Letter To My Shadow Self), write a letter. You may wish to give your shadow self a name. You can write the letter to anyone your shadow self needs to speak to. Write all that you need to say without editing."

3. When they have finished, say, "Write a conclusion and sign your letter."

4. Have participants share the letter with another safe person or with the group. Or invite a protagonist to choose an auxiliary to play him and have the auxiliary read the letter to the protagonist. Or have a protagonist choose an auxiliary to play the person to whom the letter is written and let the protagonist read his own letter.

Variations

Say, "You may write a letter from any part of yourself that feels unintegrated or that you want to release. This can include idealized projections on the part of parents, negative projections, parts of you that you fear or parts of you that you feel are in the way of your personal growth."

SHADOW-SELF DIALOGUE

Goals

1. To give voice to the shadow self and to the person.
2. To increase understanding of inner dynamics.

Steps

1. Set up an empty chair, or ask protagonist to choose someone to play his shadow self.

2. Say, "Pretend that your shadow self is sitting in the chair. Speak to your shadow self and say anything you need to say."

3. You can also ask the protagonist to reverse roles with his shadow self and sit in the chair, and then to speak to himself from the role of his shadow self. Do this as many times as is helpful.

4. Tell the protagonist to end the scene by saying the last things that need to be said for the time being from each role.

5. Have the protagonist share with another person or the group, or write in a journal to process what came up.

Variations

The same procedure can be followed for any interior role or hidden self. It can be useful as a warm-up technique to gain insight into complicated inner roles or selves, and it can be used over a long period of time as exploration.

ANGER AND RAGE RELEASE

Goals

1. To release anger or rage in a controlled, safe situation.

2. To unburden the protagonist of deeply stored historical resentment and rage.

3. To provide an arena for acting out destructive feelings so that they are not acted out in life.

Procedure

Anger and rage work can be a part of any psychodrama. Follow the lead of the protagonist, and allow her to express her anger, if and when it comes up. It is best to let the protagonist express these feelings on her own. Too much pressure from the director can make her feel that she has failed if she doesn't get her anger out, and she will turn it further inward; or, if she gets the feeling that success is defined by an explosion of psychodramatic anger, she may produce it to please the director and not get to other feelings that may be more important for her to be in touch with at that time.

If the protagonist has deep anger and built-up resentment and rage, you can ask her if she wishes to use a bataka (a soft bat) to emphasize physically what she is saying, or beat on pillows to release her rage. When using a bataka, make sure that you are aware of any physical limitations that might create a problem.

Anger can be successfully released in a wide variety of ways, and is more easily catharted than rage. If the rage is too deep to move out through psychodrama, it will need to come to conscious level slowly throughout the therapeutic process as the issues surrounding it are resolved.

DOUBLE FOR YOURSELF

Goals

1. To warm up the group.

2. To obtain a more honest reading of where everyone is within himself.

Steps

1. Ask group members to stand behind their chairs.

2. Give them questions to answer — "How are you feeling in the group?" "How are you feeling about yourself at this moment?" "What are you concerned might happen in the group?" "What are you expecting from it?"

3. Now, have them stand behind their chairs and ask them to double for themselves, that is, to act as their own inner voices and speak as they would not normally speak.

4. As director, you can interview them or ask questions of them as they double, or double for them yourself.

5. After everyone has had a chance to speak as his double, ask them to sit down and either continue to share what came up for them or move into a vignette or scene.

Variations

This can be an exercise on its own—to bond a group and deepen communication—or a warm-up to further action. It can be used, too, in one-to-one therapy as a way of getting at deeper feelings. In this situation the therapist can interview the double and ask the client to reverse roles with himself and his double, as seems appropriate. The therapist may also double for the client from either position.

WHAT'S-IN-THE-WAY ACTION

Goals

1. To get in touch with what's in the way of being successful.

2. To let go of old messages.

Steps

1. Ask participants to mill around the room.

2. Have them walk slowly and allow to come to mind whatever feels in the way of their feeling empowered and letting themselves succeed.

3. Ask participants to mill around the room and speak out words and phrases from their past, or messages from family or society that nag at them as they walk.

4. Bring them back into the large group and let them share their thoughts about how these voices keep them from moving forward, or move into vignettes, choosing one or more people to play the voices. Use role reversal and interview where appropriate.

5. Allow plenty of time for sharing.

Variations

This exercise can be used as a warm-up to several small vignettes or one large psychodrama. The milling can also be used by itself as a warm-up to discussion.

BRIEF ENCOUNTER

Goals

1. To let out held feelings related to a particular incident.
2. To gain insight into each person's point of view.
3. To rewrite history and practice an alternative behavior.

Steps

1. Ask participants to think of an argument or an encounter with one other person that they found difficult and would like to work with.

2. Set up two chairs.

3. Tell the person doing the work to give a thumbnail sketch of the situation and to describe briefly both people involved.

4. Ask the participant to re-enact the encounter, saying what he said and then changing chairs and saying the other person's part. He may have to reverse roles many times throughout this process. It is important that he change chairs each time.

5. Ask for group feedback and sharing.

Variations

When the participant is setting up the scene, ask him to show you things about himself and the other person in the situation: "Reverse roles and show me how this person would sit. How does he hold his body and use his hands?" and so on. It helps to warm the person up to the action of talking.

You may wish to give the participant "corrective time" and let him do the scene a second time, saying and doing what he wishes had happened in each role, the way he would like the encounter to have gone—an alternative behavior.

ROLE-REVERSAL INTRODUCTION

Goals

1. To bond group members.
2. To warm up group members to sharing personal information.
3. To share personal material with the group.

Steps

1. Ask everyone in the group to stand up and take a slow walk around the room, weaving around one another.
2. After a couple of minutes, ask members to look around and make eye contact with someone they don't already know, who they would like to know a little more about.
3. Ask them to slowly approach that person and, in a pair, to find a place to sit down.
4. Ask them to take several minutes each to get to know everything about one another that they can, instructing them not to share anything that would not be comfortable for the whole group to know.
5. Time them. Give each person about five minutes; then tell them to switch.
6. After they seem to have shared enough, instruct them to reverse roles with one another and to introduce themselves to the group pretending that they are their partners. For example: Michael and Ellen are partners; they reverse roles; Michael plays the role of Ellen and introduces himself to the group as Ellen,

using the information he has just learned; then Ellen introduces herself from the role of Michael.

7. Repeat this with each pair until everyone is introduced.

Variations

You may ask questions of the person speaking about the person he is playing, or other group members can ask him to provide further bonding within the group.

PROBLEM ATOM

Goals

1. To sort out and examine the various aspects of a problem.

2. To gain a variety of perspectives on a problem.

Steps

1. First ask participants to name the problem and write it at the top of the paper.

2. Using a social-atom format, ask participants to locate the problem and then themselves anywhere on the paper that feels right, using the symbols of triangles for men, circles for women and squares for the problem.

3. Now ask them to locate all other aspects of the problem as close or as far as seems appropriate, using triangles for men, circles for women and squares for genderless aspects of the problem, and to label each symbol.

4. At this point there are two options: (a) to take turns sharing the atom with the rest of the group, describing why symbols are located where they are and what feelings are associated with them, or (b) to move the atom into action by choosing group members to play the most important aspects of the problem. Ask them to stand in the same relationship to one another that appears on the paper. Ask the protagonist to mill around the various people or aspects of the problem until he finds some aspect with which he feels like speaking; then ask him to do so. Role reversal and doubling may be used. When the protagonist has spoken and reversed roles whenever he feels drawn to do so, he may end the scene any way he wishes.

5. Whichever process is used, leave plenty of time for sharing.

6. After the sharing is complete, you may wish to ask the participants to think of one important thing they learned through this process and share it with the group.

Variations

After each person has made an atom and processed it in one of the two ways, you may wish to ask him to make it over again, either (a) as it feels now that he has processed it—perhaps it has changed a little; or (b) as he would like it to be or wishes it was. Then the new atoms should be shared.

MOMENTS OF JOY

Goals

1. To get in touch with joyful feelings from the past.

2. To claim joy and use it as a building block for future experience.

Steps

1. Ask participants to find pencil and a paper.

2. Say, "Close your eyes and recall a single moment or repeated event from your past that made you feel good or joyful."

3. They should write out the experience in the first person as if it were happening in the present, or simply share it verbally without writing. "I feel the sunlight on my face. I hear the birds and smell spring in the air. I am wearing my windbreaker and going out the front door to play Kick the Can."

4. Ask them to share the memory fully with a trusted person or with the group.

Variation

The scene can be structured as a vignette and played out psychodramatically. In that case move from the imagery directly into action. In therapeutic recovery we tend to focus on painful experiences. While this is completely necessary to move toward health, it is also crucial to claim the good in our lives at an experiential feeling level so that we can become comfortable with it and feel drawn toward accepting and creating more good.

BODY DRAMAS

Goals

1. To understand the feelings that have been somatized.
2. To give the body a voice psychodramatically.

Steps

1. Allow group members to close their eyes and get in touch with themselves and then to share about any part of their bodies that is giving them trouble of any kind—stiff neck, tic, obesity, sore limbs and so on.

2. Ask if anyone wants to put his work before the group.

3. Ask that person to describe briefly what is going on with a particular part of his body.

4. Ask him to choose someone to play that part of his body or several parts of his body, as needed.

5. Let the protagonist speak to his body part and reverse roles whenever he needs to.

6. If several body parts are cast, you may ask the protagonist to put them where it feels appropriate or line them up in physical sequence.

7. After the drama, allow group members to share what comes up in the drama for them.

Variations

So much feeling is somatized that a body drama is a rich take-off point to get into feelings stored by the body. People may wish to talk to a headache or lower back pain and build psychodramas out of this by casting people in roles as they come up. They may have something to say to excess weight. If a particular person in their lives appears in the drama, you may cast the role and continue to do so for any important character-building, and move into a vignette or psychodrama.

NONVERBAL UNDERSTANDING

Goals

1. To understand how much personal information is exchanged on a nonverbal level.

2. To bond group members.

Steps

1. Instruct group members to wander around the room.

2. Tell them to notice someone with whom they feel a connection.

3. Ask them to pair off with the person with whom they feel the connection.

4. Explain that you will give about ten minutes (five minutes apiece) for people to take turns observing one another nonverbally, taking in as much as possible. Then they will share with the partner what they have observed. Allow one partner several minutes both to observe and then to share. Then have them switch and let the other person observe and then share.

5. In the large group, have them share whatever they need to that came up during the exercise.

Comments

It is amazing what people pick up on a nonverbal level. Though the exercise may seem difficult, it is surprisingly successful when carried out. (This exercise is adapted from a workshop given by Zerka Moreno.)

MASKS

Goals

1. To give the protagonist the sense of being anonymous, allowing more candid and honest expression.

2. To concretize both mood and feeling.

Steps

1. This drama game involves making a mask to represent a role each group member plays. Decide, as a facilitator, what you wish

the mask to symbolize—the inner self, the persona, the wounded child, the addict, the co-addict, the victim, the empowered aspect of self, the hero, the lost child, the mascot or whatever you wish.

2. Through brief guided imagery lead group members to identify one of these roles within themselves and to start imagining themselves in it. This is not a full warm-up to action and the imagery may be short.

3. The next step is to make the mask. This can be done in a variety of ways. Participants can use plastered gauze and actually form the mask on a person's face, or, using colors and tag board, they can cut out a mask and draw on it. It can be as ornate or simple as desired. You may even use prefabricated masks and ask the group members to choose one they are drawn to. (If you do this, you may skip Step 2 and simply lay a variety of masks on the stage, allowing participants to mill around and choose the one they are drawn to.)

4. After all group members have masks, ask them to wander around the room until they find somewhere they wish to settle and then sit down.

5. Ask them to spend some time looking at the mask and paying attention to the feelings that arise.

6. After they have had a few minutes to do so, ask them to take turns introducing themselves to the group, either from where they sit or by designating a stage area. They should say who they are, describe themselves and speak from the point of view of the role designated by the mask: "I am so and so and I look like this because . . .." Everything should be in the first person and the present, regardless of when it may have occurred. The director may wish to double to further or deepen the action, or may use an empty chair to represent the real self if the protagonist wants to reverse roles in and out between the two.

7. Allow each person to speak fully from the role as the character and to take the time to move through his feelings.

8. When everyone has worked who wishes to, ask the group to share what came up for them as a group. Or you can ask them to walk over to the person with whom they felt the most identification and share with that person. Afterwards they can come back to the larger group to continue sharing.

Variations

In schools. If you use masks as a warm-up in a school, students can make the masks during art time. They can have a writing project, consisting of writing a soliloquy, to continue the introduction.

Family of origin. For family-of-origin work, participants can make masks representing any or all family members, and then introduce them in role reversal—that is, actually be the family member behind the mask. In this case if he wants to go beyond the introduction portion of the exercise, the protagonist may wish to use an empty chair or his own mask to represent himself. He can reverse roles into the chair or mask, or stand behind the chair when necessary. He may double for each member.

Many selves. More than one mask can be made to represent aspects of the self, or more than one mask can be made to represent another person. Or you may wish to ask someone to make one mask representing the inner self and one the outer self, in order to explore the level of dissonance or integration between the two.

Addiction masks. For cases that involve addiction—either a recovering addict or the child or spouse of an addict—people can make a clean mask and a high mask, and then introduce them in role reversal, as with the family-of-origin variation.

Life stages. Masks can be made that represent different stages in life. People who are coping with major life transitions might find it useful to re-visit themselves at various stages throughout their lives in order to promote integration of the life cycle.

Idealized selves. A client might do a mask of the idealized self, the unattainable self that is always making him feel as if he is falling short, or make a mask of the idealized parent, spouse, child and so on.

In any and all of these cases, journaling might be useful as a way to follow up on feelings that continue to arise. The journaling can be done in the first person, the third person or in role reversal (journaling as another person).

Page 108: Anger can be successfully . . . R. Siroka, Psychodrama Training
        Institute, New York City (19 West 34th Street), September 20, 1993.

Page 109: What's In The Way . . . Exercise adapted from a workshop by David Swink, New Jersey, 1991.

Page 114: If a particular person in their lives . . . R. Siroka, Psychodrama Training Institute, New York City (19 West 34th Street), January 20, 1986.

Page 115: It is amazing . . . Z. Moreno, Lecture, Highland Park, NY, July 3, 1987.

Page 115: Decide as a facilitator . . . Sharon Wegscheider-Cruse, Onsite Training and Consulting, Rapid City, SD: Lecture, April 18, 1977.

6
Family-Of-Origin Games

Everyone is the child of his past.
—Edna G. Rostow

Each of us grew up in a unique family system and, deep down, we generally wish to continue to live in a similar context. If our family was nurturing, then we have had a head start in life. But if our family system was destructive, we need to find a way out of that cycle. One way is by exploring the effect of the system on us and our effect on others. Making an alcoholic father the problem, or an abusive sister the problem, is an easy way to get stuck in therapy. When we understand the full generational system, we take the pressure off one or two individuals and ultimately off ourselves. It is important, though, that this larger awareness not be premature, that it not serve to foster false forgiveness and an unconscious avoidance of the deep personal work that recovery will require.

Psychodrama offers a method of dealing with the family system *as it is stored and lives within our psyches.* Though we may not have the original cast of characters to work with, we do have the ability to concertize our inner truth and to bring our family of origin from the darkness of memory to the psychodramatic stage. The coping measures and defensive tactics that we developed as children, to help us live in a home that felt hostile, tend to surface through the action of a psychodrama. Once they are on the surface, it becomes easier to identify them and thus possible to gain some compassion and perspective about why they were necessary to begin with.

Children gain a sense of self in a variety of ways. They model parents with a sense of self. They are valued, loved and have a valued place within their families. When a parent is deeply preoccupied with a substance or activity—food, work, sex, liquor or drugs, for example—it ties up a good portion of his psychic and emotional energy. Children sense this and feel alienated by something they cannot see or understand. Their experience is one of living in an emotional vacuum, abandoned in a highly charged but ill-defined space. They sense that their parents are not fully available to themselves. Thus they internalize their parents unavailability as a dismissal or dissatisfaction with them, and they feel ashamed of themselves. They wonder what's wrong with them. The problem is compounded by the fact that parents who are not present for their children generally feel guilty—guilty for not being there and angry or even rageful toward their children for their constant demands, which act as reminders to the parents of their inability to be present and mobilize the parents' own inner pain.

As the parents feel more guilt about their angry feelings toward their child they may attempt to make up for it with effusive outpourings of attention. So the child feels out of control. On the one hand they cannot get enough attention when they need it, and on the other, they get much more than they want, in fact, an uncomfortable amount seemingly out of nowhere. The same behavior on the child's part can produce very different responses from their parents.

Children need reasonably consistent feedback in their formative years in order to build a stable sense of self; it has to be built slowly from within. And it is necessary to understand the mind of the child to conceptualize why early learning lasts a lifetime. Children do not think like adults. They live in a world of "magical" thoughts in which dresses hanging on a door can become dancing ghosts and stuffed animals have the capability of becoming real. Think then what alcoholic or depressed parents become to the minds of children. What children grow up with in these early years is stored in their brains as it is learned. When the environment that children grow up in contains secret preoccupations, misunderstood anger, anxiety, and unexpressed pain, the children pick up on it and internalize it as their own. They do not have the intellectual capability to use abstract thought. Children see their parents as representations of themselves; who their parents are feels like who they are. If their parents are strong, the children feel they are strong. If their parents feel ashamed, the children "become" that shame. If their parents are lost, the children have trouble locating themselves. The wish on the part of the children to heal their parents is an attempt to heal the self because at the deepest, earliest level, the parents are one and the same with the children. The children feel one with their parents through identification and in that sense who the parents are, is also who the children are.

The combination of inconsistent availability and feedback from the parent and the child's internalizing the parent's deep unresolved issues inhibits the growing child in his own process of exploring and building a self. The reason substances and activities are used and eventually misused is because using a substance to alter mood feels less risky than facing what lies within. To go within and truly address the pain, confusion and anger feels dangerous and frightening. Substances and activities offer an alternative mood that is at first predictable and dependable. The sad fact is that, though they initially offer relief from pain, over time they remove any real self that is there by substituting for it a false one that appears strong but is imbibed. The larger the imbibed self grows, the more insignificant the true self becomes. When that false self loses it's foothold, there is no real self to step in and take its place—hence the workaholic who throws himself out of a window when the market crashes; the mother who breaks down when the children move out; the alcoholic, cigarette or food addict who goes crazy when their supply is unavailable.

Contacting the trauma below the level of lexical thinking, accessing the symbolic and imagistic functions, allows the client to awaken the full traumatic experience, feel it in the present and release it.

THE USE OF THE SOCIAL ATOM

The social atom is a cornerstone of family-of-origin therapy. (Refer to Chapter 3, Sociometry; How Psychodrama Works, for details on doing a social atom.) In early stages you can ask your client to make a family-of-origin social atom to use as a referent throughout the process of family-of-origin work. For example, you may ask, "Whom do you need to talk to? What do you need to say to the people on your atom?" Or when a person in daily life is triggering something for your client, you can ask, "Who is this person representing for you on your atom?"

Throughout the therapy process, you and your client can explore other relevant atoms, from the perspective of adolescence or young adulthood, for example, or a client can make either of this parent's social atoms at crucial times in his life, reflecting the time of his birth, at a time when he remembers his life changing, etc. You may also ask your client to make the social atom of either parent at the onset of their alcoholism or at significant times in the parent's growing years. A client can make the social atom of siblings at relevant moments in the client's life, in order to gain perspective. Spending time in the role of someone who lives "rent free" within us helps to gain clarity on and separation from the person. The social atom is as flexible and applicable as the ability of the therapist to apply it. It can be a useful tool for exploring the original system, which has been internalized by the client, from a variety of perspectives.

The rest of this chapter is devoted to psychodrama games that deal with the wide varieties of issues present in any family system. Read the goals and apply them to specific clients and problems as appropriate. (For information on the dynamics of alcoholic and addicted families, see Chapter 11, Using Psychodrama With Addicts and ACoAs.)

SPIRIT OF THE HOUSE

Goals

1. To bring forward the unconscious atmosphere of the family.
2. To release stored feelings picked up from the atmosphere.

Steps

1. Lead a brief visualization of the atmosphere of the home. Ask group members to relax and allow their minds to go back to a time when the family was present. They should try to picture the family as clearly as possible—where they are in the house, how they look, what the atmosphere is like and so on.

2. Choose as the protagonist the person who seems to be the most warmed up. Ask him to choose group members to play family members, pets and so on, and a person to play himself. Ask him to "sculpt" the location and position of each family member, putting them in the body position that seems to represent them along with the appropriate facial expression. Ask auxiliaries to freeze in those positions.

3. Ask the protagonist to walk around the sculpture, looking at it and feeling what comes up. Then he can begin to play the spirit by saying, "I am the spirit of this house and . . ." At this point he can say whatever he wishes to say about the unconscious feelings in the atmosphere. He may wish to stand behind anyone, including himself, and double for what is going on inside him.

4. He ends the scene by saying, as the "spirit," anything that feels right.

5. Leave sufficient time for sharing.

Variations

This exercise can be a warm-up that leads into a psychodrama with the existing characters, or an exercise in and of itself with sharing at the end. It can also be done with only a protagonist doing a soliloquy as the spirit.

FAMILY RULES

Goals

1. To make conscious unspoken family rules.
2. To examine overt family rules.

Steps

1. Each group member needs paper and two colored pens.
2. To warm up, say, "Take a moment to close your eyes and let

your memories of the past surface, such as feeling about the family, or draw images of the house or family that feel important to you."

3. When participants open their eyes, say, "In one color, write the family rules that were spoken out loud within your home, for example, 'We never use bad language,' or 'We always behave like ladies and gentlemen.'"

4. Continue, "In another color, write the rules that were 'understood,' the rules that were silently perceived by everyone in the family—never spoken and never broken."

5. Have them share the rules with a trusted person or with the group.

Variations

This exercise can be a warm-up to psychodramatic action. It may also be expanded if clients wish by circling, in a third color, rules they are living by in the present and actively passing on to current family or friends.

DOUBLE MESSAGES

Goals

1. To sort out the incongruent messages and expectations given by parents.

2. To clarify crazy-making messages.

Steps

1. First, do the Family Rules exercise above.

2. Ask participants to find pencil and paper.

3. Ask participants to refer to their completed Family Rules exercise.

4. Say, "Draw a stick figure of yourself and locate around it the figures of other people in your family of origin—aunts, uncles, grandparents, pets—anyone you need to include."

5. Ask, "What were the expectations that you grew up with?" And ask participants to write out the rules that came from parents, grandparents or any other family authority.

6. Continue, "Underline the rules that your parents both expected you to follow and lived by themselves."

7. Continue, "Now circle the rules that your parents or authority figures expected you to follow but did not live by themselves."

8. Have participants share the information with a trusted person or with the group.

Comments

Dysfunctional families in "looking-good" homes tend to have expectations of children that their own behavior does not reflect, and children attempt to carry the burden of convincing the world that they are really okay. Modeling is the most powerful way of passing on behavior, and children who unconsciously model their parents' behavior but are told to behave in a different way by their parents get confused and feel inwardly dissonant. Children often mirror back to parents their own behavior, and then the parents unconsciously try to correct in their children what they cannot see or correct in themselves.

UNCONSCIOUS FAMILY MESSAGES

Goals

1. To clarify messages, both positive and negative, that are absorbed from the family unconscious.

2. To make these messages conscious so that clients can decide what to do with them.

Steps

1. Give participants paper and a pencil.

2. Ask them to draw a simple picture or symbol representing themselves—or they may use a photograph of themselves when they were young.

3. Say them, "Around the picture or over it, write the messages that were spoken, unspoken or simply a part of the atmosphere."

4. When they have done so, say, "On another sheet of paper, write a couple of paragraphs about how these messages have been carried within you and by you into your adulthood."

5. When they are finished, say, "In another paragraph write how you may be living out messages unconsciously in your own life or passing them on to other people. How do they affect the way you see other people and the way other people see you?"

6. Have them share the information with another person or with the group.

Comments

Unconscious messages that are absorbed both unexamined and unedited — that is, swallowed whole — have tremendous power. They are other people's images about themselves and about us that we accept as our own truths. It is well worth taking the time to understand these messages and liberate ourselves from them.

CARRIED FEELINGS

Goals

1. To understand what feelings were denied by other family members.

2. To separate clients' own feelings from those they carry for other people.

Steps

1. Ask participants to find paper and pen.

2. First, do the exercise above, "Unconscious Family Messages." Whether this next exercise is done alone or in a group, warm up to it with a guided imagery to get in touch with the feelings present in the atmosphere of the family.

3. Ask participants to draw pictures or symbols or write names representing family members, including themselves. Ask them to write feelings they felt that person carried but denied or refused to feel.

4. With another pen, have them draw a line from the person denying his feelings to all the people who felt feelings "for him" or carried the feelings for him, and then write the feeling words at the end of the line.

5. Have them share this information with a safe person or with the group.

Variations

When powerful family members, such as parents, deny such feelings as shame, anger, inadequacy or sexual feelings, refusing to acknowledge them openly to others and themselves, these feelings are still present in the atmosphere. Other family members receive confused messages and, without meaning to, carry these unconscious feelings as their own. When one person will not take responsibility for his feelings, other people may feel them and take responsibility for them as their own—an aspect of co-dependency and enmeshment. The diagrams that come out of this exercise make clear how the participants become enmeshed in a dysfunctional family and how difficult is the task of healthy separation and maturation: First, it is difficult to see which feelings are one's own. Next, it is difficult to separate from something one cannot locate. In an unclear system, it is difficult to differentiate,self-define and individuate.

HIDDEN FAMILY SHADOWS

Goals

1. To bring to light the hidden dark dynamics within the family.

2. To understand negative entanglements between family members.

Steps

1. Ask participants to find paper and pen.

2. Ask them to make a line sketch or any visual symbol that feels right for each family member.

3. Next to, or over, each symbol, have them write words or phrases that describe each person's hidden shadow that has power in the atmosphere but is partly or completely unexpressed.

4. Ask each participant to make a few different arrangements on different sheets of paper, locating her own shadow self and those of her family members. Locate them as they are in relationship to the self and/or cluster them in subgroupings that exist within the family on either a conscious or unconscious level.

5. Participants may use words or phrases to further describe the relationships.

6. Participants may journal about what they observe for themselves, or they may share these diagrams with a safe person or with the group.

Variations

Make sure that participants have done the personal shadow exercises before attempting this one. They may wish to draw lines between members, circles around groupings, words describing dynamics or visuals to expand the exercise. Whatever works for them is fine. (See "Shadow" Exercises, Chapter 5, Group Warm-ups).

FAMILY GROUPINGS

Goals

1. To understand how the family divides itself and who is connected to whom in particular ways.

2. To make decisions about how those alliances have affected people and explore ways to handle them.

Steps

1. Ask participants to find pencil and paper.

2. Using triangles to represent men and circles to represent women, ask participants to begin to play with different family groupings in their minds.

3. Say, "First write the constellation of the entire family as you see it."

4. When they have done so, say, "Now find as many small groups as you feel exist and use the symbols to diagram diads and triads on the same or another sheet of paper. Label your symbols with the appropriate names. You may wish to include extended family members or pets in your groupings.

5. Ask participants to share with another person or with the group their reasons for grouping people as they did, and their feelings in relation to each one.

Comments

This game may open rich discussion about newly discovered overt alliances within the family system that had an impact on the family. You may decide to structure a psychodrama that works with one of the groupings.

FAMILY-LIFE LEARNINGS

Goals

1. To understand conscious and unconscious agreements made in a family.

2. To understand how those agreements are, or are not, still in practice.

Steps

1. Ask each participant to find a pencil and two pieces of paper.

2. Ask participants to close their eyes and allow scenes from their past to surface in their minds, letting scenes roll in and out.

3. Say, "As these scenes move through your mind, make a mental note referring to something you learned from them about how the family operated."

4. Then say, "On your paper jot down words or phrases that sum up the learning from that scene. For example, 'Don't speak up,' 'Always keep family business quiet,' 'Prepare yourself for anything that could happen,' 'Ignore your pain and keep a brave face,' 'Act happy, no matter what,' 'We are a family with good values, we treat people well' and so on—both positive and negative."

5. Ask participants to write "Silent or Unconscious" at the top of one piece of paper and "Spoken or Conscious" at the top of another.

6. Have them list the tacit learning under "Silent or Unconscious" and open agreements under "Spoken or Conscious."

7. Ask them to look over their lists and underline the agreements that they are still living by today.

8. Say, "On the appropriate page jot down the current situation in which these agreements are being upheld."

9. From here there are a few options:

a. With the original characters, structure a psychodrama around the situation in which an agreement was first "understood." Choose any agreement that the protagonist is warmed up to.

b. Place the "agreement" in an empty chair and talk with it, reversing roles desired, or choose someone to play the agreement and do the same.

c. Break up into small groups or pairs and share the lists.

d. Write a letter to the agreement you would like to say good-bye to, feeling all your feelings concerning it, explaining why you need to let it to.

10. Whatever option you choose, allow time to share and process afterward.

Comments

This exercise could also apply to agreements in work situations or to family-of-origin agreements that are lived out in the workplace.

FAMILY AGREEMENTS

Goals

1. To clarify overt and tacit agreements among family members.
2. To make unconscious agreements become conscious.

Steps

1. Ask participants to find pen and paper.

2. Ask them to divide their papers into two parts—at the top half to put the word "Spoken" and at the bottom half to put the word "Unspoken."

3. Say, "Locate yourself on the paper wherever it feels appropriate along with those people with whom you had relationships. Use circles to represent females and triangles to represent males. Place these symbols in a way that shows their relationship to one another, write the names inside the symbols; and briefly state the spoken and unspoken agreements (see Figure 6.1)."

4. Share these agreements and the feelings that accompany them with a trusted person or with the group. Try to get in touch with the way in which these family agreements are currently being played out.

Variations

Unspoken agreements that have had great power in the past may continue into adulthood. A family can agree that one child is the smartest, and the rest of the children can go through life feeling dumb. The arena of the family, however small, represents the world to the child; so the role and attributes that are silently agreed upon in childhood are carried into the world as self-perceptions. This is the stuff of which self-images are made, and it is important for clients to understand in specific ways what contracts agreed to in childhood among family members are carried into adulthood. After clarifying the agreements that were harmful, clients may wish to write new agreements for each old agreement—new agreements that empower them in a positive way in the present. Affirmations can also be used: for example, "My sister is pretty, and I am smart" can be rewritten as, "I am pretty for myself inside and out, and I respect my own intelligence and the intelligence of others."

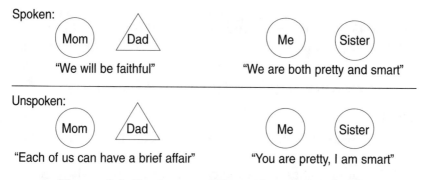

Figure 6.1. Spoken and Unspoken Agreements

IF THE WALLS COULD TALK

Goals

1. To clarify the unspoken atmosphere.
2. To get in touch with unspoken feelings or activities.

Steps

1. Ask participants to find pencil and paper.

2. Ask them to close their eyes and go within. Say, "Allow images of your childhood home to surface in your mind. Let your mind take you to a particular room. Let any images or feelings arise and simply be there with them."

3. Say, "Using the image of a wall that can talk, speak as if you were the wall and describe what you see that is going on. Describe it on a piece of paper."

4. Ask participants to share what they have written with another safe person or with the group.

Variations

This exercise can be used many times, with different rooms, and each time it will be different. It can also be used for riding in a car or living in another home that was important. Some places will hold happy and safe memories, while other places will hold unhappy or traumatic ones; it is equally important to record all of them. If any objects in the room have something to say, the object can be indicated and spoken for. The idea is to reverse roles with a wall or an object and speak "as it" in a soliloquy. This exercise can also be a warm-up to action—placing the wall or object in an empty chair and reversing roles with it or choosing a role-player.

WRITING THE SUBTEXT

Goals

1. To speak the unspeakable or give words to the unspoken atmosphere.

2. To gain insight into messages in the atmosphere that became internalized into the personality.

Steps

1. Ask participants to find pen and paper.

2. Say, "Close your eyes, relax, regulate your breathing and allow your mind to drift. Imagine that there is a stage in your mind and onto that stage let a scene appear, one in which you felt that the reality that was being acted out by others on the surface was very different from what was being felt on the inside. This was a time when you felt that the outside or inside were out of sync, making you question your perceptions, feel isolated, feel out of it or crazy."

3. Continue by saying, "Look at the characters in your scene. Look at their faces and their body postures and listen to what they are saying."

4. Continue, "Look at yourself in the scene, and allow yourself to feel the feelings that are evoked."

5. Continue, "There is a small voice inside of you trying to speak. Listen to the voice and pay attention to what it is saying. Let the voice get louder."

6. Continue, "On a piece of paper, begin to write everything that the voice is saying, whether or not it makes any sense. Write it as it comes up without trying to sound good or intelligent or correct. Just write what the voice is saying."

7. Ask participants to share what they have written with another safe person or with the group.

Variations

This exercise can be done individually or during a group session and then read aloud. It may help to play some soft background music to aid in focusing, or to dim the lights slightly. If you structure this exercise psychodramatically, you can read the material to the character of your choice and represent the person with an empty chair or an auxiliary. Then you can reverse roles and allow a response, or reverse roles as appropriate.

SCENE AND SUBTEXT

Goals

1. To make conscious the subtext of a situation.

2. To understand more fully the power of repressed feelings in the atmosphere.

Steps

1. Ask participants to close their eyes and allow a situation from their past to surface—one in which they felt inwardly split or "crazy," one in which what they were feeling did not seem to fit with what was going on outside them, for example, being pleasant and polite at a quiet family dinner while they were feeling rejected, unseen or angry.

2. Choose a protagonist, and ask her to choose people to play each part in the scene.

3. Then ask the protagonist to put the people in place, describing the character in a sentence or two or showing them the character by reversing roles and taking the character's body position. When the scene is in play, ask the protagonist to speak to whomever

she needs to. Next, have the protagonist reverse roles with the person playing her and speak the unspoken words of the subtext as she saw and felt it. She may also wish to double for herself or her auxiliaries and speak out the unconscious feelings in the situation.

4. Next, the protagonist can step out of the scene and restructure it as she wishes it had been, putting people and herself in the relationship that she would have preferred at the time.

5. Allow the group to share with the protagonist what came up for them as a result of watching the scene, and then let the auxiliary egos de-role.

Variations

This exercise can be done for many situations in which the protagonist felt impotent about not being able to speak. The idea is to give voice to the unspoken reality that was present and powerful but unacknowledged. In dysfunctional families people see one reality with their eyes, but sense another truth in feeling. When the two realities don't match up, the person feels "crazy" and begins to doubt his own perceptions. There is a great emphasis on looking good in dysfunctional families; the sicker the family gets, the wider the gap becomes between what the family looks like and what it feels like. In this exercise we give voice to that gap and gain some understanding of what was going on in that nebulous feeling space.

PARENTAL INTROJECT

Goals

1. To play out the parental introject, or the internalized parent.
2. To identify hot spots in the intrapsychic relationship with the parent.

Steps

1. Begin with a brief guided-imagery session in which you ask participants to get in touch with something about their parents that they feel they carry within them—perhaps some aspect that frightened them or made them feel bad in some way, or an aspect that made them feel good.

2. Invite group members to show or act out either one of their parents for a couple of minutes or so. Anything that comes to their minds is appropriate.

3. After each person who chooses to do so has "shown" his parent, take some time to share any awarenesses that arose.

4. Invite the group members to do the exercise again, if they choose, with the same or another parent.

5. Then ask the group to share any awarenesses that arose from this second round of acting out. What did they relive in doing the exercise another time?

6. Certain group members may wish to use this exercise as a warm-up to a psychodrama about their parents, choosing people to play their parents, or they may choose to play their parents and choose someone else to play themselves or others in the scene.

Variations

At any point these small scenes can move into larger scenes if the director and protagonist wish to follow such a path and it is okay with the group. All group members will benefit for we all carry aspects of our parents within ourselves: if one experiences a harsh, judgmental parent, for example, one will internalize that harsh parent making the parent a part of his own self system. Playing out the introject can give us a look at what we have internalized either as a critical, judgmental voice or as a positive one.

One more variation might be to attempt to face a life situation "as the parent" in order to gain insight into how the parent thinks. This can be done verbally or psychodramatically through the use of interview. Simply name the situation, set the scene or use the other above mentioned techniques.

FAMILY LOSSES

Goals

1. To get in touch with what the family as a whole has lost.
2. To identify losses so that they can be worked through.

Steps

1. Ask participants to find paper and pencil.
2. Devote some time to a guided imagery so that participants

can get in touch, first, with their families of origin and, next, with issues they feel a sense of loss about.

3. Say, "On your paper, let that voice inside of you, perhaps the voice of your inner child, speak. Write down in words or phrases what that child lost."

4. If you are in a group, you may wish to structure a psychodrama around any of these situations. Along with what was lost, the participants may wish to share what they wish had been different as a child.

5. Ask participants to share and process all their feelings with the group or with the therapist.

Variations

If you are in a large group and do not wish to do a psychodrama, you can break down into pairs or groups of three or four and share your lists, afterward returning to the large group for continued sharing.

If you are using this game in one-to-one therapy, process all the feelings with your client. You may also set up empty chairs to represent people and speak to them.

POSITIVE MESSAGES

Goals

1. To claim the good in one's childhood.
2. To understand the many places from which good can come.

Steps

1. Ask participants to find paper and pencil.

2. Ask participants to make simple line drawings of themselves as children, in any way that feels expressive and right.

3. Say, "Let yourself remember the positive messages that you heard or felt about yourself as a young person."

4. Say, "Write these messages down anywhere on the page. Next to the message, write from whom the message emanated, including yourself."

5. Finally, "Share this with a trusted person or with the group, or choose role-players to say these messages to the person in whatever way you choose."

Variations

We have all internalized positive messages about ourselves—and while it is necessary to get in touch with the negative messages, it is equally important to get in touch with the positive messages that are a part of our unconscious selves. The affirmative ways we feel about ourselves are a vital part of our well-being.

PERSONAL GIFTS AND STRENGTHS

Goals

1. To acknowledge and bring into the open strengths and gifts and to tolerate feelings that arise when acknowledging our positive qualities.

2. To take responsibility for good qualities and act on them, and also to focus on the positive.

Steps

1. Ask participants to find pencil and paper.

2. Say, "We all have qualities we feel good about. We sometimes focus on the negative and forget the positive qualities we inherited and developed. Write down some of those upbeat, character-building qualities that have brought you this far in life and that will be your strength for change and rebuilding in the future."

3. Ask participants to choose any person in their lives from whom they wish they had received a letter of appreciation thanking them for their strength and help and acknowledging their good qualities. Instruct them to write that letter to themselves as if they were that person.

4. Ask participants to share their letter with their group or a safe person, or to break up into pairs to share their letters. Alternatively, ask participants to choose someone in the group that they would like to have read the letter to them. The protagonist may also choose someone to play himself while he reads his letter from the auxiliary role.

5. Return to the large group for continued sharing.

Variations

If this exercise is done in one-to-one work, the letter can be shared and processed with the therapist. You may also structure a psychodrama with empty chairs or auxiliaries representing positive qualities. You can ask participants to talk to the quality and reverse roles with it, speaking from the role of the quality.

FAMILY GODS AND GODDESSES

Goals

1. To find a playful way to identify what the family as a whole idealized.

2. To see how the ideals played out in one's life.

Steps

1. Ask participants to find paper and colored pens or pencils.

2. Say, "Close your eyes and remember those things that were idealized by your family — work, popularity, brains, success, athletics, beauty, power, eternal victimization, failure and so on."

3. Continue, "Now, using symbols, words or colors, represent or describe the various gods and goddesses in your family."

4. Continue, "Near what you have written, try to ascertain who was the "keeper" of each ideal — whose job was it to live out a particular ideal or represent the family's interest by embodying those characteristics. There may be one person for each, or several. Write their names in the appropriate location."

5. Continue, "Next, indicate how you personally feel in relationship to each ideal — how did it work in your life?"

6. Ask participants to share their sketches and feelings in small groups or with one other person—or you can develop a psychodrama using people or empty chairs to play the various roles.

Variations

Families often assign jobs or roles to their members. In dysfunctional families the identities become rather fixed, and members come to feel overly entitled to some qualities and under entitled to others. The family lacks the fluidity of moving in and out of stages and roles in a natural way. As family members attempt to keep things stable and avoid chaos, things become fixed.

GODS AND GODDESSES JOURNAL

Goals

1. To understand how family drives were lived out.
2. To change roles with other family members in an enjoyable and interesting way.

Steps

1. Ask participants first to do the previous Family Gods And Goddesses exercise.

2. Ask them to write a journal entry from the point of view of each God and Goddess. Write in the first person and have fun: for example, "I am the Goddess of Beauty and I live in Susie's dreams. She worships me through magazines and hairdos, clips, bands and so on."

3. Participants may share these in pairs, small groups or the larger group, if desired.

Variations

Each participant might choose one Goddess to portray. She could present herself to the group in any way. She might use an empty chair to represent herself and introduce herself to the group from the role of the Goddess, standing behind the chair and talking about how she relates to "the person" in the chair. Then roles could be reversed.

DOING A PARENT'S PSYCHODRAMA

Goals

1. To understand a parent's life and emotional makeup by playing their life.
2. To get in touch with the intergenerational traits passed down and internalized from parent to child.

Steps

1. Ask participants to invite the group to share their feelings about their parents' lives, choosing something to share that they find especially poignant. Ask them to get in touch with what they

feel to be their parents' unfinished business, and to identify some piece of unfinished business that has affected them in particular - either because they are carrying a parent's pain or because they have internalized some aspect of that parent's character. You may also choose to use the Parental Introject exercise as a warm-up.

2. Ask participants to invite a group member who feels warmed up to choose someone to play himself (or use an empty chair) while he plays the parent. Then choose anyone else who may be a part of the scene.

3. Tell the protagonist to move into action with the parent's psychodrama, reversing roles where indicated.

4. The protagonist should end the scene whenever it feels finished. You may offer the protagonist an opportunity as the parent to give what he wishes he had gotten and have a moment of corrective experience. Role reversal may be useful here.

5. Allow plenty of time for sharing.

Comments

Doing the psychodrama of the parent offers an opportunity to experience what life might have felt like to the parent. There are great possibilities for insight into the parent, forgiveness and releasing passed-down pathology. It can be very healing to play out the parental introject on stage rather than in life. Playing out aspects of the parent also helps the client through the stage of individuation/separation. The same process can be followed for a grandparent, sibling or anyone that has significantly impacted a client's life.

PERSONAL NAME HISTORY

Goals

1. To learn about a person through the history of her name.
2. To share personal information.

Steps

1. Invite members of the group to introduce themselves by name and share information related to their name. This can include information about how it was chosen, its ethnic origin, whether they have ever changed it or had nicknames, whether

they like or dislike it, how they like it said, any relevant history and so on.

2. The group leader or group members may ask a couple of relevant questions to deepen the exercise.

3. Allow time for each person who wants to explore her name.

Variations

This exercise yields much personal material because so much information, history and feeling can be tied up in a name. It is a good warm-up to lead to deeper psychodramatic work with anything that comes up through the exercise. Participants can choose someone to play themselves using a childhood nickname, a name they disliked or whatever they are warmed up to.

HISTORY OF ONE'S WRITTEN NAME

Goals

1. To gain insight into a person through the history of his name.

2. To share personal information with the group and warm the group up for action.

Steps

1. Use a large chalkboard or writing board.

2. Invite participants to come up one at a time and write their names on the board. They should write their names in various long and short forms, in different writing styles they have used over the years and include name changes. They will have several versions from childhood on through the present—and they can share their memories and feelings as they write each one.

3. As the group leader, ask participants questions or allow the group to ask questions that seem relevant or appropriate to deepen the understanding of each participant.

4. Thank participants and let them sit down.

5. Share as a group what came up throughout the exercises.

Variations

Names invariably go through many changes, and those changes will show up in this exercise. It is surprising how provocative this warm-up is. The questions that you ask of the participants can be very powerful if you are sensitive to their process. The participant will hear them deeply because they are on stage while doing this exercise.

THE PSYCHODRAMATIC BABY

Goals

1. To understand what one's ideal child would be so that one can separate it from one's actual children.

2. To release the idealized baby and to make room for the real one.

Steps

1. Ask participants to find paper and pencils.

2. Ask participants to close their eyes and get in touch with their fantasies of the ideal child, to look at the child from every angle, smell it, touch it and listen to the sounds it makes.

3. Ask participants to describe and/or draw this fantasy child in as much detail as possible on a sheet of paper, and to jot down phrases that describe its personality and who or what the child might become.

4. Ask participants to write short sentences describing things they would like to do with this ideal child.

5. Next, with one or two other people or with a group, ask participants to share the ideal child fully, as if he were real, describing him and the things they do together and talking about what he means to them.

6. To psychodramatize the child, use an empty chair or have someone play the child.

7. The technique of interview may be used in either role. After the session has drawn to closure, have a period of sharing to promote more understanding in the protagonist and others present.

Comments

Some parents have many ideals that they want their children to fulfill that keep them from seeing and accepting the child for who he is. Creating the psychodramatic baby can identify and release some of that ideal so that parents can get on with the business of relating to the real child. People who have no children can have an opportunity to work through their fantasies and look for other ways of having surrogate babies in their lives. Through this exercise those who have lost a baby or do not have the capacity to have a baby can have what they yearn for so that they can release it and grieve over the loss. You may wish to ask if the ideal child has a name and what it is, making it more possible for participants not to ask existing children, spouses or others to fill the empty space.

This exercise can be geared to a child at any stage of development, from infancy to adulthood. It can also be done in role reversal: that is, the client plays one or both of her parents, creates the ideal child that she imagines her parent or parents wanted her to be and chooses someone to play that child, or plays the child herself.

THE PSYCHODRAMATIC SIBLING

Goals

1. To allow people to have the fantasy sibling they wish they had.

2. To allow people to release the fantasy sibling and accept the real one with his limitations.

Steps

1. Make sure participants have paper and pencil.

2. Ask participants to close their eyes and imagine a sibling they wish they had.

3. Ask participants to draw or write about these siblings in great detail. Are they older or younger? What do they look like? What sort of personality do they have? What are they good at? What do other people think of them?

4. Ask participants to describe with phrases the relationship between themselves and these siblings, the types of talks they have and the things that they like to do together. Ask the participants to talk about what the sibling means to them in the context of the family.

5. At this point allow time for sharing the written material with one other person or the group, or psychodramatize it by placing the sibling in an empty chair or asking someone to play

the sibling's part. Encourage clients to speak fully to the sibling about whatever they choose, and to reverse roles and speak as the sibling to them.

6. In one-to-one therapy, allow the client to share his feelings about how that drama felt and what it meant. You can then explore associations together if you choose.

7. In a group allow the members to share what came up for them as a result of watching the drama, and allow the auxiliaries to de-role.

Comments

Children often wish for a more compatible sibling. They may play out the wish either by rejecting their own sibling or, as parents, by asking their children to play out unfulfilled sibling roles. Bringing the unconscious wish forward and addressing it directly will in itself move it over or alter the object relationship. Clients can then see that they can choose surrogate siblings in their lives. It also allows the pain of less than satisfactory sibling relationships to emerge. Though much focus is given to parent relationships in recovery, the impact of sibling relationships often goes unexamined.

In dysfunctional homes where children are parentified, sibling relationships can be very powerful. This exercise may warm people up to enact other psychodramas related to sibling issues. In such cases vignettes can be structured in which the protagonist can talk to the sibling or siblings whom they need to address.

The exercise "Doing A Parent's Psychodrama" on p. 135 can also be adapted to "Doing A Sibling's Psychodrama." One can do a psychodrama, a vignette or simply take on the role of the sibling. Instruct participants to feel the sibling within, adopt their posture and attitude, then speak as them in soliloquy, interview or with other group members. At times it is easier to enter the role of a significant person rather then to enact a drama. It can be less threatening and may allow for a smoother entry into their psychic space than a more formal enactment. In doing these enactments make sure to allow plenty of time to share and de-role.

Page 122:   Who is this person representing . . . R. Siroka, Psychodrama
Training Institute, New York City (19 West 34th Street),
May 29, 1992.

Page 123:   Family Rules . . . This is an adaptation of an exercise used at
ONSITE Training and Consulting, Rapid City, SD.

Page 124:   It may also be expanded . . . Sharon Wegscheider-Cruse,
Onsite Training and Consulting, Rapid City, SD: Lecture, April 18,
1977.

Page 135:   Playing out the introject . . . R. Siroka, Psychodrama Training
Institute, New York City (19 West 34th Street), Lecture,
December 4, 1992.

Page 141:   History Of One's Written Name . . . This game is adapted from a
workshop given by Zerka Moreno.

7
Grief And Mourning Games

MR. WEBB (off stage):
Where's my girl? Where's my birthday girl?

EMILY
(in a loud voice to the Stage Manager):
*I can't. I can't go on. It goes so fast. We
don't have time to look at one another.*
(She breaks down sobbing. The lights dim
on the left half of the stage. Mr. Webb
disappears.) *I didn't realize. So all that
was going on and we never noticed. Take
me back—up the hill—to my grave. But
first: Wait! One more look. Goodbye,
goodbye world, Goodbye, Grover's
Corners . . . Mama and Papa. Goodbye to
clocks ticking . . . and Mama's sunflow-
ers. And food and coffee. And new-ironed
dresses and hot baths . . . and sleeping*

> *and waking up. Oh, earth, you're too*
> *wonderful for anybody to realize you.*
> (She looks toward the Stage Manager and
> asks abruptly, through her tears): *Do any*
> *human beings ever realize life while they*
> *live it?—every, every minute?*
>
> STAGE MANAGER: *No.* (pause.) *The saints*
> *and poets, maybe—they do some.*
> **—Thornton Wilder, *Our Town***

In the West, and especially in the United States, we have systematically removed our cultural vehicles for mourning significant losses. The rituals that used to address the intensity and depth of loss have been transformed into ways of dealing with the event rather than into a means of expressing the feelings related to it. The most obvious example is the funeral. Both in the way it is conducted and the psychological and emotional use of the event, funeral ceremonies tend to be reserved and encourage little overt mourning. Somehow we have come, as a culture, to feel compromised by the expression of deep painful feelings.

Where does all that grief go? Not so long ago, wearing black and otherwise observing a period of mourning served as a way to signal the world that things were not as usual. It allowed those in mourning the room and permission to grieve and to ask for and receive a special kind of support. After the year of mourning was over, there was another ceremony symbolizing the return to normal life.

When we do not mourn a deep loss fully, we condemn the unconscious to hold the magnitude of that pain and loss somewhere within itself. For the rest of our lives, each time we encounter an experience of intimacy that threatens, because of its depth of caring, to expose that wound to our conscious mind, we have to walk away. We walk away from ourselves, from the relationship, from our potential for love and life. We cannot go to that place of pain again, not because it hurt so much, but because we did not let it hurt enough. If we do not grieve, losing someone we love—whether through death, divorce or disease—becomes a loss of ourselves.

Living inevitably means loss. Through death we experience the ultimate loss of the person. In divorce there is the profound loss of the original family. In addiction there is the psychic and spiritual loss of a person and her terrifying replacement by someone we do not recognize. There are losses of stages of life: the loss of childhood in adolescence, the midlife crisis that brings to light our own mortality, the "empty nest" syndrome when our children leave to begin separate lives, the loss of work at retirement.

Rituals that help us deal with loss and transition are inherently psychodramatic—the visible acting out of the various components of a loss in a communal manner. Most cultures, historically, have honored such rites of passage as ways to help people move through life from birth to death. Psychodrama can help us revive our own lost rites of passage because it offers a way to move back into our lives and actively mourn any loss that needs to be dealt with and concretize transitions.

The mourning process is in itself a giving in to tragedy—to the depth of the loss, to the full extent of the pain. Only when we pass through what feels like a sort of personal death can we return fully to life. If we will experience only part of the loss, then part of ourselves remains locked in the frozen silence of unfelt sadness which will leave us shut down; we will be less alive within ourselves and our daily living. We will have that much less of ourselves available to us in our daily lives.

The need to grieve is as old as humanity. Grief, fully and purely experienced, allows us to go on with life, to pass through all the stages of anger, sadness, justifying and letting go. It creates space for new life to be born out of the wreckage of the past, and for a new person to be born out of the previous one. In mourning we reach the parameters of our soul—we die an emotional death and are resuscitated. Deep, pure grieving allows us to integrate the loss because nothing we have truly loved is ever really completely lost to us. When we refuse to grieve it, we put the loss out of consciousness; numb, we cannot gain access to either the good or the bad feelings surrounding the loss or person. When we feel all our feelings, we are able to choose what to keep alive in memory, what to continue to look at and feel nourished by.

Grief serves a number of important functions:

1. Grief releases the pain surrounding an event or situation so that it will not be held within the psyche, the emotional and physical self.

2. Grief allows the wound to heal. If we do not grieve, we build walls around the ungrieved wound in order to protect it. When a wound is not healed, it hurts. It is tender to the touch; so we push away any experience that might touch it, press on it or produce pain.

3. Experiencing the deep pain of grief makes it easier not to retreat from deep experience when it presents itself again in our lives. We reduce the fear that we will not be able to handle the potential pain that could be associated with deep feeling and caring.

4. Grief is necessary in order to release the anger that arises as part of the grieving process at feeling helpless and out of control, or at losing something or someone important, so that we can risk loving or becoming attached again in life.

If we cannot mourn, we—

- stay stuck in anger and pain.
- cannot engage in new relationships because we are still engaged in an active relationship with a person or situation that is no longer present.
- project unfelt, unresolved grief onto any situation, placing those feelings where they do not belong.
- lose personal history along with the unmourned person or situation—a part of us dies too.
- unconsciously fear losing our next similar relationship— hence any important relationship can become fearsome.

A surprisingly large number of life events go ungrieved in our futile attempt to "get on with life" or to "stop feeling sorry for ourselves." Some of these are—

- divorce, both for spouses, childrenand the family unit.
- life transitions.
- loss of job, youth, children in the home, retirement.

- dysfunction in the home, loss of family life.
- lost childhood, lost security, constant abandonment, loss of parents who were able to behave like parents.

Sometimes we feel we have no right to mourn the loss of a troublesome person—a parent, spouse, child or lover who is alcoholic addicted, mentally ill or abusive—because we are "better off without them." But painful and complicated relationships can be very hard to lose and let go of, because there is so much unfinished business connected with them. We continue to search for what we never got, trying over and over again to feel settled inside. When we can finish unfinished business therapeutically, we can release the grief and begin to move through the mourning process.

People who grew up in troubled families have much mourning to do. They often carry deep sorrow for the families they never really had or the parents who were not able to parent them, for siblings with whom they could not connect or who became too important to them because they were all that they had or for siblings who in desperation became parents in their parents' stead. The recovery process involves engaging in the cycle of grief and mourning so that the past can finally be left behind and we can begin to live again, with a fresh start.

The following exercises help people deal with all kinds of grieving and loss. Read the goals for each exercise, and use games that are appropriate for the issues your client is dealing with.

GUIDED IMAGERY FOR LOSS

Goals

1. To trace past issues, investigate what messages were received and how one was taught to handle loss.

2. To see how past losses may be affecting current losses.

Steps

1. Say, "Find a comfortable position and allow yourself to relax. Leave behind whatever outside concerns you may be carrying and bring your attention into the room. Go to your breathing. Breathe

in and out easily and completely and allow yourself to relax. Sit up straight; uncross your legs (if people are sitting in chairs); place your hands on your lap with palms facing upward; take a deep breath, hold it and blow it out slowly, as if you were blowing out through a straw. Notice areas of tension and breathe in to them, allowing them to release."

2. Continue, "Allow yourself to remember a loss, perhaps the first one you can remember—when it was, where you were, what happened, what you were told to do, what you learned about grief and loss."

3. Continue, "What have this experience and other experiences taught you about loss, and how are the lessons you learned being played out today? Whenever you feel ready, open your eyes."

4. Share what came up, in dyads and/or within the group.

Variations

This exercise is a natural warm-up to action. You may wish to put an empty chair in the center of the group. Anyone who has anything to say to someone can use the chair to represent the person, or he may choose someone to play the person or persons involved.

GRIEF SPECTROGRAM

Goals

1. To make unconscious material conscious.

2. To provide a method of action sociometry (see Chapter 3, Sociometry: How Psychodrama Works).

Steps

1. Draw an imaginary line dividing the room down the middle, showing group members where it is as you do so.

2. Explain to the participants that each end of the room represents an extreme and that the bisecting line is the midpoint: for example, hot/cold, comfortable/uncomfortable, very much/very little, good/bad.

3. Now ask a series of questions that apply to your particular subject, and ask participants to locate themselves at whatever

point along the continuum that feels right for them in response. (For example, if one side of the room represents very good, the other very bad and the midpoint on the line neutrality, the question is, "How are you feeling about your work life?" participants will go to that place in the room that best locates their feeling in the work situation or family life or whatever the subject may be.)

4. Allow people to share spontaneously feelings that come up for them while doing this exercise, either with one another or with the group at large.

Variations

In grief work one side of the room can represent very much and one side very little. You might ask, "How much grief is in your life right now?" "What is your level of loss?" "How angry do you feel?" "How tired?" "How disrupted?" "How much fear do you feel about your future?" "How much excitement do you feel about your future?"

SAYING GOODBYE

Goals

1. To say goodbye fully to someone who has left one's life.
2. To release that person and move on in one's life.

Steps

1. Allow the protagonist to share about the person she wishes to say goodbye to.

2. Allow her to choose a person or an empty chair to represent the person.

3. Ask her to set the scene.

4. Encourage the protagonist to be specific—saying goodbye to all that she will miss in detail.

5. If it seems appropriate or helpful, allow her to say what she will not miss.

6. The protagonist can reverse roles with the person whenever appropriate.

7. The protagonist can ask for something she may wish to have from the person in the form of a word, gesture or object.

8. The protagonist may wish to give something to the person as well.

9. Ask the protagonist to finish the goodbye in any way she wishes.

10. Allow plenty of time for sharing in the group.

Variations

Setting the scene can be very personal. The protagonist may wish to be in any type of setting, either real or imagined. The setting can be a funeral, a deathbed, a park scene, a field of flowers—anywhere the protagonist may choose. The idea is to say goodbye fully wherever it works best. If life did not offer an opportunity for the protagonist to say goodbye and put closure on the relationship, psychodrama can allow that to happen; goodbye may also be said in a one-to-one setting, using an empty chair.

FAMILY LOSSES

Goals

1. To get in touch with what the family as a whole has lost.
2. To identify losses, so that they can be worked through.

Steps

1. Ask participants to find pencil and paper.

2. Say, "Allow yourself to think about your family and feel the feelings that come up around happy times, sad times, secure and insecure times and so on."

3. Continue, "On your paper, let that voice inside of you, perhaps the voice of your inner child, speak. Write down in single words or phrases a list of losses."

4. Continue, "Along with what has been lost, you may choose to write down what that little person within you, or you today, wishes had been different."

5. When they have finished, participants can share their lists.

6. If in a group, you may wish to structure a psychodrama around any of the situations that has emerged, with a protagonist, protagonist's inner child and/or the relevant family members.

7. Have the participants share and process all their feelings with the group or with a therapist.

Variations

If you are in a large group and do not wish to structure a psychodrama, participants can break into pairs, or groups of three or four, and share the lists, finally returning to the large group for continued sharing.

If you are using this exercise in one-to-one therapy, process all the feelings with your client. You may also set up empty chairs to represent people and speak to them.

This exercise can also be done without pen and paper, as a guided imagery leading to psychodramatic action.

PERSONAL BURDENS

Goals

1. To bring to the surface what has been personally lost as a result of living with dysfunction.

2. To experience feelings of loss in the present, so that one can begin to let them go.

Steps

1. Ask participants to find pencil and paper.

2. Ask participants to locate themselves on the paper, either representing themselves as a symbol, a stick figure or a picture.

3. Around the drawing, anywhere that feels right, ask participants to use words or phrases to describe the burdens they felt while growing up. They may represent them in any way that they choose.

4. At this point they may share their notes with the therapist or the group, or the leader may structure a psychodrama using people to represent those burdens, speaking to them or reversing roles with them.

5. Allow plenty of time for sharing and processing feelings with the group.

Variations

In a large group, if you do not use psychodrama, you can break into pairs or groups of three or four to share the material and then return to the large group for continued sharing. In individual therapy you can represent burdens with empty chairs. The protagonist can address the chair directly, as if it were real, and talk to the burden. You may ask the client to reverse roles or speak from the point of view of the burden. You may wish to use the technique of interview to elicit more material. Then process the feelings that come up after this monodrama. The burden can also be concretized with an object such as a pillow.

ABORTION

Goals

1. To deal with the emotional pain surrounding an abortion.
2. To interact with and say goodbye to the unborn child.

Steps

1. Ask the protagonist to choose someone to play the child, or use an object that would work or an empty chair.
2. Allow the protagonist to hold, grieve for, talk to and otherwise interact with the child.
3. Allow the protagonist to reverse roles with the child.
4. Allow full time for the protagonist to share the hopes and dreams she had for the child—all that will not be, from both the viewpoint of the mother, and, if desired, from the viewpoint of the child (in role reversal).
5. Ask the protagonist to end the scene in any way she wants.

Variations

A mother often has a name for an unborn child. Ask the protagonist to use the name in the drama, if she chooses, and the child can use Mother. Often the mother will ask forgiveness from the child or will grant it to herself from the position of role reversal if there is guilt associated with the abortion. This exercise can be used with fathers in the same way. In either case the spouse can be represented in the drama, or anyone the protagonist needs to be present.

SEPARATING THE DISEASE FROM THE PERSON

Goals

1. To separate the disease from the person.
2. To allow love for the recovered person to feel less threatening.

Steps

1. Ask the protagonist to choose two people or use two empty chairs, one to represent the disease and one to represent the person with the disease.
2. Allow the protagonist to fully express all his feelings by talking to each chair.
3. Let the protagonist reverse roles into each chair and speak from both roles. Role reversal can be called in to play over and over again as necessary.
4. Let the protagonist end the scene any way that feels right.
5. Allow plenty of time for group sharing.

Variations

Separating the disease from the person can be clarifying at a variety of points. People enacting a psychodrama related to an alcoholic parent may need to express anger and hurt toward him in a safe manner. Protagonists may need to say goodbye to a "diseased" parent—either so that a relationship can continue with the parent as a healthier person, or to get in touch with the parent they did love and feel good with that part of the parent that they carry within themselves. Playing the role of the disease in role reversal can provide a vehicle for acting out the diseased introject and help the protagonist to let go of it; the technique of interview is useful here in order to bring the diseased introject fully to the surface in action. It is important to keep in mind that this exercise could encourage psychological splitting or seeing a person as all good or all bad. The ultimate purpose of this exercise is to help the client to integrate the seemingly diverse parental introjects that they carry within them. Processing with this thought in mind should aid in integration.

Page 153: How much grief is in your life right now? . . . . This and guided
          imagery for loss are adaptations developed by Ronny Halpren,
          M.S.W., Bereavement Coordinator for the Carbini Hospice in
          New York City.

8
Parenting Games

The feeling of being valuable—
"I am a valuable person"—is essential
to mental health and is a cornerstone
of self-discipline. It is a direct
product of parental love. Such a
conviction must be gained in childhood;
it is extremely difficult to acquire it
during adulthood. Conversely, when
children have learned through the love
of their parents to feel valuable,
it is almost impossible for the
vicissitudes of adulthood to
destroy their spirit.
This feeling of being valuable
is a cornerstone of self-discipline
because when one considers oneself
valuable one will take care of oneself
in all ways that are necessary.
—M. Scott Peck, *The Road Less Traveled*

Throughout the course of parenting, we are continually offered the opportunity to revisit our own childhood. The pleasant pre-occupations of youth, the wonder, excitement and fascination with a magical and exciting world presenting itself anew each day are all available to the parent vicariously, through the child's eyes. As parents we re-experience the wondrousness of our own journey into adulthood as our children's guides. We feel stirred within our souls something that had fallen asleep. We find a new meaning in life that we had forgotten, and if we are tuned in, we have an opportunity for an inner rebirth brought on by the birth of our own children.

Along with this rebirth of wonder can come a rebirth of terror. Because it is the child who lives within us who is being reborn, and not some abstracted part of ourselves, all the unfinished business, the unmet needs, the unfulfilled dreams come alive as well. We may find ourselves in a sort of exquisite pain, reaching out to touch our unmet selves but afraid to get too close.

The parent-child relationship is one of the most profoundly intimate experiences in life. Because of the genetic inheritance of characteristics on all levels, physical and emotional, we have the bewildering sense of looking in a mirror, though what we see is distinctly not ourselves. Whatever in the child reminds us of parts of ourselves that we love will give us a wonderful feeling of being "doubled" here on earth. Those parts of our children that remind us of parts of ourselves that we hate, we may deny, project onto our children and disown in ourselves. C. J. Jung once said, "The most dangerous things to children are the unlived lives of their parents." And indeed we may envy and resent those parts of our children that remind us of what we never were— "our unlived lives"—making our children feel that by being who they are they are displeasing us, or we may ask them to live the lives we never did, to fulfill our dreams and fantasies. It is only when we become conscious of these dynamics within ourselves that we will be able to allow our children to move forward into themselves with our blessings and feel supportive of them in their pursuits and interests.

The task of parenting is to move from the inner to the outer. To act as a "good enough" double in the earliest stages of life so that our children have a sense of being understood and loved. Then, to be an empathetic and helpful "mirror" so that our children learn to see themselves as others see them, and can attempt to adjust to and find their place within the world. Next comes the stage of the "auxiliary ego," wherein children learn to accept themselves as a person among people—that is, they are only the center of their own universe. There are countless "co-centers" with whom they will need to learn how to live and relate. After this comes the stage of "role reversal," where children learn empathy for others. They come to understand that not only does the world contain other people, but these other people have their own inner lives and points of view that are unique to them, and they see the world through their own eyes.

Homes where addiction and dysfunction are present do not promote a child's easy movement through the developmental stages because the principles on which the family is organized are inconsistent: the family does not have a solid "central self." Children model their sense of self on what they experience in their families, and if the family, the marriage and the individual parents do not model coherent selves, it becomes difficult for the children to internalize a secure sense of self: parents in search of a self often produce children in search of a self. In order for children to individuate or self-define, both the family and the children need a self. The family needs a self so that it can tolerate the pain of allowing the children to separate, and the children need a self to take with them into their own lives. A family that lacks a self will not foster separation and individuation; rather it will experience separation as a threat to its survival and organize to sabotage it.

Children who attempt to separate from such a family run the risk of having the door slammed shut behind them. The spoken or unspoken message may be, "If you leave, you can't come back." As a result they may just pretend to leave. Because children will connect abandonment with separation, they will, in an unconscious attempt to protect themselves from pain, not allow themselves to truly separate. Even when ostensibly on their own, they will be deeply preoccupied with the family of origin. Another possibility will be that they will separate emotionally but will pretend that they have not. They will play the role demanded of them by the family but inwardly they will be absent. In either case they will be leaving pieces of themselves behind. In the first case the self may be locked away in the unresolved past; in the second it may be unclaimed freight in the baggage room of the family of origin. In both cases it will be unavailable to them.

Such a beginning is a setup for co-dependent relationships in adult life. Children from such families are frightened of deep and meaningful attachment because attachment comes to mean pain. Some will avoid attachment by avoiding intimate relationships or fulfilling meaningful goals. Others will take hostages rather than form relationships—incorporating a person into themselves rather than living with the anxiety that comes from recognizing that all attachments in life are subject to change. Incorporating a person gives them the illusion of safety because they will not have to feel separate—and if they are not separate, they cannot be abandoned. Incorporation may also be an unconscious attempt to recreate the original feeling of oneness with the mother, the earliest sense of safety experienced by the infant.

In alcoholic or dysfunctional homes, the natural urge of the children to separate is often experienced as rejection by the parent, who punishes the children by removing love and affection. This makes the feeling of being separate intolerable, and sets up "black and white" alternatives for intimate relationships: (1) you can be incorporated into another person and not be alone, or (2) you can be your own person but then you will be alone.

A person who incorporates others feels the need to draw people, places and things into the self to fill an inner need or hunger, to sustain and feed the self. He feels a need for sameness in the others, for he has the feeling they must be the same as he to be sustaining. Difference in opinion is seen as hostile; compliance is seen as good. Because all family members are naturally different from one another, there is an enormous burden placed on family dynamics. Incorporated or enmeshed families do not take kindly to personal differences or individual likes and dislikes. What is rewarded is compliance—whatever shape that compliance may take within any given family. These families do not encourage the process of individuation, and children experience their own desire to be an individual as disloyal and hostile to the family— deep down they know that they will pay a price and that the price can be the loss of family acceptance, approval or even access.

One of the greatest gifts parents can give their children is to finish their own old business so that it is not passed on to their children to finish it for them. When adults who grew up in enmeshed families become parents, the trauma that they experienced as children is constantly reawakened. They tend toward paranoia and overreaction seemingly on behalf of their children. Really it is unresolved trauma from their own childhoods that gets mixed in with the life events of their children, causing them to misread and overreact to the normal concerns of growing up. Such parents may—

- have trouble tolerating their children's being rejected by anyone.
- tend to violate their children's boundaries by being unnecessarily intrusive and overly curious about their child's affairs.
- have a difficult time negotiating the vicissitudes of intimacy with their children and establishing an overall evenness in relating.
- overprotect their children even when it is not in their children's best interest.
- not know what normal is and consequently have trouble understanding what behavior to accept or foster as normal in their children and what behavior to discourage.
- have trouble having relaxed and easy fun with their children.
- have impulsive features that they act out in their parenting.
- feel somewhat different from other families.
- attempt to overcontrol family life and the lives of their children.
- have trouble establishing healthy boundaries with their children, positioning themselves either too close or too far.

Adults who were underprotected as children may impair their children's development by overcontrolling and overprotecting them. Maria Montessori has said, "When we do for the child what the child can do for himself, we are in the way of that child's development." Parents run a danger of getting in the way of their children's development when they are unable to allow them to struggle in ways that are vital and necessary for growth. Adults who struggled and suffered too much as children and had nowhere to go for comfort will find it difficult to allow their children to endure pain. No child can grow and develop without experiencing pain, however; so the effect will be to inhibit growth and maturation in the child. It is therefore vital for such parents to revisit their own childhoods in therapy and endure the pain that they have left behind in a frozen state—what Mardi Horowitz might call "active memory" which has a powerful hold on their inner life and their parenting style and ability.

The following games are structured to aid parents who need to heal their own childhoods and move on. Please read the goals and choose the games that are appropriate for your clients.

GENERATIONAL SOCIAL ATOM

Goals

1. To illuminate negative projections that are being carried from generation to generation.

2. To make connections between the participant's past and any projection from it onto their child's life.

Steps

1. Ask participants to close their eyes. Then say, "Allow any period of your child's life that is or has been particularly painful for you to deal with to surface in your mind's eye."

2. Continue, "Now allow your mind to float back to that same period in your own life. Open your eyes when you are ready."

3. Give participants pen and paper, and ask them to make social atoms of themselves from that period in their lives (see Chapter 3, Sociometry: How Psychodrama Works).

4. Using triangles to represent males and circles to represent females, ask the parents to locate themselves (in childhood or the corresponding period in their lives) on a piece of paper anywhere that feels right and to locate the people who were close to them in whatever size and relationship to themselves that feels appropriate. Pets can be included, and a broken line can be used for any deceased individuals.

5. When the atoms are finished, let each person share what is on his atom, from the point of view of that age, speaking in the first person, present tense: for example, "I am ten years old, and this is my father."

6. Let the person make any connections between what was going on during that period and what is going on for his child now.

Variations

When a period in a child's life is particularly painful for a parent, it is important to investigate what was going on for the parent at that same time in his own life. Overreaction as an indicator of where his own work lies. Once the work is done, it is easier to set the child free to live in his or her own experience. One can also sculpt the characters on the social atom and then have the parent walk around the characters and say what he is moved to say to whomever he is moved to say it.

DEEPEST CHILDHOOD WOUNDS

Goals

1. To identify the parent's early childhood wounds.
2. To separate the parent's wounds from what he fears for the child.

Steps

1. Ask the participants to identify two or three deep hurts or wounds that they received during their own growing up.
2. Have them choose people to represent each of those wounds, or use empty chairs.
3. Ask them to begin by taking the role of each wound and showing the group physically what that looks like. They may add sound, words or dialogue, as they wish. They may also double for the wound from behind the person playing it, acting as its inner voice and expressing the feelings underneath the physicalization. They may also begin from their own roles and then reverse roles into the position of the wound.
4. Allow them to play the scene out, with role reversals wherever appropriate.
5. When the scene feels complete, ask them to end the scene any way they choose to.
6. Allow time for sharing.

Comments

This exercise will give parents an opportunity to identify their own childhood wounds and to own their pain. It will help them not to pass on the pain, either in the form in which it was passed on to them or in the form of an opposite reaction or overprotection.

SEPARATION—
PARENT'S INNER CHILD TO CHILD

Goals

1. To distinguish the adult-parent-self from the child-parent-self.
2. To identify which self is having trouble separating.

Steps

1. Ask the participants to close their eyes. Ask them to connect with their own parent-child relationship and where they are having difficulty separating. Then ask them to see in their mind's eye if this brings up experiences from their own childhood of feeling abandoned or unprotected.

2. Choose a protagonist and ask her to structure or make a sculpture of this scene, playing herself as a child and relating to all the characters involved from the point of view of herself as a child.

3. Direct the protagonist to reverse roles at any time, with anyone, where it seems it might be appropriate or helpful.

4. When the protagonist seems finished, ask her to end the scene in any way that she wants to.

5. Allow time for sharing.

Comments

When parents have been abused or abandoned in their own childhoods, their ability to allow their children to separate can be impaired. They may feel that their children will be too vulnerable without their protection, or they may be too dependent on their children for their own emotional fulfillment to let them go. Whatever unfinished business remains unidentified can get in the way of the separation/individuation process, and without separation real rapprochement becomes difficult. This exercise can be done as many times as necessary to clear out unresolved issues.

STAGES OF GROWTH AND MATURATION

Goals

1. To help a parent to allow a child to grow up.

2. To bring to a conscious level the parts of the parent-child relationship that are enmeshed.

Steps

1. Ask the protagonist to set up a scene that is meaningful to him, in which he can say goodbye to the child he is hanging on to. The child may be at any age that feels significant to the parent and may be represented by a person, an empty chair or photograph. If a photograph is used, the protagonist can talk directly to the picture or choose someone to play the child in it.

2. Allow the parent to say goodbye fully to all that he will miss or is hanging on to. Encourage him to be specific; sometimes it's the little things that we miss the most.

3. Allow the parent at any point, if it seems appropriate, to reverse roles with his child and speak from the role of the child to himself. You can do this as many times as needed or desired.

4. When you feel the goodbye is fully expressed, ask the protagonist to end the scene any way he wants.

5. Allow time for sharing.

Comments

Separation is often seen as a permanent state, but it is really only a step on the way to individuation and autonomy and occurs over and over again throughout life. When autonomy or individuation are clearly established within the child, a new kind of relationship between parent and child is possible. The relationship can grow into one between two consenting individuals, each of whom has a separate identity and is in possession of his own personhood. It becomes a relationship in which each person is entitled to his own boundaries and individual paths. It is a relationship in which self-definition does not cost the parent and child their relationship or their mutual positive regard. This exercise is useful in allowing a child to grow up—saying goodbye to the little child at home when he goes to school or saying goodbye to the young child and making room for the teenager and so on. Each stage of parenting requires, in a sense, a different parent and it is helpful to move through feelings so that a new stage can be entered. This will help to avoid, for instance, a parent infantalizing a teenager or treating an adult child like a teenager. Children change and grow rapidly. It can be useful to have a little help keeping up.

EMPTY NEST

Goals

1. To identify fears or grief connected to an empty nest syndrome.

2. To let go of the nest stage of parenting and allow the family to evolve.

Steps

1. Ask participants to close their eyes and imagine a time when they felt their nest was full. You may have them use family photos of themselves or their children. Choose a protagonist who seems warmed up.

2. The protagonist can either select people to play the family members or simply talk to photos.

3. When the family group is assembled or the picture in hand, they should talk specifically about all they miss and feel they can't seem to stop hanging on to. Encourage them to speak directly to individuals as well as to the family as a whole.

4. Let the protagonist fully release family members into their own lives.

5. Resculpt the relationship the protagonist has with each individual member of the family, allowing the protagonist to talk to each family member as this is done. If a photograph is being used resculpting can be verbal.

6. Allow group members to share with the protagonist by way of identification.

Variations

When photos are used, the psychodrama can be a short, very moving piece. When people are chosen, the protagonist can have the option of choosing someone to play herself and can speak "to the whole picture," reversing roles with any characters, including herself. Many parents never successfully move into adult relationships with their children, but stay locked in roles that are related to parenting young children. The empty nest syndrome begins not when the children leave home, but during adolescence, when they begin to become independent, separate people. At this point the parents can fear life without their children and feel deeply rejected by them. They may also have fears about what they will do with their lives when their children need less from them. This may also be adapted for parents who lost their intact families through divorce or death of a spouse.

PARENTING ROLES

Goals

1. To identify the variety of roles that are a part of being a parent.
2. To understand which roles are comfortable and which roles need development.

Steps

1. Have everyone find pencil and paper. Then begin by saying, "Give yourself a minute to muse over which roles you feel are a part of your relationship with your child—for example, mother, father, buddy, baby-sitter, cook, breadwinner, sibling, chauffeur, disciplinarian, confidant, foe, friend and so on."

2. Continue, "As you look over the roles that you have identified, decide which roles are a satisfactory part of your relationship, which roles you are not comfortable with, which roles get overplayed or underplayed and which roles you would like to develop further."

3. Then say, "Organize these observations on your paper in any way you like, alongside the role or by category."

4. Continue, "Pull out the roles that are difficult for you by writing them on another piece of paper."

5. Continue, "List the difficult roles and, this time, jot down words, descriptive phrases or adjectives, or names that come up in connection with the roles."

6. Continue, "Now focus on one role that you would like to work on—whatever role you feel the most stuck in."

7. Continue, "Allow your feelings and thoughts about that role to surface."

8. Continue, "On a new piece of paper, write down phrases describing what is going on for you."

9. (At this point the participants may use an empty chair to represent any aspect of the role or person they would like to speak to.) Or let them simply look at the paper and write about the feelings that are coming up.

10. When they have finished, have them share the feelings they experienced with the group or with a safe person.

Variations

This process can be repeated for every role that needs work or attention in order to get what is in the way out of the way, so that the role can be played with ease and enjoyment or adjusted and made more livable.

PARENTAL ROLE ANALYSIS

Goals

1. To analyze the ways in which the role of parent changes over the years.

2. To gain perspective on how the role of parent needs to grow and evolve.

Steps

1. Participants should have paper and pencil.

2. Ask participants to choose three periods from their child's life that they feel were particularly significant.

3. Ask them to divide the page into three sections. At the top of each section, indicate one period.

4. Within each section create five categories: (1) activities, (2) feelings, (3) demands, (4) rewards and (5) overall tone.

5. Around each category write whatever words come up or describe the category, for example (1) chauffeur; (2) needed, vital, caught; (3) patience, selflessness, endurance; (4) sense of being important; (5) happy, edgy, busy.

6. After everything has been filled in, allow each person to share his chart with the group and comment on what he observes as similar and different about the stages, particularly in light of what was required.

7. Allow time for sharing among group members.

Variations

This exercise can be done at three different times, one period at each time. You can work with one stage or several, depending on the needs of the group. The idea is to understand the many aspects of one role and to come to see that each stage of a child's life requires a different parent. Tailor the exercise to the needs of the group.

PROJECTION OF NEED

Goal

1. To allow parents to own their own neediness so that they do not create false need in their children to feel safe themselves.

Steps

1. Ask participants to reflect quietly on their greatest feelings of neediness in relation to their children. What is the largest void or greatest need that their children fill for them?

2. Ask the protagonist to choose someone to play that need (or several needs) or to put the need in an empty chair.

3. Ask the protagonist to reverse roles and show what the need looks like; then reverse back.

4. Allow a short scene, talking directly to the need, expressing how the protagonist who is doubling for the need feels about having the need and so on, reversing roles where appropriate.

5. After ending the scene, allow group members to share with the protagonist what came up for them.

Comments

Parents can unconsciously create a neediness in their own children in order to cope with their own fears of rejection and abandonment. It is a way of ensuring their supply of love from their children. The idea that they will move into their own lives and no longer need their parents so much can be devastating to parents who have devoted their lives to their children. This exercise is intended to allow the parents to confront their own neediness rather than project it onto their children by seeing them always as dependent individuals.

RELINQUISHING AUTHORITY: CHANGING ROLES WITH CHANGING TIMES

Goals

1. To bring to awareness a need to alter the balance of authority in the parent-child relationship when appropriate.

2. To move authority roles over and transform them where appropriate.

Steps

1. Participants should have paper and pencil.

2. First have them divide a sheet of paper into three sections.

3. Then have them label the first section as Stage 1: 0-12 years; the second section as Stage 2: 13-24 years, and the third section as Stage 3: 24+. Under each stage have them make a list of all the areas of their children's lives that they take an active role in planning, paying for, deciding about, executing and so on.

4. At this point you can either open the group up for discussion on how the role of parent changes according to the developmental needs of the child or ask a participant to move into action with any one of the stages that the parent feels stuck in. Or, for an overview, you may choose people to represent each stage or use empty chairs to represent each stage or the child at each stage.

5. Continue the scene by allowing the protagonist to say whatever she needs to say using role reversal; then end the scene in whatever way seems appropriate.

6. Allow group members to share what came up for them from their own lives as a result of watching or participating in the drama.

Comments

Parents with growing children may find it difficult to see the children as full adults. This requires a willingness on the parents' part not to infantilize their children, either in what they expect of them or in the way that they treat them. One of the greatest gifts parents can give to their adult children is their positive regard. Adult children need to be treated as adults and allowed an adult amount of power and authority in a given situation—in a mutual letting go. Adult children then allow their parents to live freely and fully on their own without tying them to outgrown parental roles, and parents allow their children to live freely and fully without tying them to outgrown childhood roles.

THE FANTASY CHILD I

Goals

1. To bring parents in touch with all of the hopes, dreams and fantasies that they are projecting onto a child.

2. To concretize those fantasies so that they can be seen, owned and released.

Steps

1. Ask participants to close their eyes and get in touch with who they wanted the child to be or what they wanted him to become.

2. Ask them to write down two or three of their fondest dreams for the child—for example, writer, doctor, actor, famous person, wife, husband and so on.

3. Choose a protagonist and ask him to choose a person to represent each fantasy that is represented on the list.

4. Ask the protagonist to position each role player and sculpt him.

5. Now ask the protagonist to address each role player directly, sharing with him all the dreams and aspirations: for example, "I so wanted you as my son. You represent thus and such to me and I wanted you in my life," or, "I wanted you to become a doctor."

6. Ask the protagonist to reverse roles whenever it seems appropriate, allowing him, from the fantasy role, to talk about who he is, what he wanted, why he wanted it and so on.

7. You may also have someone play the role of the parent's real child behind the fantasies, so that the parent can eventually see

the child as separate from his own hopes and dreams. You can ask the protagonist to choose the child whenever it feels appropriate, either in the beginning of the drama or during it. Allow the real child to talk about what he is experiencing and how he feels about the fantasies.

8. Let the parent participate in the fantasy until he has become conscious of all that he has wanted his child to be and, if possible, some of the reasons.

9. Allow time for sharing.

Variations

Sometimes parents have many fantasies about a child that are related to their own personal needs and fears. In such a situation the child is a constant disappointment because he is not able to heal the parent's narcissistic wounds by being the person the parent wishes him to be to fill in the parent's own needs. In this exercise parents can examine what they want, not only for the child but also for themselves. Sometimes, we wish our children to be or have what we wish we were or had had ourselves. And when our wishes do not materialize, we feel let down, as if we have not been good enough as parents and the child has not been a good enough child.

You may also choose someone to play the inner child of the parent at some point, if it would be helpful for the protagonist to get in touch with unfulfilled wishes from his own childhood.

THE FANTASY CHILD II

Goals

1. To allow the parent to deal with the unfulfilled dreams of his own parents.

2. To illuminate what the parents wanted.

Steps

1. After doing the Fantasy Child I exercise, the protagonist may have come into touch with the expectations that his own parents had for him, either in terms of a parent-child relationship or in terms of who or what his parents wanted him to be. Ask the

parent/protagonist to come in touch with a scene related to these issues or to imagine a relevant conversation.

2. Ask the protagonist to choose someone to represent his parent or parents, or to use an empty chair to represent them.

3. Let the protagonist talk fully to his parents about these issues, with role reversal.

4. When the scene or conversation feels over, ask him to end the scene in any way he wants.

5. Allow time for sharing.

Variations

This scene is a natural outgrowth of Fantasy Child I and can be played out as part of that scene or as a separate one. The idea is to create awareness in the parent related to generational expectations so that they can be experienced, seen and moved aside, leaving space for a less burdened relationship between parent and child.

It is also possible to let the parent become the fantasy and act it out in as grand a manner as desired. He can cast auxiliaries as parts of the fantasy. Doing gives him the feeling of having what he desires and takes away some of the sense of loss, deprivation or frustration at never getting it.

PARENTAL FEARS

Goals

1. To make conscious parents' deepest fears related to their children.

2. To allow parents to see how their fears for their children might be related to their own childhood wounds.

Steps

1. After a warm-up, choose a protagonist and ask her to identify three or four of her deepest fears for her child.

2. Ask her to choose people to represent those fears or to use empty chairs.

3. Invite her to talk directly to the fear and then to reverse roles with it and actually be the fear, speaking back to herself from the role of the fear.

4. If the parent is finding it difficulat to speak from the place of fear, ask her to stand behind the chair and double for the fear, saying what cannot be said or is too hard to say from the chair. She can move from role to role, including the role of the double, whenever appropriate.

5. When the scene feels finished, ask the parent to end it or to say the last things she wishes to say for the time being.

6. Leave time for group sharing.

Comments

This exercise puts the parents in touch with their own fears and helps them to trace their fears back to points of origin. In this way they can discover whether their fears for their children are appropriate, or if they are primarily related to their own childhoods. The concretizing and subsequent sharing and processing in the group will help to process the fears.

CREATIVE VISUALIZATION

Goals

1. To break through psychological blocks toward a better relationship.

2. To bring comfort and reduce anxiety.

Steps

1. Ask parents to close their eyes, take comfortable positions and breathe in and out in an even, easy, relaxed manner.

2. Lead them through a brief relaxation, saying, "Relax your forehead, cheeks, tongue, jaw, neck, arms, hands, chest, hips, legs and feet."

3. Choose whatever subject fits for the moment: (a) visualizing a positive parent-child relationship; (b) visualizing a good life for the child and releasing him into it; (c) visualizing a happy life for the parent separate from the child, as the child moves comfortably in and out.

a. *Visualizing a positive parent-child relationship.* Say to the parent(s), "Go to a peaceful place within your mind, a meadow, a beach, a river, forest or whatever feels right for you. Imagine that you and your child are together interacting, doing whatever feels right and comfortable. Allow yourself to fully enter the moment. Let anything that is in the way rise to the surface of your mind. Observe what it is and let it go. Continue to deepen your experience of enjoyment and safety in this moment. Enter fully into the positive feeling accompanying this way of relating. Allow yourself to experience it as if it were completely true. Smell it, touch it, feel it. Accept this reality as the reality and take a few moments just to enjoy it."

[Brief interlude.]

"Look at the experience you have created in your mind's eye, and allow yourself to feel that it is really possible to experience it in your life. Slowly, whenever you feel ready, allow the scene to float way, above your head, far into the sky and out of view, and whenever you are ready, open your eyes."

b. *Visualizing a good life for the child and releasing the child into it.* This imagery can be used on its own with sharing afterward about how it felt and what came up for the participants. It can also be a warm-up to a psychodramatic scene related to what came up. You may use music or soft, soothing sounds to help concentration and create atmosphere.

Begin with a relaxation. Say, "Imagine your child at whatever age you wish to. Picture your child doing well in whatever activity, job, relationship or situation is desired. Be specific. See your child in full detail. What is your child wearing? Notice the hair, the body position, the expression on the face. Observe your own feelings as you watch your child functioning independently and successfully in harmony with his own surroundings. Fully experience releasing your child into his own self-reliant experience, and bless your child in your mind for the ability to live life fully and happily. Spend a few moments visualizing this scene in detail as if it were absolutely true."

[Brief interlude.]

"Now, gradually allow the scene to move away from you and release it into the clear, blue sky. Watch as it disappears over the clouds, the horizon, up, up and out of view. Slowly, whenever you feel ready, open your eyes."

(c) *Visualizing a happy life for the parent separate from the child.* This can be used as a warm-up to action. The therapist can put out an empty chair and allow the parent to address her child in whatever way feels right. You may also wish to allow each parent to write a letter to her child, expressing the feelings the imagery evoked. The letter is for use in therapy, not for mailing.

Begin with a brief relaxation. Say, "Visualize yourself in your mind's eye. Allow yourself to come fully into view, engaged in activities that you particularly enjoy and that give you a good sense about yourself. Fully participate in this activity as if it were actually happening. Experience it in great detail. Look around yourself and notice all your surroundings. What are the smells, the sounds, the sensations, the emotional atmosphere? How do you feel when you are fully engaged in your own life? Allow yourself to continue to participate in this scene as if it were real."

[Brief interlude.]

"Experience yourself as autonomous, exploring and pushing on the boundaries of your very self. Move freely into your self and enjoy the experience of being there. Simply be there in a relationship with yourself. Slowly, whenever you feel ready, allow the scene to drift up and out of view. Then, gradually bring your attention back to the room and open your eyes."

Page 163: When we do for the child . . . Maria Montessori Lecture, Meca-Seton Clarendon Hills, Illinois, 1975, June 6.

Page 164: "active memory" . . . . Mardi Horowitz quoted in *Trauma and Recovery*, Basic Books, 1992.

9
Games For Work-Related Issues

*Man must evolve for all human
conflict a method which rejects revenge,
aggression and retaliation.
The foundation of such a method is love.*
—Martin Luther King, Jr.

As children, each of us held a unique position in the family—
the star, the black sheep, the savior, the mediator. When we enter
the workplace, this childhood role—along with all its accompanying feelings—is activated by the new "family" experience of the
organization. Sometimes we can turn former roles to good advantage: the family mediator can become a successful diplomat; the
childhood leader can become a fair and balanced manager. But
many times we take our less successful experiences to work with
us as well. The daughter's need for approval from her parents
translates into the need for approval from her boss. The son's feelings that no matter what he does it will not be enough feeds the
compulsion to do too much, which can lead to workaholism. A

child's erroneous belief that, if she did not take care of things, nothing would get done comes with her to work in or out of the home and is lived out on the organizational level.

Men and women who grew up in severely dysfunctional homes were not taught how to set boundaries in their own homes. As a result their ability to take care of themselves in a job situation is often impaired. As adults, according to Janet Woititz, author of *Adult Children of Alcoholics*, they may carry one or more of these myths into the workplace:

1. If I do not have a good relationship with my boss, it is because of a deficiency in me.

2. If I am not productive, I am worthless—if I don't do it, it won't happen.

3. I am afraid that you will find out that I am not capable of doing this job—that you will figure out the real me. (I'm going to work harder to keep you from figuring me out.)

4. I don't say "no" because I feel so replaceable.

5. I should be able to do whatever is asked of me.

6. Anything that goes wrong is my fault.

7. Anyone who is unhappy is unhappy with me.

8. I shouldn't have to ask my boss for what I need; my boss should be clairvoyant about my needs.

9. I should be able to fix anything that goes wrong.

People who carry a sense of shame and failure because of what went on in their families find it very difficult to communicate with other people, to get help and to share responsibility. They feel that, in some magical way, they should be able to carry the whole load. When they can't, they feel unsupported, misunderstood and used. They may decide to escape to avoid the painful feelings that are being stirred up, a route that leads to a disorganized life and difficulty in earning a living. Or if they can't leave, they may simply work harder, a route that leads to burnout and/or workaholism.

Many people set unreachable goals and standards. Children who were never able to correct a sick family or make their parents better tend to set unreachable goals and standards for themselves as adults. They have trouble tolerating being beginners. They feel they should walk in knowing it all. This either inhibits them from learning how to do a job and slowly becoming competent, or it keeps them locked in the cycle of doing too much in order to protect themselves from the core feeling of failure. They are constantly productive and responsible, but they feel as if they are working in vain to surmount the insurmountable. They rarely feel satisfaction at a day's work well done because they have never accomplished their original task—correcting the sick family. They may find it difficult to break tasks into manageable parts that they can finish and let go of; so every task tends to take on overwhelming proportions. Ironically, those overwhelming proportions are seductive to the person who is locked in the cycle of working for approval that will never be granted, for the promise of approval is always somewhere out there.

Family-of-origin work, as described in Chapter 6, Family-Of-Origin Games, can enable people to work through their early feelings of despair until they are able to release themselves from the feeling that they will never be adequate. Once their compulsions and tensions are dealt with and they can generate feelings of self-acceptance, forgiveness and approval without having to seek them from work relationships, they can walk into the workplace without asking it to heal them.

The games in this chapter are intended for therapy groups dealing with work-related issues or for one-to-one counseling on issues that arise in or around the workplace, whether it be professional, volunteer or domestic.

INNER FACE VERSUS WORKPLACE FACE

Goals

1. To understand how what is going on inside dovetails with one's outward presentation.

2. To make conscious the inner subtext.

Steps

1. Ask participants to find pencil and paper.

2. Have them divide the paper into two columns and write "Outer" at the top of one and "Inner" at the top of the other.

3. Under "Outer," ask them to write any words or phrases that describe the way that they feel they are seen at work.

4. Under "Inner," ask them to write the feelings that are underneath this outer face.

5. Have them break down into pairs or groups of three and share what they have written.

6. Restore the large group, to share any new awareness.

Variations

Set up two chairs and have one person first sit in the outer-self chair, talking to his inner self. Then he can reverse and sit in the inner-self chair, talking to his outer self—the order is up to him.

PERSONAL OVERVIEW

Goals

1. To understand feelings related to work.

2. To create an opportunity to reinforce the positive and let go of the negative.

Steps

1. Ask participants to find pencil and paper.

2. Have them warm up by mentally reviewing the past month, the month before that and so on for a few months.

3. Ask participants to divide their paper into two columns. Say, "In the first column, jot down situations at work that you feel went well, that worked for you, that you felt good about or proud of. In the other column, write things that happened that did not work for you, that you didn't feel good about and that you still carry some uncomfortable feelings about."

4. Have participants divide up into pairs or groups of three and share their feelings about what they have written.

5. Next, have each participant make two lists: "Three things I would like to build on and reinforce," and "Three things I would like to address." Keep it to three items in each column so that the list doesn't become overwhelming.

6. You can have participants move into a large discussion group or small discussion groups to continue, or go on to another exercise. Make sure that you allow sufficient time for sharing

feelings in this exercise so that no one goes away feeling discounted or unheard.

Comments

This exercise can stimulate a lot of sharing and needs to be handled sensitively; it is desirable to address the issues involved in small groups or in one-to-one work, if it is available. Some issues may come up that are not work-related, and participants may jot those down on still another sheet of paper as information for continued personal work.

ROLE REVERSAL ON PAPER

Goals

1. To gain insight into the concerns and needs of someone in another role.

2. To take a break from one's own narrow perspective.

Steps

1. Ask participants to find pencil and paper.

2. Have them close their eyes and allow to come to mind any person in their work life with whom they feel a charge or intensity of any kind.

3. Ask them to reverse roles with that person (to act as if they were that person) taking on his body positions and mannerisms.

4. Now have participants ask a series of questions and let them answer the questions from the point of view of the person they have chosen to be—silently or outloud. Such questions might include—

- How do you feel about your job?
- How do you feel about the people you work with?
- If you could have any other job in the organization, what would it be?
- What direction would you like to see the organization take?
- If you could wave a magic wand, what would you change about this organization?
- What is the most difficult thing you have to deal with at work?

- When would you like to retire?
- What would you do after retirement?
- What is your favorite thing to do at work?

5. Now ask the participants quietly to come back to themselves and do what they need to do to let go of the roles they have assumed.

6. You can have a general discussion about what people learned from trading roles, or break down into small groups for ten minutes and share more personally.

Variations

If the group members are very comfortable with one another and the group is not too big, you can invite the entire group to ask questions, and they can take turns answering as the character. If you do this, let them know ahead of time that you will be answering questions out loud in the group.

ACCOMPLISHING A TASK

Goals

1. To create team spirit.

2. To become sensitive to the variety of roles that are played out in working together.

Steps

1. Form groups ranging in size from six to eight.

2. In step 3, you will be assigning a task to be accomplished. Now, write on the blackboard or large paper the roles that are relevant to the task (the roles must equal the number of people in each group). Ask each person to assume one of the roles. Use any roles that pertain to the particular task—for example, CEO, middle manager, insurance salesperson, facilitator, social worker, fundraiser, teacher, director, assistant, floor manager, police chief, priest, nun and so on.

3. Now give each group the same task to solve. Perhaps the district manager is coming to check on the group, or perhaps one member is resigning and the group needs to decide who gets the

open job. A specific task can be used, like deciding on a direction for a particular group. Do anything that works for you, and whisper the task to each group as they are taking a few minutes to choose roles and getting to know each other in these roles. Though the task is the same for all, they need not know that.

4. Allow the groups to really get into it so that they can feel what it might be like to be in the shoes of the person they are playing.

5. Check on the groups if necessary, and ask them how they are doing and how much more time they need.

6. After the groups wind down, or after giving them ten minutes or so, ask them to share (from where they are sitting together) what came up and what they learned.

Variations

After doing this exercise with a pretend task and pretend roles, you can do it with a real task and pretend roles, and eventually with a real task and real roles.

WORK ROLE ANALYSIS

Goals

1. To understand the variety of ancillary roles within the large role.

2. To see where these roles work for and against each other.

Steps

1. Ask each participant to find a red pencil, a blue pencil, a black pencil and a piece of paper.

2. Say, "Using a triangle as a symbol for male and a circle for female, locate yourself anywhere on the paper that feels right."

3. Say, "Write your job or role title on your symbol."

4. Continue, "Now, using circles, locate on the paper as many ancillary roles as you can think of that are a part of your job, and label them: for example, main role—salesperson; ancillary roles—listener, talker, chauffeur, scheduler, researcher, accountant, long-range planner, entertainment supervisor and so on."

5. Say, "Now draw a red line from your main role to a role you feel tension in and a blue line to a role that you feel okay about."

6. Continue, "On another sheet of paper, jot down any feelings that come up when you look at your chart."

7. Break the group into subgroups of two or three and ask group members to share whatever feelings are present for them.

8. Restore the large group and continue with the relevant discussion.

Variations

This exercise would be a useful warm-up to a discussion of a person's role within an organization and the importance of the effect of role interaction and group dynamics. We are hoping to give each person the feeling that he counts; also to help him to find alternatives when roles that are not working well and to empower himself in roles about which he feels positive. This exercise might be particularly useful in one-to-one counseling situations.

WORK ATOM

Goals

1. To clarify one's personal relationship to people in the workplace.

2. To understand where one fits into the work environment.

Steps

1. Ask participants to find paper and pencil.

2. Say, "Using a circle to represent female and a triangle for male, locate yourself anywhere on the sheet of paper that feels right."

3. Then, "Using the appropriate symbols, locate people at the workplace where you feel they are in relation to you. Place them as near or far as feels right in any direction that you choose. Anyone who has passed away can be represented by a broken line symbol."

4. Continue, "Write in the name of the person each symbol represents."

5. When they have finished, say, "Share your atom with the group or just look it over on your own. On another sheet of paper, you may wish to jot down any thoughts that occur to you when you look at it."

Variations

After the atom is finished, instruct people to look at it and observe where they placed themselves and in what relationship to others. What is their size as compared to the size of others? Are they comfortable with the distance or closeness? Are some symbols incomplete or lined many times, indicating tension or unfinished business? How do they feel when they look at their atoms?

GROUP WALK

Goals

1. To get group members on their feet and mixing.
2. To release feelings in a safe way.

Steps

1. Ask group members to stand up and begin to move around the room.

2. Ask them to take in each person as he goes by—and to avoid bumping into one another.

3. Depending on the group, you may ask them to move quickly or slowly, or to focus on letting tension go in hands, shoulders, neck and so on.

4. Now ask participants to establish eye contact with one person, to walk up to him and to share one thing with him, either something from the following list of suggestions or something that is personally relevant. Repeat this process of walking, establishing eye contact and sharing for each question.

- One thing I like about my job is . . .
- One thing I don't like about my job is . . .
- This is exactly what I wanted to do when I "grew up" . . .
- This person _____ would never believe I do what I do . . .
- One person who does not understand why I do this type of work is . . .
  - I identify with my fellow workers in this way . . .
  - I feel different from my fellow workers in this way . . .
  - On a scale from one to ten, I rate my job satisfaction at . . .

• If there were a genie at our workplace, I would have him magically . . .

5. At this point you can return to walking and move directly into another exercise, break into small groups and let people share what came up for them as a result of this exercise, or reconstitute the large group. Allow time for sharing, but make sure that sharing is always only about personal experience, that there is no cross-talk or advice.

Variations

This game is a good warm-up for further work. It is a natural lead-in for breaking a large group up into smaller groups and then moving on to another exercise.

GETTING-THE-JOB-DONE ATOM

Goals

1. To define the job that needs accomplishing.
2. To delineate its various components.

Steps

1. Ask participants to find pencil and paper.
2. Say, "Using triangles as male symbols, circles as female symbols and squares as neuter symbols, first locate yourself and your project anywhere on the paper that feels right."
3. When participants have finished, say, "Now add symbols for the various aspects or elements of the project and for the people involved. Place them in whatever relation to yourself and one another in which you see them to be, and label each symbol."
4. Continue, "Now that you have your project laid out in front of you, on another sheet of paper list, vertically, each person and element. As headings for two adjacent columns write 'Current State,' and 'What it Needs.' Fill in each of these columns with a sentence or so after each person and element."
5. Continue, "On another sheet of paper, make a simple project time-line showing the order in which you want to accomplish tasks, noting those involved, and estimate overall time required.

Have one sheet of paper next to this to act as a wastebasket, and jot down on it any extraneous things that you can eliminate immediately to make the job less complicated."

6. Finally, "Redo your project atom to reflect your current sense of how you want to organize the job. Refer to it and the other papers as you move along, crossing out things that have been taken care of and adding to your wastebasket page whenever you can."

Variation

If you don't wish to fill out the interim sheets, you can make only one or two atoms and cross out and write phrases on the first. This can also be adapted for home related tasks.

FANTASY ATOM

Goals

1. To allow people to open up and dream a little.
2. To gain a greater comfort with reality by making unconscious fantasies conscious.

Steps

1. Ask participants to find pencil and paper.
2. Say, "Using the symbols of a circle for a female and a triangle for a male, locate yourself anywhere on the paper that feels right to you."
3. Continue, "Place anyone from any part of your workplace, not where he actually is, but where you wish he was in relation to you." Anyone can be included on the atom from any level of the workplace—top management, food services, janitorial staff and so on.
4. When participants have finished say, "Now look over your atom, and label each symbol by name."
5. Now ask them just to look at the atom and notice what feelings come up when they look at things as they wish they were.
6. Ask participants either to share those feelings or to jot them down on another piece of paper, depending on what would be more comfortable.
7. Discuss the purpose of the atom, which is to let them compare their work and fantasy atoms and to more fully understand the hopes and dreams that they carry around with them.

Variations

Encourage people to see if there is anything on the atom that may be actually possible, that they could take steps toward bringing about. This exercise is best done in a one-to-one counseling situation or in a small, trusting, well-supervised group.

PROJECT ATOM

Goals

1. To understand the various components of a project and how it affects one's work life.

2. To improve project performance.

Steps

1. Ask participants to find paper and colored pens or pencils.

2. Say, "Using the symbols of circles for females, triangles for males and squares for objects or project elements, first locate yourself anywhere on the paper that feels right."

3. Continue, "Now locate the people and elements that are a part of this project as it affects you. Place them in any relation to you that feels right or accurate."

4. "Using a red line for tension, a green line for neutral and a blue line for positive feelings, draw lines from yourself to all the people and elements on your atom."

5. Finally, "Now look at your atom, and share any awarenesses that arise in you."

Variations

This exercise is for personal use or use in one-to-one counseling situations. The idea is to process and move beyond work or project-related issues. It can also be adapted for work-related issues in a therapy situation or in the home.

WHAT'S IN THE WAY OF SUCCESS

Goals

1. To get in touch of what's in the way of being successful.

2. To let go of old messages.

Steps

1. Ask participants to find pencil and paper.

2. Say, "Sit quietly, and allow to come to mind anything that feels in the way of your feeling empowered and letting yourself succeed."

3. Continue, "Write these things down in any way you wish—all over your paper—pictures, voices and phrases from your past or messages from family or society that nag at you."

4. When they have finished, have participants break up into pairs or groups of three or four and share with one another whatever they would like about their discoveries.

5. Restore the large group and share, or structure a vignette or psychodrama, addressing whatever is in the way of the protagonist's success.

6. Allow further sharing among group members.

Variation

This exercise is a good springboard for discussing personal empowerment. You can talk about all the things that we put in our way that can be let go of, the concept of empowering ourselves rather than waiting to be empowered by someone else and our ability to change many things in our personal attitudes toward our jobs. This exercise is best used in group therapy or in one-to-one work. It may also be adapted to a successful home life.

10
Games Within The Classroom

The Risk Of Birth, Christmas, 1973

This is no time for a child to be born,
With the earth betrayed by war & hate
And a comet slashing the sky to warn
That time runs out & the sun burns late.

That was no time for a child to be born,
In a land in the crushing grip of Rome;
Honour & truth were trampled by scorn—
Yet here did the Savior make his home.

When is the time for love to be born?
The inn is full on the planet earth,
And by a comet the sky is torn—
Yet Love still takes the risk of birth.

—Madelaine L'Engle

Each student comes to school from a home, and each student carries the system of her home into that of the school. The lessons children learn at home—how to relate to authority, how to deal with siblings or peers, how to tolerate discipline, how to connect with other people—enter with them into the educational system. A child who does not learn to relate well at home will not arrive at school with that skill magically in place; a child who has learned that authority is insensitive or harsh will arrive at school expecting such treatment and even behaving in a way that engenders it.

Along with a family system, each child brings a cultural system. Every culture has its own set of rules, rituals and behaviors. The school itself reflects the culture in which it exists, which may or may not be compatible with the culture from which the child comes. A child from a culture that differs from the school's culture can feel misunderstood or isolated from the whole, regardless of what his home life is like.

The most popular child in the classroom tends to be silently chosen by the majority of students to represent them; he reflects the qualities the group most values. The least popular child tends to represent qualities that the students reject or are afraid to know and express within themselves, or he may exhibit characteristics they see as antisocial or otherwise undesirable. The broader the level of acceptance and comfort, the less extreme these two positions are and the stronger the recognition of the wide variety of roles possible within the class. The best adjusted child tends to be that child who most accurately perceives, knows and accepts his position within the group.

The school system is not generally the place to use psychodrama because its orientation is to heal the intrapsychic system, which is too rigorous a therapeutic goal for the school environment. More generalized sociodramatic goals are helpful, however. The primary goal of action techniques in schools should be to help the children make positive connections with one another and with authority figures. Once children learn how to really connect, many things are possible. It will enable them (1) to alter or accommodate their status in the class; (2) to reach out for positive activities, which in turn will alter their self-concept; and (3) to make constructive use of the authorities available to them in order to learn and grow as people. All this will continue to help them as they make their transition between school and the world at large, because they will take their sociometric status and their new learning with them and apply it to whatever situation they move into after school. In summary, the use of action techniques in a school system can—

1. Help students to connect to one another in positive supportive ways rather than negative, competitive ones.

2. Help students to connect with authority in a constructive manner.

3. Elucidate the nuance and meaning in the situations presented, through watching and participating.

4. Make students aware of the options in behavior that they might make use of themselves.

5. Provide role-training and practice in learning how to handle a variety of situations.

6. Provide a situation in which all have an equal opportunity to participate.

7. Provide a forum through which school-based issues and related feelings can be explored in a safe and structured manner.

The challenge is to provide young people with a place in which they can explore themselves, to encourage a meaningful growth experience without opening up more than can be brought to adequate closure.

Many of the young people school psychologists see have low self-esteem. Children who hear and internalize negative messages at home or in their social networks take them in as truths and form a negative self-image. In helping these children, we first need to alter their image of themselves. One way to do so is by meeting them where they are and then slowly bringing them to a new place. It is the first task of action techniques, then, to double—to speak "as if" from the inside of these children or act as an inner voice—allowing them to feel that they are not alone. Only when the self has been able to incorporate a "good enough" double (acting as the self) will they have the ability to make use of the corrective information that may come to them from the outside. In other words, they will need to have a secure inside before they can use what is available to them on the outside.

Action techniques offer a concrete method for role-playing the double. Simple role-plays can be set up that allow students a new and challenging way in which to explore themselves and one another. Many of the exercises in this book (as well as in this chapter) can be adapted to use with young people, at the discretion of the therapist.

BASIC METHOD

The following is the basic method for setting up a role-play of a situation in a school or youth group.

Steps

1. Ask the students to name the scene or the issue they wish to work with.

2. Ask them to name the people in the scene or the roles in the scene.

3. Ask the students to think of words that describe characteristics of each person in the scene and write those down on the blackboard next to the characters.

4. Ask for volunteers to play each role.

5. Ask each role-player to take a position that seems to embody the characteristics that the group came up with. Invite group participation for this.

6. Ask group members to say what these role-players might say, and write it down if you like.

7. Open the scene. Move into action by saying some of what was suggested or whatever the characters come up with.

8. Allow the scene to progress in whatever way it unfolds.

9. At any point you can freeze the action to discuss what is going on with the audience or group, and then continue the action again.

10. When the action is frozen, ask for doubles if you choose to—students who identify with any role or who feel they might know what is going on inside a person. Ask these doubles to take turns standing behind the person playing the role for which they choose to double and to speak the inner life of that character, and then to sit down again.

11. This freezing and moving back into action can take place as often as seems appropriate.

12. End the scene by asking characters to say the last thing that needs to be said for the time being.

13. You may choose to enact more than one ending. After one

ending ask the group what other endings or resolutions may be possible, and then act them out.

14. Allow plenty of time for group sharing: what came up for participants as a result of watching the action; how they may have identified or understood the scene for themselves; and how it felt to play their roles.

FOLLOW-UP EXERCISES

Follow-up exercises allow the students both to further the healing process and share their feelings and to open up new creative methods of expression. For example—

1. Ask students to write a poem about the scene or feelings elicited relating to the scene or any aspect of it.

2. Do a role analysis of any character within the scene (see Chapter 3, Sociometry: How Psychodrama Works, for an example of role analysis.)

3. Ask them to discuss or journal about any character's "shadow side" or, in the first person, to write or act out a monologue, that would reflect the inner life of that character.

4. Invite the students to mentally reverse roles with any person in the sculpture and write a monologue in the first person from that person's point of view.

5. Ask them to write a letter from one person in the sculpture to another person in the sculpture.

6. Ask them to write a story with these characters in it.

7. Say, "With any or all characters, draw out what you feel each person might be thinking, saying or feeling. Do this by dividing a piece of paper into three columns. Label one column Thinking, label the next column Saying and label the third column Feeling. In each appropriate column you may include a line relating to what each person from the above might be wishing could be or could happen."

8. Ask students to make cartoon drawings of each of the characters in the scene and to draw above each character two bubbles—a speech bubble for what the character is saying and a thought bubble for what the character might be thinking.

9. Ask students to divide a piece of paper into two columns. Title one column Outer Person and the other column Inner Person. Ask the students to reverse roles mentally with any character they

choose or with all the characters in the scene. Then have them write in the first column what the outer person seems like or how they present themselves, and in the second column what they imagine might be going on within the inner person.

ROLE-PLAY OF BEING MUGGED

Goals

1. To practice appropriate responses to being mugged.

2. To reduce anxiety about being mugged so that the student or person being mugged has a better chance of being alert and spontaneous in difficult situations.

Steps

1. Ask two or more students to volunteer, depending on how many are involved in the mugging.

2. Let one (or more) be the victim(s) and one (or more) the mugger(s), preferably by their choice.

3. Ask the group to define a situation—walking home from school, waiting for a bus and so on—and have the role-players enact what they would do in that situation.

4. Ask the mugger to observe the victim, check out the situation and then make his move to ask for whatever he wants from the victim—leather jacket, watch, money, walkman and so on.

5. Allow the victim to respond in a variety of ways. Encourage the victim to play out several responses.

6. Freeze the action and ask the group to identify (1) the safest responses and (2) the responses most likely to get the victim into further trouble.

7. Now ask the students to role-play the scene so that the victim can practice responses that are most likely to keep him safe. You may invite people to double for either role if you choose.

8. End the scene in any appropriate way.

9. Allow plenty of time for sharing.

Variations

At any point you may freeze the scene and ask participants either to stand up behind any character to double for him or to take turns in offering a variety of options on how to act.

DEPRESSION

Goals

1. To provide a way to concretize the inner experience of depression and bring it out of hiding.

2. To provide a format for talking about depression.

Steps

1. Ask for a volunteer who would like to do a role-play with depression.

2. Ask that person to choose someone to play the role of depression, or use an empty chair.

3. Ask the protagonist to reverse roles with depression and physicalize, that is show with his body, what depression looks like.

4. Reverse roles, and begin the role-play by allowing the protagonist to talk to depression—for example, "I'm sick of living with you," "I hate the way you look and act," "I wish I didn't feel you" and so on.

5. Reverse roles throughout the role-play, whenever it feels appropriate.

6. As the leader you can double behind the protagonist and express what feels true but unspoken or invite other group members who identify with either role to double as they choose.

7. When you feel the scene is drawing to a close, ask the protagonist to say the last things he wishes to say to depression.

8. Invite other group members to share what came up for them watching the drama, and ask depression how it felt to play the role.

Variations

If you wish to do this exercise in a one-to-one situation, you can use an empty chair to represent depression and reverse roles with the protagonist, then process the experience with the client. Processing may continue through journaling or any artistic mode available. Any mood, concern or part of the self can be role-played in this way—the part of the self that feels shy, unpopular, popular; feelings of happiness, anger, sadness, fear and so on. The role-playing can be followed up with journaling, writing, poetry or artwork if desired. (see Follow-up Exercises under Basic Method).

PRESSURE TO USE DRUGS

Goals

1. To role-play high-pressure situations before they occur in life.

2. To practice dealing with pressure to use drugs in a variety of ways.

Steps

1. Ask group members to come up with a situation in their lives in which they have felt pressured to use drugs.

2. Ask for volunteers to play the various roles.

3. Set the scene by asking—

a. "What is the situation?"

b. "Where are people standing or sitting?"

c. "What is their body posture and body language?"

4. Ask each player to take on the physical posture of the role that he is playing.

5. Let the scene begin, and ask the characters to start interacting.

6. Allow the characters to play out the scene fully, using role reversal and doubling whenever it seems appropriate.

7. When the scene feels as if it is coming to a closure point, ask the characters to say the last things they need to say to one another to finish the scene.

8. Allow plenty of time for sharing.

Variations

You may wish to have a student play the role of the double and stand behind the person who is feeling pressured (or any character) and speak his inner feelings throughout the scene. If you do so, ask him during the sharing phase to talk about how he was feeling while playing the double.

PERSONAL DOUBLE

Goals

1. To bring hidden thoughts and feelings to a conscious level.

2. To make it safe for the protagonist to come to the threshold of her own feeling.

Steps

1. Ask a person who wishes to work either to choose a person to play her or to use an empty chair.

2. Next ask her to describe herself—how she is standing or sitting and why, what she is feeling and so on. If a person is being used instead of an empty chair, she should take on the appropriate body posture. First she sits in the chair and plays herself. Have her introduce herself and say a bit about herself.

3. Now ask the protagonist to stand behind herself and say from the position of the double the real truth about how she feels inside.

4. You may wish to ask her to reverse roles wherever it would seem helpful, or she can play out the whole drama from the double position.

5. When you feel that the drama is coming to a close, ask the protagonist to end the scene any way she wants.

6. In a group allow others to share what came up for them while they were watching; in one-to-one work, continue to process feelings and thoughts. Invite any role-players to share how playing the role felt.

Variations

This exercise constitutes deep work and should be undertaken only when appropriate role-players can share from the role in the first person during the sharing phase. The protagonist can continue to process what comes up through journaling, poetry, art, music or whatever creative form she has access to. The journaling can be in the first or third person.

HIDING BEHIND A NEGATIVE ROLE

Goals

1. To help students realize that they do not need to get stuck in playing negative roles.

2. To bring a negative role out into the open where it can be seen for what it is.

Steps

1. Ask the group members to come up with a negative role that they play or see played around school, such as that of a bully or noncooperative disruptive student and so on.

2. Place a chair in the middle of the group.

3. Let the kids take turns sitting in the negative chair, where their purpose will be to exaggerate the negative role as much as possible.

4. Ask other group members to do two things:

a. Stand behind the chair and, whenever they feel inspired, double for the feelings they sense are being hidden by the negative role-player.

b. Ask questions of the person playing the negative role.

5. When the scene seems played out, ask the person playing the negative role to end the scene with a few sentences about how he is feeling.

Variations

If you wish to do this exercise in a one-to-one situation use an empty chair to represent the negative role. Ask the student to talk to the negative role and reverse roles wherever appropriate. You may wish to double for the student or the empty chair representing the negative role. If you double for the empty chair, do so sparingly so that you do not get too much negative projection. This approach can also be used in a group situation and then processed by the group when appropriate.

PART III

PSYCHODRAMA IN THE TREATMENT OF ADDICTION AND TRAUMA

*"Like a baton in some grotesque
generational marathon . . . ".*
—from a New York Times book Review of
Alice Miller's *Prisoners of Childhood*
describing generational dysfunction

People affected by trauma, alcoholism or addiction have special issues in common that the director of a psychodrama will need to consider. Chapters 11 and 12 address the needs of these groups and how they relate to the psychodramatic process.

Twelve-step programs have a significant impact on the therapeutic process. Their format offers support and a holding environment for feelings that come up throughout recovery, and provides new models for behavior with other people. Group

203

interaction is highly structured, with a strictly adhered to format. The rule of no cross-talk, for example, assures that a speaker will not have to fear attack. By listening to other people's stories, members feel identification. This breaks down the walls of isolation and the feeling that no one understands them, and fosters self-acceptance. People tell their stories in an environment that provides unconditional acceptance and understanding. This is a primary therapeutic function and a vital part of the process of inward reconstruction. The very strict rules in 12-Step groups make it safe for people to stop hiding behind their masks of "looking good."

Experiential therapy allows the traumatized "inner child" to literally come back from the dead and learn to feel, talk and be alive again. It creates a space in which the unspeakable can be spoken, and additionally offers the help of a caring guide and group, encouraging experimentation with new roles and alternative ways of being. Through these two approaches, participants can place themselves on the continuum of the disease and thus come to understand what happened to them as children, adolescents, teenagers and adults, blazing a trail for wellness.

The addictions field primarily uses a therapist-centered medical model, treating according to diagnosis and using the concept of disease. The therapist will treat "issues"—for example, shame, abandonment, denial and so on—or will have a clear idea of where the client should go and will use experiential techniques to get him there. This differs from the way psychodramatists work, essentially letting the protagonist lead the way. This does not, however, render a marriage between the two fields unsuitable.

Working a 12-Step program can fit in beautifully in conjunction with psychodrama, group psychotherapy and sociometry. There are countless opportunities for new sociometric alignments and connections within 12-Step rooms, reciprocal pairs (sharing after meetings and during breaks, and telephone therapy), dyads, triads and overall group identification, as well as other aspects of the developmental process described as follows.

The Double

The format of no cross-talk allows the doubling process to take place without fear of attack. Listening to other people's stories makes us feel understood from the inside, which strengthens a sense of self-acceptance by offering an environment that loves, accepts and understands unconditionally. This is a primary therapeutic function and a vital part of the process of inner reconstruction. Without successful doubling the mirror will feel harsh and disconnected. When this function is provided by both therapist or group and a 12-Step program, there is substantial support. Through meetings or telephone therapy, 12-Step support is constantly available, so that help can be found when it is needed.

The Mirror

The mirror enters naturally through both the group process and the program. Interaction mobilizes feelings and issues; and in the course of exploring them, we see a variety of points of view reflected back to us. The mirror need not necessarily be confrontational, it can simply be another point of view, an alternative perspective.

In 12-Step work this is handled in a very structured way, so that the amount of mirroring remains safe and tolerable. In the psychodramatic process the mirror enters through sharing, when people say both what came up for them as a result of watching or participating in the action (which is a mirror in that it reflects variety on the same theme) or in the process of giving group members honest feedback. Group process in a therapeutic setting constantly mirrors in one way or another.

The Auxiliary Ego

The function of the auxiliary ego is to recognize that there are people in this world wholly different from and outside of one's person and personal reality. These goals are met in 12-Step work, where the wide variety of participants provide many auxiliaries who are different but still connected. They are from many walks of life, but they share a common program. They are separate but connected. This is the third developmental stage as it is reproduced in these therapeutic environments, that is to individuate or separate, but to retain a psychological and emotional connection to others.

Role-Training

The role-training or behavior aspect of psychodrama is useful to recovering people who have not had the opportunity to work out issues in adequate ways. They have grown up with models who alternated between erratic, impulsive, or controlled and rigid behavior. Addicted families lack spontaneity. Members do not feel free to express thoughts and feelings as they occur. They fear judgment and attack so they edit their speech and action, removing any personal expression that might get them into trouble with others in their highly-stressed family.

Being able to experience strong feelings in the context of a psychodrama, either as the protagonist, auxiliary ego or audience, is very healing for the adult child of an addict, the addict or the co-dependent. Having the opportunity to tolerate a feeling within a controlled environment is an important part of recovering the self that went under for protection. Psychodrama offers a safe situation in which the self can re-emerge and learn to be spontaneous again.

11
Using Psychodrama With Addicts And ACoAs

In search of my mother's garden,
I found my own.
—Alice Walker

Addicts, alcoholics and adult children of alcoholics (ACoAs) have grown up in environments with many common features that cross both cultural and economic barriers. It is no accident that those who grow up with these similar influences shaping their lives tend to choose one another as friends and later as marriage partners. In their homes looming problems were managed through various types of denial behavior from rigid and controlled discipline to ungoverned chaos — a sort of "survival of the fittest" atmosphere. The family experienced erratic behavior; often they achieved "normalcy" by denying their pain and entering a cooperative delusion.

THE ALCOHOLIC FAMILY SYSTEM

Alcoholic family systems are characterized by denial, repression and delusion. Because family members rightly sense that alcohol is a threat to their very survival (coupled with the insidious slow onset of the disease of alcoholism), they silently close ranks and attempt to ride out the storm. But alcoholism is not like most other problems that befall families: it is socially mortifying; it destroys the consistency and trust of close relationships; it turns otherwise functional people into frightening, out-of-control monsters; and it renders those involved senseless with pain. It cannot be stopped by getting a prescription from a doctor or going to a hospital for an operation. The alcoholic family, when it does not know how to stop the drinking behavior or how to look at its own underlying pathology, is forced to sit back and watch itself be destroyed.

Because the helplessness and hopelessness of this situation are too painful to endure, these families deny that they have a problem. They delude themselves into thinking that the bizarre and twisted behavior that they live with is normal, and they repress their ever deepening feelings of shame, rage, despair, desperation and isolation. Spouses in these families learn to focus the problem onto the alcoholic and can develop and unwillingness to look at their own behavior. They are caught in the emotional bind of feeling like martyred victims while overflowing with self-recrimination and self-loathing. J. Sexias describes the situation succinctly:

If you listen to an articulate adult tell how it was to be raised in a family in which one or both parents regularly and/or continually drank too much, you become outraged and mystified. The account will sound like a nightmare because time is distorted and reality challenged. Alice in Wonderland had it easy! At least she eventually awakened from her dream. But the child of an alcoholic lives unremittingly with the illogical.

For family members to allow themselves actually to feel what Sexias describes would be intolerably threatening. They may choose one child as a scapegoat and project their unconscious feelings of self-hatred onto that child; they may choose a hero to live out the family dreams and aspirations that they feel are now lost to them. Other roles may emerge—that of the lost child who silently goes about taking care of herself and becomes spiritually invisible within the family or that of the mascot who constantly sacrifices his own needs and identity on the family altar of dysfunction, flying into action to make people feel better and take away their pain. Children in these families grow up being systematically trained to lie to themselves and others about how they really feel. Of such a child, psychoanalyst Karen Horney has said:

> *To the extent that safety has become paramount, his innermost feelings and thoughts have receded in importance — in fact, have had to be silenced and have become indistinct. (It does not matter what he feels, if only he is safe.) His feelings and wishes thus cease to be determining factors. . .*
>
> *He idealizes, to begin with, his particular "solution" of his basic conflict: compliance becomes goodness; love, saintliness; aggressiveness becomes strength, leadership, heroism, omnipotence; aloofness becomes wisdom, self-sufficiency, independence. What — according to his particular solution — appear as shortcomings or flaws are always dimmed out or retouched. Imperceptibly he becomes this image: the idealized image becomes an idealized self. And this idealized self becomes more real to him than his real self. . .because it answers all his stringent needs. This transfer of his center of gravity is an entirely inward process; there is no observable or conspicuous outward change in him. The change is in the core of his being, in his feeling about himself.*

Men and women who walk into adulthood with an idealized self rather than a real self are not equipped to live life spontaneously, for in order to be spontaneous, we need access to our core feelings, likes and dislikes. Children of alcoholic families who have an idealized rather than a real self unconsciously look for the ideal job, the ideal mate and an ideal family, rather than real people and professions. They become bonded with the fantasy of who they are rather than the reality of who they are and feel incapacitated when confronted with real-life situations and relationships.

Part of the process of therapy for these people is a process of dismantling this idealized self so that the hidden core self can emerge. It is generally full of rage and tears. And when they finally come into contact with it, they may not recognize what they are seeing; they may be angry at the therapist who has put them in this vulnerable, defenseless position. They will have to take the time it will take to rebuild a self.

Often in alcoholic families, bonding among members is distorted. Instead of bonding with the real parent, a child may bond to what they wish their parent was: a fantasy bond. Siblings may form bonds based not on friendship and mutuality, but on the need for comfort and safety in the face of danger or the playing out of painful family dynamics: a traumatic bond. Children who have formed such bonds actively seek them out as adults. Therefore, when treating the ACoA in therapy, it is necessary to understand both the intrapsychic system of the child who grew up in an alcoholic home and the alcoholic system itself. According to P. Steinglass:

> *In recent years a more empathetic view of families with alcoholic members has been emerging. Family-oriented clinicians and researchers have drawn on the burgeoning interest in family systems theory and on findings from family interaction research to suggest that families with alcoholic members constitute highly complex behavioral systems with remarkable tolerance for stress as well as occasional bursts of adaptive behavioral inventiveness that provoke wonder and admiration in observers.*

ACoAs carry this "tolerance for stress and adaptive behavioral inventiveness" into adulthood. Steinglass also found that the "stress attendant on alcoholism is spread uniformly throughout the family rather than being restricted either to the person who is drinking or to the nonalcoholic spouse." Such holistic thinking, which is central to a systems perspective, is expounded by Michael Patton:

> *A system is a whole that is both greater than and different from its parts. Indeed, a system cannot validly be divided into independent parts as discrete entities of inquiry because the effects of the behavior of the parts on the whole depend on what is happening to the other parts. The parts are so interconnected and interdependent that any simple cause-effect analysis distorts more than it illuminates. Changes in one part lead to changes*

among all parts and the system itself. Nor can one simply add the parts in some linear fashion and get a useful sense of the whole.

Moreno, one of the earliest systems thinkers, left us with the science of sociometry: tools to study and measure dynamics within a given system. We can use the social atom in innumerable ways to examine many aspects of multigenerational systems and to provide a firm anchor for concretizing one's position in the family or personal network. We tend to take our status in our original family into other areas of our life—work, school, relationships, marriage—living it out over and over again.

Children from alcoholic families grow up keeping secrets. The biggest secret that they keep is that they hurt inside. ACoAs often suffer silently. Claudia Black tells us,

> *They weren't always the ones who had adjustment problems, nor were they the angry ones. The majority of these people indicated, instead, that they had strong tendencies to appear "normal" and to be from "typical" American families. They did not exhibit problematic behavior, and they rarely or never talked about the alcoholism in their primary family . . .*

Karen Horney has said,

> *Through a variety of adverse influences, a child may not be permitted to grow according to his individual needs and possibilities. . . . the people in the environment are too wrapped up in their own neuroses to be able to love the child, or even to conceive of him as the particular individual he is; their attitudes toward him are determined by their own neurotic needs and responses.*
>
> *As a result, the child does not develop a feeling of belonging, of "we," but instead a profound insecurity and vague apprehensiveness, for which I use the term* basic anxiety. *. . . The cramping pressure of his basic anxiety prevents the child from relating himself to others with the spontaneity of his real feelings, and forces him to find ways to cope with them. He must (unconsciously) deal with them in ways which do not arouse, or increase, but rather allay his basic anxiety.*
>
> *In a healthy human relationship the moves toward, against, or away from others are not mutually exclusive. . . . But in the child who feels himself on precarious ground because of his basic*

anxiety, these moves become extreme and rigid. Affection, for instance, becomes clinging; compliance becomes appeasement. Similarly, he is driven to . . . keep aloof, without reference to his real feelings. . . . The degree of blindness and rigidity in his attitudes is in proportion to the intensity of the basic anxiety lurking within him.

In time, he tries to solve it by making one of these moves consistently predominant—tries to make his prevailing attitude one of compliance or aggressiveness or aloofness.

THE EFFECTS OF GROWING UP WITH CHAOS

Children from alcoholic homes have little sense of certainty about what the day will bring. Family members walk gingerly, tiptoeing around anything that they fear might become explosive, while at the same time waiting hypervigilantly for the bottom to fall out of the situation and the yelling, insults, shouting of orders and general abuse to begin. Talking things out in a constructive manner is not possible under either of these circumstances, and so people tend to:

- hold feelings in until they become numb
- act feelings out—do inappropriate things to "get rid" of the feeling rather than identify and experience it
- disappear within themselves, yet remain physically present
- leave the situation and isolate themselves in an attempt to gain safety

During early childhood years, this turbulent emotional environment sets up a fear of feeling. As children, the only thing ACoAs had any control over was themselves, and many discovered that shutting down their own feelings was the most effective way to control their inner experience of chaos. Unfortunately, life is full of ups and downs, and real relationships and families are seldom the way they looked on the Donna Reed show. When ACoAs attempt to have families and relationships in adulthood, they overreact to the vicissitudes of daily living, not so much because they feel strongly about a given situation, but because they are afraid of the potential strength of their own feelings. Feeling their own feelings puts them into a state of fear in which they see chaos, out-of-control behavior and abuse looming around the corner—because this was their early childhood experience. They are so convinced that distress is at hand that they experience mistrust and suspicion if problems are solved smoothly. Often they will push a situation in a convoluted self-protective attempt to ferret out potential danger until, through their relentless efforts to avoid it, they actually create it. And so the pattern of strong feeling leading to chaos, rage and tears is once again reinforced.

While the ACoA is well defended and may present as tough or inaccessible, he is covering up deep wounds; the reason the defenses are so strong is that he is protecting and shoring up so much vulnerability. The ACoA has never really had the opportunity to get to know himself in a supportive family environment. Letting down his guard would mean deep connection and love one day and emotional annihilation another, for inconsistency is the hallmark of a family where addiction is present. Because the ACoA has not been able to develop a self safely he has trouble inwardly locating or describing a self when asked to be self-examining in therapy. Psychodrama, by putting the inner reality of the protagonist on stage over and over again in a safe way, where it is not attacked, allows a self to emerge. Then it can be examined after it is seen and observed by the protagonist himself. Seeing the self in action affirms the self for the client and opens the door for the process of rebuilding the self.

Breaking destructive patterns is one of therapy's treatment tasks. Groups, because they mobilize feeling or become the surrogate family, are ideal vehicles both to bring these patterns forward and to create the opportunity to heal them. Psychodrama, because it allows the original cast to be present through role-play, presents the client with the opportunity to resolve transferences by working them through in a controlled environment. The child who could not speak says what she needs to say; the adolescent who hid in his room comes out and talks to the people he ran from; and the wife who silently poured bottles of liquor down the sink confronts her alcoholic husband.

Being part of group therapy sessions over a prolonged period of time helps the addict or ACoA learn to "sit with" painful feelings or anxiety-provoking situations without running from them or acting out in inappropriate ways. When the person can consciously acknowledge and feel his feelings—when he can own them—then he can make informed choices as to what to do with them.

Low self-esteem is a core issue for addicts and many ACoAs who have internalized confusing messages about themselves from their home environments. Following is an overview of some of the factors that contribute to low self-esteem and some of the common feelings and issues addicts and ACoAs share.

- shame
- isolation
- unresolved grief and mourning
- developmental distortion
- Post Traumatic Stress Reaction
- sober vs. nonsober thinking and behavior
- emotional numbness
- disorganized thinking
- distorted internalized family system
- distorted parental role models
- difficulty in forming empathic bonds
- incomplete separation from parents
- parentified children
- internalized marital dysfunction
- inflexible ego structure
- physical and sexual abuse in childhood
- dissociation
- grandiosity
- difficulty clarifying needs

SHAME

For the addict or the person in an addicted environment, shame becomes not so much a feeling that is experienced in relation to an incident or situation, but rather a basic attitude toward and about the self. It can be difficult to identify because it is so pervasive, a part of the very fabric of the personality. It is experienced as a lack of energy for life, an inability to accept love and caring on a consistent basis or a hesitancy to move into self-affirming roles. It may play out as impulsive decision-making, or an inability to make decisions at all.

Shame can keep people stuck at an early stage of development, and it can also be the fuel behind compulsions and obsessions. Some will never feel they can achieve enough to offset their deep sense of shame, and some will use alcohol, drugs, food, sex or work compulsively to mediate emotional pain and shame.

How Can Psychodrama Help?

One of the most important steps in relieving shame is to break the lock that imprisons the secret behind the shame and bring it to the attention of others. The group acts as a powerful witness to the material being shared. The person who role-plays a situation with which shame is associated has the chance to give back to the perpetrator the shame that she has internalized as her own. In psychodrama this can happen spontaneously, in just the way the protagonist needs it to take place.

Unconscious feelings of shame will exert a powerful control over the psyche until they are made conscious and felt in the present moment: when shame arises, an effort is made to allay it— by controlling the self or others, by acting out behaviorally or by ingesting substances. Psychodrama offers the opportunity both to mobilize shame through direct enactment and to watch the enactment of others, so that shame can be brought from the inner depths to the surface of the mind where it can be seen and felt in the present; its origins can be understood and insight can come. Psychodrama provides previously hidden pieces of the puzzle so that the whole picture can be seen.

ISOLATION

In the addicted family, where real feelings and issues are being denied, children who are in pain have nowhere to go for understanding, comfort or reality confirmation. They feel crazy—as if they are overdramatizing the situation or creating unnecessary trouble. To make matters worse, family members who are steeped in denial will confirm their distorted self-perceptions, because the reality is too painful for the family to live with and denial feels safer. The child's opportunities for genuine connection within the family system decrease because the system itself is living a lie, silently committed to maintaining the status quo.

In such a closed system, no one tells the truth about how he feels, and no one escapes from his pain. The inability to talk safely about reality forces everyone to go "under" with his real feelings—which means there can be little support and empathy. The result is that everyone feels isolated in his own pain.

How Can Psychodrama Help?

Our status within a group rises when we make a sincere self-disclosure. Our sense of isolation diminishes, and our altered status brings new and meaningful connections with other individuals in the group.

Psychodrama calls on people to work together toward the common goal of role-playing the protagonist's drama or their own. Group members are asked to play important roles in the protagonist's life and, through this, have an opportunity to experience themselves in different roles. They also feel important to the action because they come to see how helpful they are to the catharsis and resolution of the protagonist's work.

All these factors draw people from their isolated positions toward interaction, which continues to diminish their sense of isolation. In the group sharing, the director can bring in isolates simply by asking how they experienced the psychodrama and what it touched for them in their own lives.

UNRESOLVED GRIEF AND MOURNING

Addicted families suffer profound losses. There is the loss of the addict to his substance and the enabler to her co-dependency. For children there is the loss of parents to rely on, the loss of a free and untroubled childhood, the loss of a feeling of safety, the loss of the secure family unit, the loss of trust, the loss of a stable and smooth early development. There are the losses of comfortable family events, rituals and holidays, and for children the loss of the security of knowing that their parents are in a position to parent them and meet their changing needs.

Many members of addicted families experience a sort of inner death or psychic numbing as a way to cope with an overload of fear, pain and anxiety—and one task of therapy is to provide a safe arena in which they can undergo a process of mourning in a supportive, emotionally connected group.

How Does Psychodrama Help?

Psychodrama, unlike other methods, offers an opportunity to speak what needs to be spoken and do what was left undone. We can finish old business in the context of an enactment. The final goodbye, the thing we never had a chance to say, the love that went unspoken, the tears that were never shared, the anger that was held in quivering silence—all can be role-played psychodramatically so that we can work through the unresolved loss, bring it to satisfactory closure and move on with our lives.

DEVELOPMENTAL DISTORTION

Parents who are more preoccupied with their own problems than with parenting cannot adequately meet their children's needs. The child's sense of basic trust and security is threatened, which makes it difficult to build self-esteem and move through developmental stages freely and with the necessary support. If a child, for instance, needs to move away from the parent and the parent is not secure enough to allow that, or interprets it as a personal rejection, the child's strivings for autonomy will be blocked—and later developmental stages will be affected as well. A teenager especially needs to believe that separation from home will not mean banishment. If, instead of putting his energy toward becoming his own person, he constantly uses this energy to make sure his home is still intact, separation will be seriously hampered.

How Does Psychodrama Help?

When a scene or situation that has been locked within a person's psyche is placed upon the psychodramatic stage to be lived out again, unhealthy behaviors that surface in action are often seen and identified as "crazy" or "sick"—both by the protagonist and by the group. Distorted behavior that one has lived with for so long that it came to feel normal becomes easier to see for what it is when it is fully enacted. Later, with the sharing and processing within the group, nuances of the internalized distortions can be examined and replaced with new awarenesses, and insight can occur. Long-term therapy allows the client to move slowly through and rework the stages of development that he missed.

POST TRAUMATIC STRESS REACTION

Children who grew up in addicted homes are survivors of a wide range of early childhood trauma. Their traumas were often sustained over a long period of time, and they were helpless in the face of them, never knowing when to expect abuse, what caused it or how to prevent it from continuing. As adults they may bear many of the symptoms of Post Traumatic Stress Syndrome experienced by combat soldiers.

ACoAs have a tendency to over-react, overmanage, or withdraw and hide. They learned as children to become hypervigilant for any sign of distress—and would swing into action to placate, manage, avoid or take on the abuser in order to protect themselves. So it is no wonder that many of them court crisis and choose high-stress professions and partners. They have come to gain a certain sense of self-worth from managing the unmanageable. Even when there is nothing particularly threatening to take care of, they will perceive that there is. According to Claudia Blackburn,

> ACoAs with Post Traumatic Stress Reaction (1) have a hard time setting emotional boundaries; (2) are very well defended; (3) have numbed out and avoided pain for so long that they feel "something is missing"; (4) experience other people setting limits and boundaries as rejection or even abuse; and (5) may report that they "have had a trauma but moved through it quickly and are just fine now."

How Does Psychodrama Help?

The action component of psychodrama accesses the same areas of the brain that are accessed through everyday behavior. In other words, if trauma happens through action, it can be healed through action. Old traumas, such as growing up with an alcoholic parent and a painful family system, are carried into adulthood. Normal life provokes anxiety because the traumatized self waits for the crisis to come. ACoAs who have bonded with crisis rather than normalcy hesitate to bond with what feels good as a way of protecting themselves against the pain of their original loss. Unfortunately, this way of living does not protect them but keeps them in a constant state of free-floating inner tension.

When hurts and pains are brought out of hiding (through

sharing, role-playing, journaling, art or whatever will reach into the shadowy depths and bring out the truth), the story can be told and witnessed, and the person is enabled to find meaning in the pain. Psychodrama is particularly well suited to reach past the defenses and activate, both through identification with others and through one's own drama, the material that needs to be self-disclosed.

SOBER VERSUS NONSOBER THINKING AND BEHAVIOR

Addicted homes function with two alternating realities, one sober and one substance affected by the addict's substance abuse. When a substance is being used, its use has to be protected by the person using it. This requires minimizing and denying the impact the user has on the system. Whether the substance is alcohol, drugs, food or sex, its compulsive/addicted use will alter family dynamics. The addict will put energy into preserving the supply of the substance, often in secrecy, and the family will put energy into preserving the normal look of the family.

The system organizes itself differently when the addict is using and when he is not, differing realities that live on within children and are triggered throughout their adult lives. Normalcy triggers mistrust, and pain triggers early fears of abandonment and/or dependency that can bring the past into the present in the form of defensive, passive-aggressive or aggressive behavior.

How Does Psychodrama Help?

People can play out both sober and nonsober realities in psychodrama. Through psychodrama they can raise the level of awareness about each and bring what has been confused and colluded in the unconscious to the conscious level, where it can be separated into two distinct atmospheres. They can come to see where the nonsober inner world may be polluting their current lives.

Psychodrama can also help clarify what comes from the past and what belongs to the present. For instance, if a wife is screaming at her husband and saying things that she unconsciously wishes she could have said to her alcoholic father, the director can ask her to choose her father and speak directly to him. Doing so can make her aware in actuality of how feelings carried over from her addictive family are where her past is overwhelming her present, and where habits developed in a relationship where addiction was present get played out in a relationship where addiction may not be present.

EMOTIONAL NUMBNESS

Children who grow up in painful situations learn how to numb themselves emotionally in order not to hurt. They can accomplish this numbness through compulsive behavior, distracting the hurt into an activity, repressing or dissociating from the painful feelings, using a substance to bury hurt or learning how to shut down emotionally. Shutting down can effectively stop pain, but it also stops other feelings. It puts the person using numbness out of touch with his real feelings and inhibits his ability to make meaningful connections between circumstances and his emotional responses to them. Feelings of isolation and disconnection result.

How Can Psychodrama Help?

Thawing out these frozen feelings during therapy can feel very disorienting, frightening and confusing—but ultimately it gives the person back to himself. Psychodrama models the opposite of emotional numbness by encouraging engagement in emotionally charged activity. Watching other people's dramas and identifying with them gives the person an opportunity to lower defenses and warm up to his own feelings. Through the process of identification with the psychodramatic action, feelings that have been buried rise to the surface. Often memories that were previously out of reach come into the foreground. It is difficult to remain completely shut down in a psychodramatic environment without having the shutdown become obvious. Over a period of time, psychodrama will gradually help a person restore the ability to feel and behave in a spontaneous manner.

DISORGANIZED THINKING

One of the survival tactics of dysfunctional families is to look good, and because the emotional undercurrent can differ radically from the surface image, children experience their inner reality as out of sync with their outer reality. Their feelings are not corroborated or validated, and so they feel disconnected and confused. Addicted people do not think clearly. Children who try to speak rationally with their nonsober or dysfunctional parents do not arrive at rational understandings. They are made to feel that their perceptions are inaccurate, and consequently they come to doubt their ability to reason. When feelings and thinking are at odds with what is acceptable, thinking can become disorganized. And so children in addicted families eventually experience thinking and feeling as detached both from each other and from the children's internal reality, which comes to seem meaningless and irrelevant. Deep, unresolved pain and anxiety are carried at the expense of the inner person.

How Does Psychodrama Help?

Emotion and thought are connected. Often we organize thinking around strong emotions to in some way accommodate, manage, validate or rationalize them. When emotional pain has nowhere to go, it builds emotional pressure and distorts the way we experience ourselves and our worlds. We organize our thinking around erroneous perceptions because the emotions that come to the surface in present-day living are not about present-day circumstances. Many are historical emotions looking for a place to go for release, but we do not identify them as such; rather, we think the pain we are experiencing is about whatever circumstance triggered it. When emotional loads are held in silence and secrecy within the psyche as deep, untouchable wounds, a network of false reasoning grows up around them to protect them and keep them from being known, seen and felt. When they are released in psychodrama, they no longer have that effect on thinking.

DISTORTED INTERNALIZED FAMILY SYSTEM

The addicted family system is build around denial, delusion, repression and distortion. The principles upon which the family is organized are based on living with addiction or dysfunction. When this dysfunctional family is internalized early in life by the growing child, he carries this system internally into adulthood which mean that the ACoA's "inner family" is also dysfunctional. In adult life this system is lived out and becomes an organizing principle in relationships and families where addiction and trauma may or may not be present. ACoAs and addicts tend to be hypervigilant in relationships—waiting for trouble even when trouble is not there. The closed-system rules—"Don't trust, don't talk, don't feel"—are triggered and the adult uses these ways of behaving and surviving in the new family.

How Does Psychodrama Help?

In a psychodrama group, family dynamics and transferences become felt and acted out. Resolving these transferences is the road to healing. The group sociometry brings the internalized family of each group member to the surface. Social atoms and action sociograms offer each participant endless opportunities to examine and reexamine the family from his own position, as well as from the positions of others. Role reversal allows the participant not only to see another person's point of view within the system but also to experience it.

Over and over again in the group, through dramas and in sociometric exercises, family roles and family systems are examined and explored. Making the unconscious dynamics of the family system conscious is the first step toward evaluating and sorting out the distortions from the point of view of the protagonist, as it is the protagonist's truth that is being told. This process helps to reduce the cognitive dissonance within the self by bringing reality and distorted perception and expectation into greater balance.

DISTORTED PARENTAL ROLE MODELS

In dysfunctional homes the child's normal developmental needs are often neglected in favor of coping with addiction and compulsion. What the child sees are parents who are lost to him and unable to be fully present as parents. Later in life, when he becomes a parent himself, he does not have healthy parental roles to use as models.

Modeling is one of the deepest forms of learning. Our own parents teach us more about how to parent than anyone or anything else. We tend to parent either in the style that we were parented or in a style that is in some form a reaction to that. Therapy offers an opportunity to relive the pain of inadequate parenting and to be reparented in healthier ways.

How Does Psychodrama Help?

In psychodrama the person can play out the introjected parents both from his point of view and from theirs. Spending time in the role of the parent helps to bring the personality of the parent that lives within the protagonist to a conscious level. Then the director can use the technique of interviewing the protagonist in the role of his parent, both to keep him in that role and to elicit information. Spending time in the role of the parent allows for playing out the introject in a safe clinical environment where destructive internalized roles can be examined, experienced and released. Spending time in the role of the protagonist helps that person to give back to the parent such feelings as shame, anger and even love, which he has carried in silence within him because the empathic bond between the parent and child was not sufficiently intact to contain these emotions.

DIFFICULTY IN FORMING EMPATHIC BONDS

Children learn whether or not the world can be trusted by the way they are treated by their primary caretakers. If caretakers perceive their needs with reasonable accuracy and respond to them, children come to see the world as a friendly place that can meet their needs. When children have not had an empathic caretaker, when their development of self is incomplete and there is a sense within them that they have not gotten enough of what they need, it becomes difficult for them to give from what feels like an empty place. A person who was unable to separate emotionally from the parent will find it difficult to have a sense of other because, to some extent, she is still incorporated within the parent.

Empathy is present when we are able to reverse roles with another person, seeing and feeling things as the other person might see them. The person who has not had enough development and satisfaction in the self finds it difficult to let go of the self and reverse roles. According to Robert Siroka, "There is a sense that the self is not intact enough to leave in favor of empathy with another, that some part of the self might be lost or compromised if it is not constantly guarded or even withheld." In this climate of a lack of self-trust, it becomes difficult to extend outwardly toward another.

How Can Psychodrama Help?

Psychodrama has the power to access early pain and rejection, and opens the protagonist up to very raw emotion. At those moments the protagonist can work through the pain that has blocked him and the defenses that numb the pain. Once they are out of the way, the protagonist is able to let people in, in a more positive manner. New bonding experiences can occur, and the self can be lived in and rebuilt. Once the self is intact, an awareness of the other is possible; once empathy is incorporated into the self, it can be extended to someone else.

INCOMPLETE INDIVIDUATION/SEPARATION FROM PARENTS

The stages of separation and individuation from the parent allow an eventual rapprochement or return to take place. Some parents view separation as rejection and withdraw their love and break their connection with a child who they feel is moving away from them. In this case separation comes to mean loss of the parent, which often feels like too high a price to pay. For example, the adolescent girl who brings friends home rather than going out with them, so that she does not leave her mother alone too much, will not be able to move through her developmental task of separating; she feels she must take care of her parent's needs before exploring her own.

One of the tragedies of this situation is that the child confuses separation with incorporation. The lesson is, "When I feel a need to move away, I have to move toward instead—I have to incorporate within me that which I wish to leave and lie about my wish to leave it, even to myself, because it is intolerable to my parent. My parent would die without me." The developmental task of individuation becomes too frightening and painful to undertake. And as a result the child learns to meet her needs through a kind of emotional and psychic fusion: "I meet my needs through meeting yours, and I allow you to meet your needs through meeting mine."

How Can Psychodrama Help?

We must first successfully bond before we can successfully individuate. Psychodrama helps protagonists experientially to "get what they never got." After concretizing, for instance, the feeling of aloneness, it moves in to fill the void by using surrogates to provide a feeling of love, acceptance and support. Because psychodrama can mobilize deep feeling, the protagonist can come to be fully in touch with areas of unmet need or open wounds, letting down defenses against feeling pain. Once the pain is felt, it can be healed.

For individuation to take place, we not only have to locate the parent, but we also have to locate the parent within ourselves. For this to happen, we need to work through and resolve the parent-child relationship. When the parent is intact within the child, the child can then move out into the world with an inner point of reference—a sense of being loved and held; he can learn to love and hold himself and recognize other people and experiences that provide that same feeling. But if this deep feeling is not intact, he is condemned to a lifelong search for the love and acceptance he never got. Sadly, without actually experiencing and learning that feeling, we do not know what we are looking for and confuse love and acceptance with just about anything that feels good.

PARENTIFIED CHILDREN

Dysfunctional homes do not just happen. They are created by parents who themselves were not adequately taken care of and nurtured. These parents tend to look toward their own children to meet their unmet emotional needs for security and safety.

When children are called upon to meet an excess of their parents needs and their parents are not able to reach out in larger ways, they become little adults too soon. Little adults in dysfunctional homes tend to (1) try to be perfect to make their parents look good; (2) think of what would be best for their parents before what they would like; (3) consider their parents' needs before their own; (4) gain their self-worth from being good rather than feeling good; (5) put their own needs aside so regularly that they lose their ability to identify them; (6) feel inadequate because they cannot make their parents happy; (7) are called upon to supply their families with self-worth; and (8) internalize an overwhelming sense of failure at not being able to fix their parents and families.

While meeting another's needs is natural and healthy, it becomes dysfunctional when neither party has an awareness of whose needs are being met and neither party can identify his own needs. In such cases people may feel their own needs and feelings through identifying them in someone else, and they miss or even deny them within themselves. Depending on someone else's neediness to gain one's own emotional relief creates a co-dependent relationship.

How Can Psychodrama Help?

Some of the wounds of being a parentified child are (1) the loss of childhood; (2) assuming adult roles beyond one's capability and the resulting sense of failure; (3) the loss of the parent as a person by whom to be nurtured and mentored; (4) the day-to-day learning to fill someone else's needs before one's own and the lesson that the way to get love and approval is by caretaking another person; and (5) the loss of time to wonder, struggle and focus on one's own developing self. Through psychodrama the adult children act out desires and unfinished business so that they can become conscious and be resolved, and through the sociometry of the group he can resolve transferences and practice new behaviors.

INTERNALIZED MARITAL DYSFUNCTION

Into extrafamilial personal relationships ACoAs inevitably bring the internalized marital dysfunction of their parents. For most the model is a marriage in which partners were unable to talk things out honestly and openly, to reach resolution and to move on. Or they may have had parents who used the children to play out unresolved hurt and competitive issues, actually pitting the children against the spouse to gain power in the relationship. They take in, at a deep level, the reality of two people who were disappointed in one another and hurt each other profoundly.

With such a model, marriage may not only look dangerous but actually become dangerous; with the relationship skills that ACoAs have learned, they may continually recreate the pain and misunderstanding that they grew up with. Learning to be in a functioning relationship means revisiting that pain and bringing it into the present to be seen, felt and released, and then forging new and constructive relationship skills.

How Can Psychodrama Help?

The atmosphere of a marriage is a primary force in the atmosphere of a home, and psychodrama offers an opportunity to recreate that atmosphere on the stage so that it can be entered and experienced from the point of view of the child who lived in it, of the parent who lived it and of the adult who can now see it as it really was. Bringing out through role-play the way in which one's parents related, and re-experiencing it in the present, can help the protagonist to see how he may be unconsciously living out his parents' script. Psychodrama helps to illuminate destructive patterns and aid in understanding them.

INFLEXIBLE EGO STRUCTURE

ACoAs learn not to share their real feelings or discuss what is really going on within them. They come to understand that if they let their guard down, they leave themselves vulnerable to possible hurt. They also learn not to tell the truth about what they see going on around them, because if they do, they risk being attacked and put down by those in the family who are in denial about the family illness and invested in "looking good" as a survival strategy.

When people who use denial to survive are challenged, they experience the challenge as life-threatening. As a consequence ACoAs and addicts come to lead a double life. All of the members of the family system are leading double lives, either consciously or unconsciously, because their inner and outer worlds are not in sync. They become frightened and self-protective. They learn that they need to be on guard at all times, either to avoid abuse or maintain a momentary safe edge.

In an environment where "the best defense is a good offense," being spontaneous, vulnerable or even casually interactive feels unsafe, and often is. Rigid and inflexible roles are developed. Even fun and humor have an unnatural intensity about them because they are used as much to release painful feelings or to control through sarcasm masquerading as humor as they are for enjoyment. People take their positions and guard them; behavioral roles become survival roles. Then roles learned in the system become the internal organization of the self-system and are played out in group situations throughout life.

How Can Psychodrama Help?

The therapeutic group is a safe place for people to learn new roles and practice new behavior. The sociometry of the group allows for transferences and projections to be resolved through making them conscious and working them through. Flexibility of mind is an important component of mental health, and psychodrama offers direct experience in a variety of roles—strengthening roles that one feels insecure in, discarding or reworking roles that are no longer serving the self-system well and spending time in and practicing new roles and/or new behavior. Examining old and new roles from a variety of perspectives—directly in the role, in role reversal, as an auxiliary, as part of the audience or as an observer—is a concrete way to alter internal organization.

PHYSICAL AND SEXUAL ABUSE

Because of the reduced inhibitions that result from alcohol and drug use and the poor impulse control of the addict, children of addicts run a high risk of being violated physically and/or sexually. A deeply internalized sense of helplessness, defeat and terror results from being subjugated in such ways by an authority figure or a parent. When the abuser is a parent, confusion at the core of the personality about boundaries and proper behavior in intimate relationships results. Trusting other people feels foolish, compromising or dangerous. And trusting the self is equally difficult because the victim may feel a deep sense of guilt or complicity: "What was my part in this? Why did I want/deserve for it to happen?"

Part of healing is accepting that one was truly an innocent victim. Unfortunately, along with this comes the tragic realization that the parent or authority figure was the perpetrator, that he really did put the child at terrible risk with apparently no thought of the child's welfare or future well-being.

No child really wishes to know this about a parent or elder. This may account for why these memories so often do not surface until the victim feels independent enough to survive on her own. The disease concept is helpful because it is more acceptable and forgivable to think that a parent did this because he had a disease—that his disease had taken him over and he was "out of his mind"—than to feel that he deliberately inflicted pain.

How Can Psychodrama Help?

The brain, when traumatized, does not work normally; it generates a frozenness rather than a context. Consequently, traumatic memories are stored in an unfinished, unresolved state. Each time a memory stored in this way is called to the surface (because something has triggered it, such as an intimate relationship, loud anger, sexual interaction and so forth), it emerges in this unfinished, frozen state and blocks normal participation in the experience at hand.

By using psychodrama to bring traumatic memories to the surface, and then enacting a metaphor of the situation with safe surrogates and clinical control, a context for the event can be supplied. The story can be told and the frozenness can be walked, spoken, acted, cried, raged and worked through. All the emotions that were arrested can surface and be experienced in the body so that they can be integrated and viewed while they are actually being felt. In this way the natural paring down and discarding of irrelevant brain cells and the inclusion of new ones can occur; the trauma memory will be restored in a new cell assembly, with some information discarded and new information added, and new awareness can foster a move from helplessness to empowerment. Thus traumatized people can begin to see that they were actually a victim of their size and situation; that they need not feel responsible for what happened as if they caused it; and that they can take care of themselves in a way they could not as children, so that living and loving and risking is again possible.

DISSOCIATION

When life becomes too frightening or painful, one possible reaction to that trauma is to dissociate from it—to psychically move away. People often recall trauma, such as physical or sexual abuse, as an out-of-body experience, as if they were watching themselves from another location.

The most extreme form of dissociation is Multiple Personality Disorder—when the person generates one or more alternate personalities who are assigned to deal with the pain. In a lesser form of dissociation the person simply drifts, mentally, far away, not to any particular place, but away from the present moment. This habit of never being fully present is a defense against feeling, only here there is no substance, just a sort of psychic absence. Dissociation also serves as a defense during trauma, allowing some individuals to experience painful events as though they had happened to a different "self." This defense trades awareness of immediate physical helplessness during trauma for a subsequent sense of psychological helplessness, with intrusive recollection of the events (absorption), the loss of pleasure in usually enjoyable activities (dissociation), and extreme sensitivity to stimuli reminiscent of the trauma (suggestability or absence of criticism).

People who dissociate regularly can feel "fake" or inappropriate because their actions in the present are not connected to real feeling. They "think" their feelings instead of feeling them, making a mental effort to come up with what looks to them to be the right response to a situation because they lack access to the information that would inform and guide appropriate responses.

How Can Psychodrama Help?

To heal dissociation a person has to re-enter the self to make a real connection with his inner life. And to effect the return, he has to feel, experience and reintegrate all the feelings that lay unfelt during the flight from the self. Psychodramatic warm-ups and viewing of or participating in another person's drama are useful in putting him in touch with repressed feelings. The enactment phase, whether he is protagonist, auxiliary role-player or audience member, offers him the opportunity to experience frightening feelings in a safe setting. Once they are felt and reviewed by the inner observer, they can be integrated in a new way. Then the sharing phase allows him to see that he is not alone in having sought a way out of feeling more pain than he could tolerate. Psychodrama's emphasis on spontaneity training is useful here because it helps to retrain people to live inside of their own minds and bodies and to learn to tolerate strong feelings without dissociating.

GRANDIOSITY

Because of the magical thinking of childhood, coupled with the child's fervent wish to bring peace and harmony to her unhappy family, she comes to feel that she knows how to cure her family—*if only everyone in their family would listen to her.* Later in life this kind of magical thinking can translate into grandiosity—the feeling that she alone really saw and understood what was going on in her family.

A different kind of grandiosity develops as a defense against feelings of helplessness, inadequacy and despair. Because the reality of a situation is too overwhelmingly painful for a child to live with, he constructs a false reality full of special reasons and rationalizations for his family's difference from others. Rather than feel like an underdog, he tells himself that his is a special lot—he is misunderstood by outsiders. All the while, beneath this illusion of being exceptional, lives a wounded little person, terrified to let himself know that which he suspects he already knows, that this family is slowly falling apart.

The parentified child also has an exaggerated sense of his own importance. He truly feels that without him the family would not operate. He carries this illusion into adulthood, where he believes that it is he and he alone "who keeps it all together" and understands what is really needed. It is difficult for him to become comfortable with his rightful size.

How Can Psychodrama Help?

Psychodramatic enactment allows an authentic self to emerge. The wounded, frightened child can come out of hiding and connect, through his pain, with others. Connecting with others and moving out of isolation reduces the need for a grandiose defense system. Through identification with others who have also been hurt and who have felt different from other people, he learns that he is not alone in having survived painful, often mortifying, childhood experiences: others have also been abused and made to feel bad about themselves. This identification with others helps to depersonalize the feeling of being somehow defective and encourages an acceptance of a more real self. When the shame is reduced, the need to compensate with grandiosity lessens.

DIFFICULTY IN CLARIFYING NEEDS

A person whose needs are continually unmet in childhood can become frightened of asking for what she needs. First, she becomes unable to tolerate her own neediness. Being needy feels weak, stupid or dangerous, and so she hides the feeling from herself by denying it or projecting it onto another person.

Next, the idea of being clear about needs and asking for something on behalf of the self creates a paradoxical dilemma. On the one hand, the fear of asking and not receiving brings up the pain of the childhood disappointment of needing and not getting and then feeling humiliated for feeling needy. On the other hand, if a need is requested and met, the satisfying of the need brings up the pain of separation because the met need is by nature finite, and because while she is asking to have a specific need met, her real hunger is far deeper and more difficult to define.

The ACoA learned in childhood to depend on no one. She met or did not meet her own needs in painful isolation, never taking the risk of asking. Consequently, the deep, irrational position is, "I will not ask for anything that will prove to me what I already know, that my parent is not there. This is how I will stay connected, by suffering my neediness in silence. If I were to make my needs known and out in the open, I would risk being cut off for being too needy, and then I would be all alone." Because of this inner dynamic, ACoAs seldom risk being upfront about needs, as it brings up fears of abandonment and separation.

How Can Psychodrama Help?

Group interaction mobilizes feelings of neediness because it recreates the original family dynamics; it can induce a person to feel isolated, threatened, unheard, unseen, rejected, competitive and so on. Over time, being able to tolerate the feeling of neediness, to own this feeling, to express it and to process the discomfort associated with it will help to make the behavior and dynamics resulting from it conscious. Once these elements are made conscious, they can be worked with and understood.

Page 208: If you listen to an articulate family . . . Steinglass, Peter, *The Alcoholic Family*, Basic Books, 1987.

Page 209: Other roles may emerge . . . Wegscheider-Cruse, Sharon, 1986, *Another Chance*, Health Communications, Deerfield Beach, Florida.

Page 209: To the extent that safety . . . Horney, Karen. *Neurosis and Human Growth*. Norton, 1970.

Page 210: In recent years a more empathetic view . . . Steinglass, Peter. *The Alcoholic Family*. Basic Books, 1987.

Page 210 "Stress Attendant on alcoholism" . . . Steinglass, Peter. *The Alcoholic Family*. Basic Books, 1987.

Page 210: "A system is a whole" . . . Patton, Michael. *Qualitative Evaluation and Research Methods*, London Sage Publications, 1980.

Page 211: "They weren't always the ones" . . . Black, Claudia. *It Will Never Happen to Me.* Medical Adm. Co. 1981.

Page 211: Through a variety of adverse influences . . . Horney, Karen. *Neurosis and Human Growth*, Norton, 1970.

Page 218: "have had a trauma" . . . C. Blackburn, 1993, February 22. Lecture, Caron Foundation, Warnersville, PA.

Page 221: "Don't trust, don't talk" . . . Black, Claudia. *It Will Never Happen To Me*, Medical Adm. Co., 1981.

Page 224: "The stages of separation and individuation" . . . Mahler, Margaret, *The Psychological Birth of the Human Infant.* Basic Books, New York, 1975.

Page 229: Dissociation also serves . . . According to Spiegel, 1986.

12
Trauma

Experience, which destroys innocence,
also leads one back to it.
—James Baldwin

Trauma is an emotional experience or shock that does not get processed normally and has a lasting psychic effect. According to B.A. van der Kolk,

> *Sudden, terrifying experiences which explode one's sense of predictability can have profound short-term and long-term effects on one's subsequent ways of dealing with emotions. . . . The helplessness and rage which usually accompany these experiences may radically change a person's self-concept, and interfere with the view that life is basically safe and predictable, a precondition for normal functioning. People seem to be psychologically incapable of accepting random, meaningless destruction and will search for any explanation to make meaning out of a catastrophe, including blaming themselves, or their loved ones: helplessness asks for a culprit. This may be either turned against the self, for having been unable to prevent the inevitable, or against others.*

The child who has watched a parent change before her eyes from a kind and present person to a stumbling, angry drunk has been systematically traumatized. The child who has been repeatedly physically beaten, and has developed methods of coping to deal with the terror, pain and loss of safety, has been traumatized. The child who has been used to gratify the sexual needs of a parent while she has lain helpless will emerge from the experience as a casualty of trauma, feeling disempowered, enraged and guilty. So will the child who has been ignored by his caregiver, who has been asked by the unconscious of the parent to disappear, for though this child will have no event or set of obvious circumstances to point to, he will be left with a sense of being lost in space, of being there but not there. Reaching out to touch another person or allowing himself to be touched will feel fraught with anxiety and danger.

Children who have grown up in addicted homes, who have a history of abuse and neglect, grow up with a predisposition for trauma. Later on in life, experiences that other people would be able to cope with in the course of a day will return them to their early coping strategies and unresolved pain. Attempts to have intimate relationships as adults can make them feel that their lives are at risk. Having a child who is ignored or rejected by peers can be extremely painful for them, since, as children they felt they had nowhere to go. Moreover, committing to a life's work and moving methodically toward it—with full risk of making mistakes, failing or succeeding—can feel like an impossible task. In fact, just about any of these normal life events can act as triggers that bring up pain, fear and anger.

"People with PTSD [Post Traumatic Stress Disorder] organize their lives around dealing with the aftermath of trauma in one or both of two seemingly contradictory ways," says van der Kolk (see Chapter 11, Using Psychodrama With Addicts And ACoAs, for more on Post Traumatic Stress Disorder).

[their lives] are dominated by recurrent intrusive, overwhelming memories related to the trauma in the shape of . . . nightmares, flashbacks or anxiety attacks, and/or they show extreme avoidance of involvement in life, in fear that any intense feelings may trigger a re-experience of trauma. . . . When exposed to issues

dealing with intimacy, trust, dependency, or anger they often react to current situations as if they were traumatized all over again: they either blow up, withdraw or both. Aware of the effects of their behavior or their surroundings, but unaware where these feelings come from, they feel guilty and angry, and are prone to dull these feelings with overwork and/or alcohol.

When we are traumatized, we have one or more of the following responses: fight, flight or freeze. Any of these responses precludes working through a situation, confronting it, assessing options and making choices. When life experiences are not worked or lived through, they are incomplete. Events stored by the brain in this manner become a part of our storehouse of unfinished business, what John Moreno would call "open tensions' and "act hungers." They form what comes to be the root of Freud's "repetition compulsion," an early hunger that cries out for action or completion.

Psychiatrist Mardi Horowitz has postulated a "completion principle" that "summarizes the human mind's intrinsic ability to process new information in order to bring up to date the inner schemata of the self and the world." Trauma, by definition, shatters these inner schemata. The unassimilated traumatic experiences are stored in what Horowitz calls "active memory," which has an "intrinsic tendency to repeat the representation of contents." The trauma is resolved only when the survivor develops a new mental schema for understanding what has happened.

According to Guy Taylor, traumatized infants suffer a decrease in attachment to the primary caregiver. This leads to denial of need, erosion of trust, total emptiness. They, and other victims of trauma engage in a process of selective perception: they begin to focus on what they need to survive to the exclusion of what they need for personal development, and they tend to elaborate and condense early memories, losing a sense of context and time. They experience memory, imagination and fantasy as a minefield and consequently, as a defense, avoid fantasy, imagination and dramatic play.

Psychodrama offers a unique opportunity for healing in several ways. Working through early traumas with real people gives a lost context back to the survivor. He can resolve the trauma both

by releasing or catharting the associated emotions and by reconstructing and reworking the scene. The protagonist can not only
tell his story but also show his story and have it witnessed.

DISSOCIATION AND REPRESSION

Repression is generally of two kinds. In one instance a person
consciously recognizes something as threatening or anxiety-
provoking and so represses it in order to avoid feeling or experiencing fear and anxiety. In the other threatening material is
relegated to the unconscious before the person registers it consciously as threatening. David S. Holmes writes: "(1) Repression is
the selective forgetting of materials that cause the individual pain;
(2) Repression is not under voluntary control; and (3) Repressed
material is not lost but instead is stored in the brain and can be
returned to consciousness (as postulated by Freud) if the anxiety
associated with the memory is removed. The assertion that repression is not under voluntary control differentiates repression from
suppression or denial with which it is sometimes confused."

Dissociation as a defense against painful material spans the
spectrum from actually assigning another personality or personality state to take control of a situation, as in MPD to simply removing one's consciousness from a threatening situation. In the theory
of Parallel Distributing Processing (PDP), the brain is seen as stor-
ing memory in separate cells which may or may not be overseen
by global consciousness. In this sense all memory has a dissociative component.

*"McClelland and Rumelhart (1986) note that the distributed mem-
ory model fits traumatic amnesia well, for two reasons: (1) The
fact that context learned may persist despite dense amnesia to the
episode in which it was learned can be accounted for by the acti-
vation of weightings in the net despite the loss of the weightings
associated with the episode itself. (2) Large changes in connection
strengths analogous to the effect of one traumatic experience do
not always assist learning. Such memories are kept out of consciousness and yet exert effects that can be modeled using PDPs.
The point is that such memories need not be integrated, and, if
they involve self-concept, they may indeed be mutually exclusive
of one another and/or compete with one another, yielding in the
aggregate a dissociative disorder in which there is a discontinuity*

in personal identity and memory. It is the distributed nature of memory and its context dependence that makes dissociation potentially the rule rather than the exception."

In using experiential techniques with traumatized populations great caution should be exercised in order to reduce the risk of retraumatization and dissociation. (See Chapter 4, guidelines for Therapeutic Safety.) The work should be undertaken only with highly trained clinicians and in well supervised clinical situations. The greater the sense of safety and support in the clinical situation, the more likely it is that the protagonist will experience the painful feelings being held and contained throughout the three phases of the enactment.

INFORMATION AND THE BRAIN

Information is recorded in brain cells and stored in cell assemblies. Learning is a process of paring down and building up cells. Because traumatic memories tend to be repressed, they come to the surface unconsciously, affecting personality and behavior. When we bring them to the surface consciously and release the strong emotions associated with them, we can discard what we no longer wish to keep and add on new insights, thus coming to see the traumatic situations with new awareness and perspective. The new learning will actually alter the cell assembly. A new cell assembly, different in structure from the previous one, will be reintegrated by the brain.

At this stage it is the task of treatment to help the survivor find meaning or learn something positive from the trauma. The expression "every cloud has a silver lining" is not just a cliché: it is also an important coping tool that enables survivors to restore a sense of beauty and order to their lives so that they can move forward with positive energy toward themselves and others. They have the information necessary to separate the past from the present, and the dysfunctional, self-sabotaging behaviors can be seen for what they are. They can understand inappropriate over-reaction and unhealthy behavior patterns as an unconscious wish toward mastery of the traumatic experience or ridding the self-system of the stored trauma and the anger, rage and helplessness associated with it.

Because of the way in which memories are triggered by association, an experience, odor, texture, sound or object reminiscent of any part of a memory stored in the cells of the brain can stimulate associated memories. Also, because memories with a high emotional content, pleasant or unpleasant, are more easily recalled by the brain, traumatic memories have a sort of hierarchical power over other less emotionally laden ones. Thus it follows that when they are triggered, they feel larger than life or unmanageable. Because they overwhelm our present, we tend to engage defense systems in order to make them less threatening. Experiencing them in the here and now and seeing them for what they are and where they come from helps to reduce the anxiety associated with them and has a freeing affect for the client.

In the rapid eye movement (REM) dreaming state there is, according to J. Allan Hobson, a "scanning of the brain for undesirable information . . . that the system wishes to discard, much like the 'forgetting' that is observable after the sleep of latency age children." And it is this writer's suggestion that a similar scanning, selecting and repatterning process may be taking place in deep states of psychodramatic enactment (see psychodramatic trance Chapter 11). It may help to account for the fact that the psychic healing effect takes place even when the client does not recall the psychodramatic enactment. The question then is to what extent can we effect and clinically encourage this particular sort of healing. Also applicable here is what Marshall Edelson calls "effective imagination," or the use of imagination to "gratify wishes or to avoid painful states using such devices as condensations as are employed by the scriptwriter, where one element in the script can simultaneously allude to many events or objects because, for example, it has played a part in each of them or resembles each of them in some way." This healing work is done by primary process functioning and can be effective in reducing anxiety. Both of these natural psychic healing processes must certainly impact the clinically structured psychodrama and its three phases: warmup, enactment and sharing.

TRIGGERS

Trigger events—events in the present that trigger memories or emotions from the past—often bring survivors into treatment.

According to Claudia Blackburn, common triggers include relationships, new stressors and exposure to a developmental stage for which the person is not ready.

Relationships

For the ACoA who has been traumatized in the home, early feelings of dependency and responsibility can be aroused by intimacy with another person or the responsibility of raising children. These deep emotional responses feel as if they are relevant only to the present, but in fact they are often projections. The therapist needs to examine the client's early history to determine why the emotions are so intense and where they truly stem from.

New Stressors

For survivors most meaningful attachments bring up a fear of loss. An actual loss causes them to re-experience their early losses; attaining success brings up the fear of losing something that may become meaningful. Rather than make healthy attachments, they either avoid commitment to a person or circumstance or experience people, places and things as extensions of the self rather than as separate from the self. The incorporation creates an illusion of safety because it keeps them from having to experience feelings of separateness and isolation, which bring up profound fears of loss and abandonment.

An intimate relationship, a new job, a child, marriage or any situation that causes stress can bring up deep fear and anxiety. Life experiences that other people might find stressful but manageable can feel unmanageable for the survivor, for whom they may stir up old fear, pain and anxiety that are still in an unresolved, free-floating state.

Exposure To A Developmental Stage
For Which The Survivor Is Not Ready

Children who are asked to be little adults may also be, paradoxically, infantalized by parents who do not want them to grow up and separate. They lead double lives, simultaneously being responsible co-parents and obedient youngsters. They may not be allowed the freedom to move through normal developmental stages, in which they would naturally be, at times, difficult and demanding. These children often enter adulthood feeling ill-equipped, as if they are actors in a play who don't know their lines as other people seem to, perhaps because they do not have an easy, open channel between their cognitive and feeling selves. Their feelings tend to be unavailable or confusing to them, or they may feel flooded with undifferentiated emotions.

This lack of connection between their cognitive and feeling selves is part of "not knowing what normal is." It is an aftermath of trauma. In order to know "normal," one must experience "normal"—and the experience of normal is not consistent with dysfunctional households.

TRAUMA EXERCISES

The following exercises should be used with caution and only by an experienced therapist or psychodramatist. (Refer to Guidelines For Therapeutic Safety: First, Do No Harm, Chapter 4.)

TRAUMA TIME LINE

Goals

1. To bring to consciousness how trauma breeds trauma.

2. To connect related traumas so that one can see the full impact, not just of one traumatic event, but of a string of related traumas.

Steps

1. Ask participants to draw a time line of their lives. Divide the time line into blocks of twenty years or whatever division is appropriate.

2. Draw lines in between to represent five-year intervals.

3. Ask group members to recall events, situations or behaviors from their families that have felt traumatic to them. Have them locate these events on their appropriate place along the time line.

4. Ask participants to look at the time line and notice how one event may have created fertile ground for, or opened the door for, another.

5. Either in the large group, in small groups, in pairs or one to one, share the feelings that come up around viewing these events as connected.

6. The Trauma Time Line, followed by sharing, is complete in and of itself, since the real goal is to see the interrelatedness of the traumas. However, you can choose to continue, using one of the variations listed below.

Variations

The purpose of the Trauma Time Line is to map out the inter-relatedness of the traumas in one's life so that they can be lifted from one's psyche. When only one event is seen as the trauma, some recovery can be missed because the feelings and develop-ment that did not take place are not seen as connected to the trau-matic situations. The repetition compulsion supersedes the pleasure principle. All of the traumatized feelings need to be seen through investigating the compulsions so that the ability to feel good can be restored. This does not necessarily mean that each and every trauma has to be counted—only that there are gener-ally a string of events that a person experiences as traumatizing when that person has been traumatized early in life. One event may not tell the whole story.

The exercise can be a warm-up to telling one's "trauma story." You can work with the incidents along the Trauma Time Line in any of the following ways:

- *Psychodramatic action:* Move into action (a vignette), i.e., "Who would you talk to when you look at your time line?"
- *Journaling:* Journal about the feelings that arise when looking at the time line.
- *Sharing:* Share feelings that arise when looking at the time line in pairs, subgroups, group or one-to-one.
- *Sociometry:* For example, ask, "Who in this room do you feel has been where you have been or who might best understand your traumas? Go over to that person and share with them why you chose them."
- *Role reversal:* Reverse roles with one's self at any point along the time line and share with her from that time, in the first person, how you feel (for example, "I am six and I don't know what is happening around me."). The person can sit on the stage, adopt a physical posture and soliloquize.
- *Letter writing:* Participants can write a letter to someone to whom they feel a need to express themselves, or write a

letter to themselves that they wish they had received from someone at any point along the trauma line.

TRIGGER ATOM

Goals

1. To identify situations in present-day life that trigger old pain.
2. To explore the pain that gets triggered.

Steps

1. Begin with a brief guided imagery in which you ask participants to relax and allow them to identify life situations that they feel they overreact to.

2. Following the format for a social atom (triangles to represent males, circles to represent females, squares for genderless items), ask participants to choose one of these situations to work with. Next, have them locate themselves on the paper wherever it feels appropriate, and then to locate the people, places or things which trigger large responses in them.

3. Allow people to share their atoms in groups or pairs (for example, "I am here and my boss is on top of me and larger than me because it feels . . ."). The goal is to become conscious of historical feelings that are being played out in the present and to identify and connect underlying feelings from the past that are being triggered from present-day interaction.

Variations

This exercise should help to separate the past from the present and illucidate how present day overreactions may belong to the past. It may be useful to journal, both from the point of view of the inner child and the point of view of the adult, in order to further work out feelings brought up by the exercise.

CYCLE OF TRAUMA

Throughout the therapeutic process, as clients work through their early traumas, a cycle of trauma will be engaged, a model for which has been created by Claudia Blackburn. Engagement in this cycle is a sign that the client is in "the process" and that treatment is working. (see Figure 12.1)

Hypervigilance. A person who carries unresolved trauma becomes hypervigilant. Psychologically and physiologically, she is geared up to react to trauma at all times. Some of the characteristics of hypervigilance are sleep disturbances, restlessness, difficulty in falling asleep, nightmares, high-content dreams, irritability, anger, outbursts, difficulty in concentrating, exaggerated startle response and persistent arousal. When she is confronted with an event or situation that triggers old pain, she will re-experience the trauma: the pain, anger and fear associated with the early trauma will surface, and it will feel as if it is happening in the present. Usually this re-experiencing takes the form of a projection, and the trauma victim will not be aware of where her feelings are coming from; they will seem to stem only from the trigger event.

Shame. A child who is traumatized experiences a great deal of shame, because a child's natural egocentricity causes him to interpret all events as personal, as being about him. When the feelings associated with painful or traumatic events are accessed in therapy, the old shame is mobilized and may flood the client. In an effort to get rid of his feelings of shame, the client may act out through compulsive or impulsive behavior. He may become angry, blaming or violent, and he may project his painful feelings onto someone else. He may impulsively pick up a drink, overeat or act out sexually to stop the hurting, uncomfortable feelings. He may turn to compulsive medicating behaviors that have worked in the past to quiet or numb painful feelings—smoking, exercise, work, tightly controlling events or others, being perfectionistic, picky or judgmental. In such an event a client may find it difficult to stay with the therapeutic process.

Avoidance. The next stage of the cycle is avoidance or numbness. Avoidance can take the form of emotional withdrawal from other people or situations in an effort to "stay safe." The rationale: "If it hurts, I can protect myself by not going there again." "There" can be any life situation or relational attachment that arouses early pain. At this stage the client may wish to leave therapy, or he may leave a relationship or whatever he fears is bringing up uncomfortable feelings.

Numbness may take the form of emotional removal or disengagement. It is often accompanied by a blank sort of smile. The advantage of numbness is that it is extremely effective at taking away painful feeling while allowing the person to continue to function. The disadvantage is that, like novocaine, which is so effective in removing pain, it also removes all other sensation. The person will go on living with little access to his real feelings. Paradoxically, he will be tender to the touch, because he is protecting a wound, while also being insensitive to what is going on around him, because he is out of touch with the affective atmosphere. As a client he can be difficult because he is both hypersensitive and difficult to penetrate.

Figure 12.1. The Blackburn Cycle Of Trauma

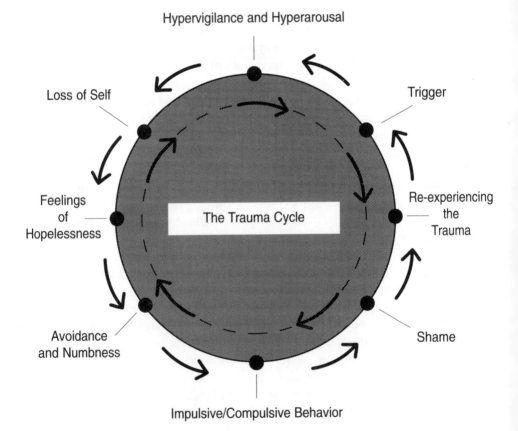

Editor's Note: *The Blackburn Cycle of Trauma as it appears in this book was reproduced incorrectly. The correct diagram is shown below:*

Figure 12.1. The Blackburn Cycle Of Trauma

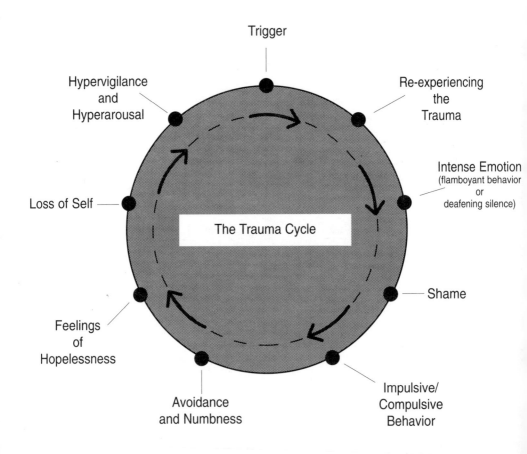

Despair. Next comes despair. It is the despair that the child in a pain-filled home felt when all her attempts to cope, fix and oblige still did nothing to make things better—when no effort of will or wish took away the deep sense of pain and the fear of doom that hung like a threatening storm cloud over the family she loved and that, for the child, was her entire world. It is the despair that comes with a feeling that life, after all, was not meant to work out. It is the despair she felt living in a home that she could not make better, in a system that could not meet her needs and with parents who were not able to parent her adequately. She carries this sense of gloom and doom around with her as a quiet sadness that nothing can make better. In the treatment of trauma, this despair is both a sign of engagement in contacting the trauma and a necessary part of healing.

Loss Of Self. After the sense of despair and helplessness, and the feeling of powerlessness, there is a profound loss of self. "This notion of the self as a mediating function rather than a collection of attributes means that awareness of self emerges from processing, from choosing among experiences. In this sense, self is not an ordinary object of consciousness but rather a subject of consciousness." An important part of our sense of self is built on a feeling of mastery over our lives, a sense of being in the driver's seat, of having choices and the will and ability with which to exercise them. When this is removed by circumstance, we lose a sense of personal empowerment and connection between our volitional nature and our ability to act or exercise our competence. David Spiegel says, "For example, during and after a trauma, the awareness of self becomes extremely painful. The rape victim who was made into an object to be humiliated during the assault finds the notion of self contaminated by fear and pain. Suspension of this view of self becomes a welcome rather than a frightening experience." This, along with the many defenses she has adopted in order to feel safe, erode and subsume a basic sense of self. This is why the survivor begins to search outside the self for inner sustenance. It is a failed attempt to locate the self where the self does not exist—in other people, places and things.

In conclusion we can say that experiential therapy and psychodrama work on four levels: emotional, cognitive, behavioral and spiritual. On the emotional level it relieves the self system of accumulated anxiety, stress and pain by bringing it to the surface and giving it concrete form through role-play. By replaying the situation as it was, or as we wish it had been—saying what went unsaid, doing what went undone, altering and reworking the experience—we can begin to be freed from the repetition compulsion or the unconscious need to continually act it out in life.

On the cognitive level psychodrama encourages new ways of thinking. It allows a situation to be seen through a variety of perspectives often affecting a shift in perception within the client. Through role-reversal it even offers the opportunity to see a situation through the eyes of another person. Because from the perspective of the brain "to do is to know" the action component of psychodrama anchors new learning on a cognitive level.

On the behavioral level, psychodrama provides the opportunity to explore and change old behavior and practice new behavior. Feeling, thought, perception and behavior tend to be role specific; we tend to organize these aspects of self around playing a particular role. If we can explore and play out the role and observe it in action we can begin to make meaningful corrections between the role and the thoughts, emotions, behaviors and perceptions that were an outgrowth of, and motivated by, playing it.

On the spiritual level, role-playing is a form of spontaneity training. It trains us to open up to different ways of living and perceiving and requires us to act without planning the outcome—to make split-second decisions. This, in turn, warms us up to our own creativity and spontaneity. Spontaneity, creativity and openness form pathways into the spiritual self, they are the attributes of the gods.

Page 235: Sudden, terrifying experiences . . . Van der Kolk, in Judith Herman, *Trauma and Recovery*, 1993.

Page 236: are dominated by recurrent . . . Van der Kolk, in Judith Herman, *Trauma and Recovery*, 1993.

Page 237: "completion principle" . . . Mardi Horowitz, in Judith Herman, *Trauma and Recovery*, 1993.

Page 237: traumatized infants . . . Guy Taylor, Conference, American Society of Group Psychotherapy and Psychodrama, New York City, Lecture, May 18, 1991.

Page 238:   "(1) Repression is the" . . . David S. Holmes, "The Evidence for
            Repression: An examination of sixty years of research.," *Repression
            and Dissociation: Implications for Personality Theory,
            Psychopathology & Health*, Chicago, University of Chicago Press,
            1990.

Page 240:   Trigger events . . . Claudia Blackburn, 1993, February 22. Lecture,
            Caron Foundation, Warnersville, PA.

Page 242:   "not knowing what normal is" . . . J. Woititz, *Adult Children of
            Alcoholics*, Pompano Beach, FL: Health Communications, 1983.

GLOSSARY

act hunger: A deep inner drive that hungers for action and completion, an impulse searching for action.

action sociogram: A social atom put into action.

audience: The members of a psychodramatic group who, while not directly participating in the enactment as auxiliaries, participate internally as spectators who identify with, support and *hold* the work.

autodrama: A drama that is enacted without a director; that is, the protagonist chooses the auxiliaries and directs the drama himself.

auxiliary egos: The people playing the characters in a psychodrama other than the protagonist.

concretization: The act of giving shape and form to the intrapsychic objects and dynamics of the protagonist.

cultural conserve: According to J.L. Moreno, a once spontaneous act that has become in some way fixed in the culture, for example, Beethoven's Fifth Symphony, a funeral or a wedding.

director: The person directing the psychodramatic action, usually the therapist.

double: The inner voice of the protagonist.

drama game: A structured experiential exercise with a pre-designated focus, which can be used as a warm-up or a complete exercise.

enactment: The action phase of psychodrama.

family sculpture: A living picture of a family, in which a protagonist and auxiliary role-players are used.

future projection: A scene that has not actually happened but is anticipated, feared or wished for in the future.

interview: The investigation by a therapist of a protagonist to discover further relevant information of a protagonist or an auxiliary ego.

mirror technique: The employment of a double or stand-in for the protagonist to play him so that he can watch the scene from another perspective.

monodrama: A drama in which there is only one person representing all the parts, and a director.

multiple auxiliaries: The protagonist may choose to have more than one auxiliary represent a role or a person.

multiple doubles: More than one double may be used for the protagonist or other roles being doubled.

open tensions: Areas within the psyche or self system that feel unfinished, incomplete or left in a state of anxious closure.

protagonist: The person whose story is being enacted in the psychodrama.

psychodrama: A therapeutic method that uses action and role-playing techniques as therapeutic agents.

reformed auxiliary ego: An auxiliary who, after the conflict or drama has been played out, is offered to the protagonist as the protagonist might wish him to be, that is, in a reformed state.

role analysis: The taking of one role played in life and analyzing it in depth.

role-playing: The acting out of an aspect of the self or of a significant person in one's life within the context of psychodrama.

role reversal: A technique that allows the protagonist to play any role in the drama, in order to see the self from the outside and to experience the role from the position of the other.

scene setting: The process that the protagonist goes through in setting the scene for the enactment as he sees it or wishes to have it.

sharing: The portion of psychodrama, after the enactment, in which role-players and auxiliary egos share what comes up for them throughout the enactment.

social atom: The nucleus of people in a person's life that help that person to remain in social balance and connection.

sociometry: The network of connectedness through attractions, repulsions and neutrality that forms the social grid for all social actions.

soliloquy: The speaking out in the first person of the inner goings on of the protagonist at any given point in a psychodrama or group process.

spectrogram: The allotment of personal values, intensities or definition along a designated line: for example, 1-10, hot-cold or very much-very little.

surplus reality: What is carried in the psyche as personal history, which affects the whole of who the person is and how he relates: the intra-psychic personal material that a person carries within the psyche in reference to the self and others pertaining to the self.

time regression: Any enactment that represents or concretizes a scene, or a metaphor from the past.

vignette: A small scene enacted with only one or two role-players chosen by the protagonist.

BIBLIOGRAPHY

Ackerman, R.J. *Children Of Alcoholics: A Guidebook For Educators, Therapists And Parents* (2nd ed.), Holmes Beach, FL: Learning Publications.

A Course In Miracles, Choose Once Again, Celestial Arts, Berkeley, CA, 1981.

Alcoholics and other dysfunctional families, *The 12 Steps For Adult Children*, Recovery Publications, San Diego, CA 92110. Biddle, B. J., & Thomas, E. J., (eds.). (1966). *Role Theory: Concepts And Research.* New York: John Wiley & Sons.

Black, C. *It Will Never Happen To Me*, Denver, Medical Administration Co., 1981.

Blatner, A. (1987). *Acting-in.* New York: Springer Publishing.

Blatner, A. & Blatner, A. (1987). *Foundation Of Psychodrama: History, Theory And Practice.* New York: Springer Publishing.

Bradshaw, John (1988). Healing the shame that binds you. Health Communications, Inc., Deerfield Beach, FL.

Buchanan, D. R. (1984). Psychodrama. In T. B. Karasu, (ed.). *The Psychiatric Therapies.* Washington, D.C.: The American Psychiatric Association.

Campbell, Joseph (1968). *The Masks Of God: Creative Mythology.* New York: Viking Press.

Campbell, Joseph (1990). *Transformations Of Myth Through Time.* New York: Harper & Row.

Cousins, Norman, (1979) *Anatomy Of An Illness As Perceived By The Patient.* New York: Norton; New York: Bantam (1981).

Curtin, Paul, J., M.A., CAC (1985). *Tumble Weeds.* Stroudsburg, PA: Quotidian.

Curtin, Paul, J., M.A., CAC (1987). *Resistance And Recovery For Adult Children Of Alcoholics.* Delaware Water Gap, PA: Quotidian.

Dass, Ram and Gorman, Paul (1987). *How Can I Help?* New York: Alfred A. Knopf.

Dayton, Tian (1990). *Drama Games.* Deerfield Beach, FL: Health Communications, Inc.

Denning, Melita and Phillips, Osborne (1980-1983). *Creative Visualization.* St. Paul, MN: Llewellyn Publication.

Estes, Nada, J. & Heinemann, Edith, M. (1982). *Alcoholism.* St. Louis, Toronto, London: The C. V. Mosby Company.

Faber, Thomas, F. (1986). *Alcohol And Culture Comparative Perspectives From Europe And America.* New York: New York Academy of Science.

Feuerstein, George (1978, 1989). *The Yoga-Suttra Of Pantanjali.* Rochester, VT: Inner Traditions International, Ltd.

Fine, L. J. (1979). Psychodrama. In R. J. Corsini, (ed.). *Current Psychotherapies* (2nd ed.), Itasca, IL: F. E. Peacock.

Fisher, Ruth (1988). *Time For Joy - Daily Affirmations.* Deerfield Beach, FL: Health Communications, Inc.

Fox, Emmet (1938). *The Sermon On The Mount.* New York: Harper & Row.

Fox, J. (ed.) (1987). *The Essential Moreno: Writings On Psychodrama Group Method And Spontaneity By J. L. Moreno, M.D.* New York: Springer Publishing.

Franklin, Jon. (1988). *Molecules Of The Mind.* New York: Dell Publishing Co.

Freedman, D., Pisani, R. & Purves, R. (1978). *Statistics.* New York: Norton.

Fried, M. N. & Fried H. (1980). *Transitions: Four Rituals In Eight Cultures.* New York: W. W. Norton.

Fuhlrodt, R. B. (ed.) (1990). *Psychodrama: Its Application To ACOA And Substance Abuse Treatment.* (Available from Perrin & Treggett Booksellers, P.O. Box 190, Rutherford, NJ 07070. 1-800-321-7912.

Gawain, Shakti (1989). *Return To The Garden.* San Rafael, CA.

Goertz, C. (1973). *The Interpretation Of Cultures.* New York: Basic Books.

Goldman, E. E. & Morrison, D. S. (1984). *Psychodrama: Experience And Process.* Dubuque, Iowa: Kendall/Hunt.

Goodman, Elaine and Walter (1979). *The Family Yesterday, Today, Tomorrow.* New York: Farrar-Straus and Gidroux.

Greenberg, I. A., (ed.) (1974). *Psychodrama Theory And Therapy.* New York: Behavioral Publications.

Guilford, J. P. (1977). *Fundamental Statistics In Psychology And Education.* (3rd ed.) New York: McGraw Hill.

Hale, A. E. (1986). *Conducting Clinical Sociometric Explorations: A Manual For Psychodramatists And Sociometrists.* (Available from Ann E. Hale, 1601 Memorial Avenue, #4, Roanoke, VA 24015).

Hay, Louise, L. (1984-1987). *You Can Heal Your Life.* Santa Monica, CA: Hay House.

Hayes, W. L. (1973). *Statistics For The Social Sciences.* New York: Holt, Rinehart & Winston.

Hobson, Allan, J. *The Dreaming Brain.* New York: Basic Books, Inc. Publishers.

Hoel, P. G. (1960). *Elementary statistics.* New York: Wiley and Sons.

Hollander, C. E. (1978). *A Process For Psychodrama Training: The Hollander Psychodrama Curve.* Denver, CO: Snow Lion Press.

Kuman, V. K. & Treadwell, T. W. (1985). *Practical Sociometry For Psychodramatists.* (Available from Tom W. Treadwell, West Chester University, West Chester, PA 19380).

Marineau, R. F. (1989). *Jacob Levy Moreno 1989-1974: Father Of Psychodrama, Sociometry And Group Psychotherapy.* London and NY: Tavistock/Routledge.

Meyerhoff, B. (1977). *We Don't Wrap Herring In A Printed Paper.* In S.

Moore, B. Meyerhoff, (eds.) Secular Ritual (pp. 199-226). Amsterdam:Van Gorcum.

Miller, Alice (1981). *The Drama Of The Gifted Child.* New York: Basic Books, Inc. Publishing.

Moreno, J. L. (1946). *Psychodrama: Volume One.* Beacon, NY: Beacon House.

Moreno, J. L. (1941). *The Psychodrama Of God: A New Hypothesis Of The Self.* (Also called The Words Of The Father.) Beacon, NY: Beacon House.

Moreno, J. L. (ed.). *Sociometry And The Science Of Men.* Beacon, NY: Beacon House.

Moreno, J. L. (1951). *Sociometry: Experimental Method And The Science Of Society.* Beacon, NY: Beacon House.

Moreno, J. L. (1947). *Theater Of Spontaneity: An Introduction To Psychodrama.* Beacon, NY: Beacon House.

Moreno, J. L. (1978). *Who Shall Survive?* (3rd ed.). Beacon, NY: Beacon House.

Moreno, J. L. & Moreno, Z. T. (1959) *Psychodrama: Volume Two.* Beacon, NY: Beacon House.

Moreno, J. L. & Moreno, Z. T. (1969). *Psychodrama: Volume Three.* Beacon, NY: Beacon House.

Nunnally, J. C. et. al. (1925). *Introduction To Statistics For Psychology And Education.* New York: McGraw Hill.

Nunnally, J. C. (1959). *Tests And Measurements: Assessment And Prediction.* New York: McGraw Hill.

Nunnally, J. C. (1978). *Psychometric Theory.* New York: McGraw Hill.

Oliver-Diaz, P. (1985). *Self-Help Groups Through Children's Eyes, Focus On Family And Chemical Dependency,* vol. 8, no. 2.

Presnall, Lewis, F. (1977). *Alcoholism, The Exposed Family.* Salt Lake City, Utah: Utah Alcoholism Foundation.

Schechner, R. and Appel W. (1990). *By Means Of Performance Intercultural Studies Of Theater And Ritual.* Cambridge: Cambridge University Press.

Spiegel, M. R. (1961). *Schaem's Outline Series. Theory And Problems Of Statistics.* New York: McGraw Hill.

Starr, A. (1977). *Rehearsal For Living: Psychodrama.* Chicago: Nelson Hall.

Steinglass, P. (1980). *A Life History Model Of The Alcoholic Family,* vol. 19, no. 3.

Sternberg, P. & Garcia, A. (1989). *Sociodrama: Who's In Your Shoes?* New York: Praeger.

Strauss, R. (1976). *Conceptualizing alcoholism and alcohol problems.* In O'Gorman, P. Smith, I. and Stringfield, S., (eds.). *Defining Adolescent Alcohol Use, Implication Toward Definition Of Adolescent Alcoholism* (pp. 106-107). New York: National Council On Alcoholism.

The American Psychiatric Association (1987). *Diagnostic And Statistical Manual Of Mental Disorders.* Washington, D.C.: American Psychiatric Association.

Turnbull, C. (1990). *Liminality: A Synthesis Of Subjective And Objective Experience.* In Richechner and Willie Appel, (eds.). *By Means Of Performance: Intercultural Studies Of Theater And Ritual.* Cambridge: Cambridge University Press.

Warner, G. D. (1974, 1982). *Psychodrama Training Tips,* vols. 1 and 2. (Available from G. Douglas Warner, 326 Summit Avenue, Hagerstown, MD 21740).

Werner, H. & Kapan B. (1963). *Symbol Formation.* New York: Wiley.

Williams, A. (1989). *The Passionate Techniques: Strategic Psychodrama With Individuals, Families And Groups.* London/New York: Tavistock/Routledge.

Yablonsky, L. (1976). *Psychodrama: Resolving Emotional Problems Through Role-Playing.* New York: Basic Books.

Yalom, I. D. (1975). *The Theory And Practice Of Group Psychotherapy* (2nd ed.), New York: Basic Books.

Articles

International Journal Of Small Group Research Special Issue. Psychodrama as a field of systematic small group research. (1989). 5(1).

Buchanan, D.R. (1989). The central concern model, a framework for structuring psychodramatic production. *Group Psychotherapy, Psychodrama And Sociometry*, 33, 5-17.

Kellerman, P. F. (1983). Resistance in psychodrama. *Group Psychotherapy, Psychodrama And Sociometry*, 36, 30-43.

Weiner, H. B. (1975). Living experiences with death—a journeyman's view through psychodrama. *Omega*, 6(3), 251-274.

INDEX

H.

I.

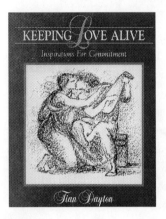

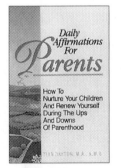